I Know What It Says . . . What Does It Mean?

CRITICAL SKILLS FOR CRITICAL READING

MAJOR CONCEPTS

(Chapter indicated in parentheses)

Critical Reading as Active, Reflective Problem Solving

- Each reader is the author, in the sense of creator, of his or her own understanding. **(Introduction)**

- Reading is ultimately an act of inquiry, a search for meaning. Although our eyes may scan a page word after word, line after line, our minds move "up, down, and sideways." **(Introduction)**

- A text is read at various levels—as words, sentences, and paragraphs—and as a whole. Analysis is a tool for understanding at each of these levels. **(1)**

- Readers read punctuation as well as words. Punctuation reflects the writer's analysis of a sentence. **(1)**

- Communication relies on shared knowledge. Writers rely on their readers to recall information and ideas and to draw on that knowledge to infer unstated meanings. **(2)**

- Readers must "read" ideas as well as words to make sense of the text. **(2)**

- What we don't know influences our understanding as powerfully as what we do. **(2)**

- We cannot literally read "between the lines." But we can reason about what a text does say, and in so doing find a deeper or hidden meaning. **(3)**

- To find meaning in a text, readers construct images of the author, audience, purpose, and context. **(3)**

- The forms of discussion—restatement, description and interpretation—reflect different kinds of understanding and different images of the text. **(4)**

Critical Reading of a Text as a Whole

- Critical reading sees each text not as an object to be worshipped, but as an expression of one person's understanding; not as objective truth, but as the subjective understanding of a fellow human being. **(5)**

- Choices of content, language, and structure shape the thought of the text. **(5)**

- Conclusions are more a reflection of initial beliefs than of the reasoning by which they are reached. **(6)**

- Critical reading focuses not on the examples, but on what the examples are examples of. Like the individual frames of a movie, the examples are meaningful only insofar as they contribute to the whole. **(6)**

- Pattern identification depends on isolating "differences that make a difference" while overlooking superficial variations. **(7)**

- Readers infer meaning by recognizing how specific parts, in a certain relationship, convey a particular meaning. **(8)**

- The inference equation model offers, in effect, a "grammar" of meaning. **(8)**

- Any word choice represents a conscious decision to portray a topic one way instead of another. Although we may debate whether the words within a text accurately portray the topic as we know it, we must assume that those words accurately portray how the author wishes that topic to be viewed. **(9)**

- Authors draw on a broad arsenal of devices to make their portrayals convincing. In most instances, the motives and techniques are forthright and honorable: the product is of value and the claims are legitimate. In other instances, things are not as they are made to seem. **(10)**

- Readers must distinguish when a label is useful for descriptive purposes and when it serves more to reduce the level of discussion. **(10)**

- Authors persuade by endowing assertions with acceptable or unacceptable qualities. **(10)**

- Although important, critical reading is not an end in itself. We do not read simply for the sake of reading, but to discover information and ideas for future actions and decisions. **(11)**

- To protect themselves from being led down a path of outlandish claims to seemingly reasonable conclusions, readers evaluate the assertions on the basis of their prior knowledge and experience—what they have come to believe to be true. **(11)**

- Critical reading often involves little more than bringing to all written texts the same skeptical questioning and analysis, the same sensitivity to nuance, that we commonly employ with speech. **(11)**

DANIEL J. KURLAND

I Know What It Says . . . What Does It Mean?

CRITICAL SKILLS FOR CRITICAL READING

Wadsworth Publishing Company

I(T)P™ **An International Thomson Publishing Company**

Belmont • Albany • Bonn • Boston • Cincinnati • Detroit • London • Madrid • Melbourne
Mexico City • New York • Paris • San Francisco • Singapore • Tokyo • Toronto • Washington

English Editor: Angela Gantner
Editorial Assistant: Lisa Timbrell
Production Editor: Carol Carreon Lombardi
Managing Designer: Carolyn Deacy
Designer: Wendy Calmenson
Print Buyer: Diana Spence
Copy Editor: Tom Briggs
Cover Design: Madeleine Budnick Design
Compositor: Fog Press
Printer: Malloy Lithographing, Inc.

 This text is printed on acid-free recycled paper.

COPYRIGHT © 1995 by Wadsworth Publishing Company
A Division of International Thomson Publishing Inc.

I(T)P   The ITP logo is a trademark under license.

Printed in the United States of America
1 2 3 4 5 6 7 8 9 10—01 00 99 98 97 96 95

For more information, contact Wadsworth Publishing Company:

Wadsworth Publishing Company
10 Davis Drive
Belmont, California 94002, USA

International Thomson Publishing Europe
Berkshire House 168–173
High Holborn
London, WC1V 7AA, England

Thomas Nelson Australia
102 Dodds Street
South Melbourne 3205
Victoria, Australia

Nelson Canada
1120 Birchmount Road
Scarborough, Ontario
Canada M1K 5G4

International Thomson Editores
Campos Eliseos 385, Piso 7
Col. Polanco
11560 México D.F. México

International Thomson Publishing GmbH
Königswinterer Strasse 418
53227 Bonn, Germany

International Thomson Publishing Asia
221 Henderson Road
#05-10 Henderson Building
Singapore 0315

International Thomson Publishing Japan
Hirakawacho Kyowa Building, 3F
2-2-1 Hirakawacho
Chiyoda-ku, Tokyo 102, Japan

Library of Congress Cataloging-in-Publication Data

Kurland, Daniel J., 1939–

   I know what it says— what does it mean? : critical skills for critical reading/
Daniel J. Kurland.
     p.   cm.
Includes bibliographical references and index.
ISBN 0-534-24486-6 (acid-free paper)
1. Reading (Higher education). 2. Reading comprehension. 3. Critical thinking.
I. Title.
LB2365.R4K87 1995   1994
428.4'07'11—dc20

                                       94-9452

9-8-03

To my father, who taught me to pursue dreams
and
to Gail, for helping to make them so

CONTENTS

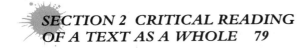

xii • Contents

TEXTS FOR ANALYSIS

xvi • Text for Analysis

PREFACE

To survive in the modern world, all agree, students must learn to think and read critically. Ideally, that's what education is all about.

For decades, however, students have been left to their own devices to intuit critical reading behaviors. They are told what the outcome should be, but not how to obtain it—where to go, as it were, but not how to get there.

I Know What It Says . . . What Does It Mean? offers the first comprehensive response to that need. The text has been designed for use in a wide range of settings, from introductory composition courses, to first-year seminars, critical thinking classes, and developmental reading or college skills workshops. It may also be assigned as a companion text in content courses across the curriculum.

A Method to Empower

This text has been created to empower teacher and student alike:

- to enable teachers to offer students a method of investigation
- to enable students to approach texts systematically, certain of what to look for and how to think about what they find

The innovative inclusion of distinct tactics and techniques enables both teacher and student to focus on process, not product—on reading behaviors rather than "correct" answers.

Critical Thinking and Critical Reading

Critical reading involves more than thinking critically about what one has read. To think critically, one must first read critically. The discussion therefore emphasizes concepts essential to a critical approach to reading:

- reading as a reflective, problem-solving activity
- reading ideas as well as words
- reading a text as a whole

Throughout, the text examines the role and responsibilities of the reader in constructing meaning from evidence within the text.

The Approach

The text examines the behaviors underlying the reading and interpretive process:

- recognizing the sequential development of a discussion
- analyzing patterns of content and language throughout a text, and recognizing their role in shaping the thought of that text
- inferring meaning on the basis of prior knowledge, cultural understanding, and a variety of mental frameworks for comprehending the world

Concepts are introduced in an order that makes sense conceptually and pedagogically but still recognizes reading as a continuous flow of recognition and exploration, of discovery and problem solving.

Unique Features

The text introduces a number of unique elements essential to critical reading:

- the image of the text as portrayal, rather than fact—an outlook that frees students from the necessity of rote responses and encourages the interpretative effort
- emphasis on classifying patterns of evidence—recognizing what the examples are examples *of*—to limit personal responses and ensure a consistent analysis of the complete text
- the introduction of inference equations—that meaning is implied by specific parts in specific relationships—as a framework for both inferring meaning and presenting one's understanding in written or oral form

Traditional Features

Although original in outlook, the text incorporates topics common to more traditional texts, including denotation and connotation, figurative language, logic and logical fallacies, and techniques of persuasion.

Conceptual Frameworks

Throughout, the discussion of reading behaviors is based on an understanding of how meaning is conveyed by texts, of how texts "work."

Traditional frameworks of understanding emphasized in the text include the general/specific relationship, standard rhetorical models of discussion, common conceptual relationships (e.g., cause/effect), levels and bases of analysis, and the notions of assumptions, perspective, and consistency.

Original frameworks of understanding include the role of inference in the interpretive process; the implications of choices of content, language usage, and structure on the meaning of a text; the notion of conceptual ingredients inherent in a topic; and specific frameworks for reading ideas as well as words.

Reading and Writing

Although manifestly about reading, the text is, in many ways, a composition text as well. An increased understanding of how readers interpret texts has obvious implications for the way students shape and edit their own writing.

The Structure of the Text

The text is divided into three sections, followed by Texts for Analysis and an Appendix of Resources for Critical Reading.

Section One, Critical Reading as Active, Reflective Problem Solving, examines the processes involved in recognizing what a text "says," "does," and "means" on the sentence and paragraph level. This section offers teachers an opportunity to test and reinforce initial skills in grammar, punctuation, and general comprehension.

Section Two, Critical Reading of a Text as a Whole, examines the skills, strategies, and perspectives underlying critical interpretation of a text as a whole. It focuses on the influence of patterns of content and language and the effects of various persuasive devices. The discussion offers guidelines for both reading and writing about texts. These first and second sections contain numerous exercises that extend and reinforce ideas within each chapter.

Section Three, Tactics and Techniques—Putting It All Together, reviews earlier discussion with the aid of additional illustrations, offering concrete examples of the processes in action.

Texts for Analysis offer a diverse and provocative collection of non-fiction readings for discussion. The readings include multiple views of the same topic, as well as contrasting approaches within the same genre.

Appendix: Resources for Critical Reading contains extended discussion and illustrations of basic concepts for general review.

Critical Reading 101

Finally, it is hoped that *I Know What It Says . . . What Does It Mean?* will encourage greater emphasis on critical reading throughout the curriculum and establish a place for courses in critical reading per se.

INTRODUCTION

An expert can make a complex skill look easy. But the apparent effortlessness of a chess master or concert pianist does not deceive us. What we sometimes fail to appreciate is that skilled reading is an intellectual feat no less complex than chess playing.

• M. A. Just and P. A. Carpenter
THE PSYCHOLOGY OF READING AND
LANGUAGE COMPREHENSION[1] •

All reading is an active, reflective, problem-solving activity.

Legend has it that someone once asked Willy Sutton, the famous bank robber, why he robbed banks. "Because that's where the money is!" he replied. People in search of knowledge consult written material in much the same way—because that's where the information is. From written texts* we learn everything from ways to bake a cake to theories of the origin of the universe, from the history of ancient Africa to the workings of the human brain. While television may provide up-to-date information on our society and environment, written materials remain a major source of information, ideas, and inspiration for our future actions. Like Willy Sutton, we go to the source to obtain what we need. All we have to do is take it out. Or so it would seem! But most reading is not that simple. Often, the words may be clear, but the idea is not. We may see what a text says but have little understanding of what it means.

READING: SYMBOLS AND MEANING

Reading involves finding meaning in a system of symbols. Consider the following symbols:

We read the time from the position of the hands of a clock; we read a warning from the markings on a traffic sign; we read the relationship between physical properties in a physical equation—here, the relationship of area to length and width. In each case, we observe visual symbols and grasp some **meaning**.

Initially, reading may appear simple. We seemingly strip meaning from the page, like peeling tape from a box. This image, however, greatly oversimplifies the

---

Text is used throughout as a general term to indicate *any* work of nonfiction: textbooks, essays, letters, newspaper or journal articles, petitions, leaflets, laws and regulations, transcriptions of speeches and radio commentary, and reports of all kinds.

reading process. Above all, this image fails to recognize the reader's role in finding—or, more accurately, in constructing—meaning. We read, in other words, not only with our eyes, but with our minds as well. Much of what we obtain from the reading experience, then, depends on what we bring to it. We do not simply "withdraw" ideas like money from a bank. Rather, each reader is the author, in the sense of creator, of his or her own understanding.

EXAMPLE: Reading for Meaning

The following news item, from *Time* magazine, offers an initial opportunity to examine the reading process.

A Graduation Gift from Uncle Sam

Armed-forces recruiters are catching flak for paying schools to get scouting information about students. The city of Los Angeles board of education passed a measure last week that stops the district from selling the names and addresses of high school students to military recruiters. The board was responding to complaints from parents, who consider the practice an invasion of student privacy. Since 1971 the district has been selling the names of juniors and seniors for 3¢ apiece. Last year it made $8,081 from the list, which school officials say was used to cover clerical costs. The Pentagon acknowledges that buying lists from high schools is a common way for the military to target potential recruits.[2]

Reading sentence by sentence, you recognize statements about events in Los Angeles. You see what the text says. But because the article seems simple enough, you are hardly aware of the complex interpretive processes you have carried out to see what it means. To illustrate some of the activities involved in making sense of the article, consider the same article with one reader's thoughts printed in italics. (Other readers would, of course, respond differently.)

A Graduation Gift from Uncle Sam

"Uncle Sam" refers to the United States government. It is a name normally found on recruiting posters or in political cartoons. What kind of gift does this refer to?

Armed-forces *images of the army, war . . .* **recruiters** *who try to enlist youth . . . patriotism . . . "Be the best you can be" . . . glory* **are catching flak** *war image, but playful . . . maybe the article isn't all that serious* **for paying schools** *what!—since when do schools get paid by the military?* **to get scouting information** *like with football players?* **about students.** *Either they're resourceful or devious.* **The city of Los Angeles** *oh . . . kooky California!* **board of education passed a measure** *saying what?* **last week that stops** *they're against it* **the district from selling** *the army wants names bad enough to pay for them . . . the school board would sell kids to the army* **the names and addresses of high school students to military recruiters.** *Now the title makes sense . . . the "gift" is being approached by a recruiter.* **The board was responding to complaints** *PTA pressure . . . parents . . . maybe it's more local politics than a real issue* **from parents,** *Save my son!* **who consider the practice an invasion of student privacy.** *That* *comma, it indicates that all or a whole bunch of parents consider it an invasion of privacy, not just a few complainers.* **Since 1971** *background, precedent . . . is it trying to justify?* **the district has been selling the names of juniors and seniors for 3¢ apiece**. *Sounds like small change, but maybe . . . 1000 at 3 cents apiece is $30 . . . make that 10,000 kids, it's LA . . . $300 . . . for twenty years or so, $6000 . . . getting up there.* **Last year it made $8,081** *hey, that's money* **from the list, which school officials** *bureaucrats* **say** *not "insist" or something stronger . . . does the text want us to believe this?* **was used to cover clerical costs**. *In other words, it wasn't to make a buck, but then again it wasn't patriotism to charge them.* **The Pentagon acknowledges** *aha, they admit it!* **that buying lists from high schools is a common way for the military to target** *another war image, and this "targeting" can hurt later, but the article is being playful in its use of language again* **potential recruits**. *Is this legal? Fair? Against freedom of privacy? Is it what a public school should be doing? If I shouldn't be bothered by it, why tell me about it? Does* Time *magazine want me to be outraged?*

The above comments document an active, reflective, problem-solving approach to reading.

READING UP, DOWN, AND SIDEWAYS

Reading is, ultimately, an **act of inquiry**, a search for meaning. While our eyes may scan a page word after word, line after line, our minds move "up, down, and sideways." We recall information and ideas from our prior experience. We anticipate arguments and imagine possible conclusions. We fill in references and make associations. We experiment with different analyses of sentences and draw inferences from the information before us. We examine *how* ideas are expressed as well as *what* ideas are expressed, what a text *does* as well as what it *says*.

The reader's thoughts while reading the *Time* magazine article include all manner of thinking: inferring, questioning, predicting, evaluating, reacting, second-guessing, calculating, speculating and deciphering. Overall, these processes involve three areas of concern:

- **Analyzing** the text to understand the sentences and their roles in the discussion—reading "down" the page
- **Drawing on prior knowledge** to infer unstated meanings, including making sense of references and figurative language—reading "up" from the page with one's mind
- **Inferring an overall meaning** from patterns of elements throughout the text—reading "sideways" across the text as a whole

In practice, readers engage in all three processes at once, whatever the reading material—whether casually reading a magazine in a dentist's office or poring over a physics textbook in a library. Additional care and concentration are required, however, when more complex texts are involved or when more than a casual understanding is desired.

READING IMPROVEMENT: THE NEED FOR A METHOD

The ultimate goal of critical reading is to understand a text as completely as possible. This goal is often described in terms of discovering an overall or underlying meaning beyond what is actually stated within the text. Because such a meaning is not stated, however, it can be subject to debate.

In academic situations, students can often rely on outside assistance to direct their investigations. Teachers may direct attention to significant aspects of a text. Questions at the end of the chapter can guide an analysis of a text. Outside of school, the situation is different. There are no introductions suggesting an underlying meaning, no "questions for analysis" to point the way. Readers are on their own.

As the chapter-opening quotation suggests, reading is as complex an activity as playing chess or the piano. Whatever the endeavor, students seek ways to improve their performance. "Just doing it!" is usually not enough. Plodding through a difficult piano piece error after error may provide additional practice, but it will not necessarily improve one's playing. Losing a chess game to someone far more skilled than you can be a learning experience, but it will not necessarily result in personal improvement. In all such endeavors, good students try to assure their grasp of basic skills. Pianists practice musical scales; chess players review different moves to ensure the necessary response when the occasion arises. In much the same way, simply reading more, or more difficult, texts will not improve the depth of one's understanding. Readers must know what they can expect to discover in a text and how to think about what they find. They must have techniques to check their progress and to evaluate their final understanding. To make sense of complex texts, they must have a method. Only then can they, on their own, investigate texts of various difficulty in a variety of circumstances.

THE APPROACH OF THIS TEXT

This book is not about memorizing definitions or learning grammar rules. It is about understanding an approach to examining and discussing written material. This approach is based on an investigation of how texts "work"—how meaning is conveyed by the written word—and of how readers make sense of what they find. The discussion looks at the influence different aspects of a text have on the overall meaning. It reviews common thought processes and suggests how those processes can be applied more successfully to complex texts.

Critical Reading

"Critical reading" means different things to different people. For some it suggests any close reading of a text. For others it implies an effort to "detect the possibly crafty purpose of the author"[3] or to defend against "the seduction of eloquence."[4] Critical reading often includes issues of critical thinking. Other times, it suggests a more specialized linguistic endeavor. Courses in critical reading may be designed to overcome weaknesses or to encourage advanced interpretation. In all cases, the term *critical* should *not* suggest the negative evaluation often associated with criticizing something. Critical reading is reading with an open mind—not to agree or disagree, but to discover. Above all, it sees written texts not as authoritative pronouncements, but as human creations subject to interpretation and evaluation.

In the first section of this book, "Critical Reading as Active, Reflective Problem Solving," *critical reading* is used as a general term for a careful reading at the sentence and paragraph levels. In this section, we discover the degree to which all readers read even the simplest of texts "up, down, and sideways" to go beyond what a text says to see what it does and what it means.

As noted earlier, *critical reading* can also refer to reading for an understanding that goes beyond what it stated. In this context, the text is seen not as a window on the world though which one has a direct view of the reality, but as one person's views and understanding. Here, critical reading is not simply to acquire information, but to understand the underlying values and assumptions of a text as a whole. The ultimate goal is an interpretation, the discovery of a deeper meaning. Does the *Time* magazine article, for example, take sides? Does it justify the actions of the army recruiters? Does it condemn them? It is this meaning of critical reading that underlies the second section of the book: "Critical Reading of the Text as a Whole." This section examines both what we mean by the "meaning of a text" and the specific processes readers follow to reach an understanding.

The Scope of the Discussion

While the discussion that follows is concerned with nonfictional texts, essentially the same processes are involved in the analysis of fictional works—novels, short stories, plays, and poetry. And while the focus here is on reading, the discussion has implications for writing as well. The better you understand how writing communicates ideas, the better you can employ the same processes when creating texts yourself.

Finally, we should note that the barriers to critical reading have little to do with linguistics; rather, they involve closed-mindedness, passivity or rigidity of thinking, sloppy work habits, and a lack of imagination. To that extent, a book on critical reading can only do so much. It can explore how texts are structured and how texts use language to manipulate thought. And it can suggest ways in which we can read more closely and more reflectively. The will and patience to apply these tools must be your own.

• WHY AM I READING THIS? •

A newspaper is not read in the same way as a service manual, nor is a text-book read in the same way as a personal letter. Your **purpose** and **expectations** affect your reading style.

Before reading any text, ask yourself:

- Why am I reading this?
- What am I looking for, and how will I test my understanding?

In a hurry, you may scan a text, skipping sections that are not of interest at the moment. You may read to catch the general drift, to find specific information, or to gain in-depth understanding. You may read a text through once or reread it time and time again, and then test your understanding by doing exercises. You might simply read for pleasure until a story no longer holds your attention. No form of reading is necessarily wrong. Reading styles should be judged primarily on whether they are appropriate for the task at hand.

EXERCISES/DISCUSSION

A. Does a Falling Tree Make a Noise in a Forest?

There is a classic philosophical debate as to whether a tree that falls in a forest makes a noise if no one is there to hear it. In the same vein, one can ask if a text has meaning without a reader. Even with a reader, what we mean by the meaning of a text is not necessarily clear.

Evaluate how realistic each of the following definitions of the meaning of a text might be. What would each suggest about the obligations of the reader? In each case, consider whether your reply might be different were the text a history textbook, a newspaper editorial, or a news article.

1. What the author intended to mean
2. What a reader thinks the author intended to mean
3. The feelings, thoughts, or actions the author hoped to inspire
4. The feelings or thoughts actually inspired in a reader
5. A single meaning inherent in the text
6. What an unskilled reader thinks it means
7. What a skilled reader thinks it means
8. What a community of like-thinking readers might take it to mean
9. What someone in authority tells us it means

CRITICAL READING AS ACTIVE, REFLECTIVE PROBLEM SOLVING

If we consider men and women generally . . . there is only one situation I can think of in which they almost pull themselves up by their bootstraps, making an effort to read better than they usually do. When they are in love and are reading a love letter, they read for all they are worth. They read every word three ways; they read between the lines and in the margins; they read the whole in terms of the parts, and each part in terms of the whole; they grow sensitive to context and ambiguity, to insinuation and implication; they perceive the color of words, the odor of phrases, and the weight of sentences. They may even take the punctuation into account. Then, if never before or after, they read.

• Mortimer Adler, HOW TO READ A BOOK[1] •

CHAPTER

Analysis—
Making the Complex Simple

*There is probably no more urgent need in education than that students
learn how to apply such language abilities as thinking, reasoning, judg-
ing, and so on to the experiences they have with the written page.*

• Neil Postman and Charles Weingartner
LINGUISTICS: A REVOLUTION IN TEACHING[2] •

The primary tool for understanding language is the process of analysis. This tool can be applied to words, sentences, paragraphs, and the text as a whole.

ANALYSIS

Reading, it has been suggested, involves a complex combination of mental activities. How does one go about examining and understanding such a complex phenomenon? Consider this traditional Jewish tale celebrating the powers of reasoning:

> War was on the horizon. Two students in the *yeshiva* [school] were discussing the situation.
>
> "I hope I'm not called," said one. "I'm not the type for war. I have the courage of the spirit, but nevertheless I shrink from it."
>
> "But what is there to be frightened about?" asked the other. "Let's analyze it. After all, there are two possibilities: either war will break out, or it won't. If it doesn't, there's no cause for alarm. If it does, there are two possibilities: either they take you or they don't take you. If they don't, alarm is needless. And even if they do, there are two possibilities: either you're given combat duty, or non-combatant duty. If non-combatant, what is there to be worried about? And if combat duty, there are two possibilities: you'll be wounded, or you won't be wounded. Now, if you're not wounded, you can forget your fears. But even if you are wounded, there are two possibilities: either you're wounded gravely, or you're wounded slightly. If you're wounded slightly, your fear is nonsensical, and if you're wounded gravely, there are still two possibilities: either you succumb, and die, or you don't succumb, and you live. If you don't die, things are fine, and there's no cause for alarm; and even if you do die, there are two possibilities: either you will be buried in a Jewish cemetery, or you won't be. Now, if you are buried in a Jewish cemetery, what is there to worry about, and even if you are not . . . but why be afraid? There may not be any war at all!"[3]

At each step in the discussion, an apparently complicated problem is broken into parts to facilitate its solution. This is the process of **analysis**.

ANALYSIS AND SYNTHESIS

Analysis is a formal process of examination. Analysis involves dividing a whole into parts so that an apparently complex phenomenon is reduced to simpler form.

The goal of analysis is not simply to break a complex topic into smaller pieces, but to fully understand the whole. As a result, analysis is followed by **synthesis**, an examination of how the parts are related to one another within the whole. This second step brings to mind the adage "the whole is greater than the sum of its parts." A bicycle is, after all, more than a frame, wheels, handlebars, and so on. Disassembled in a heap, these component parts are merely junk. Only when assembled a certain way do the parts form a vehicle one can ride. In this sense we begin to understand something only when we see its **structure**—when we recognize its parts and the ways in which they are interrelated—how the parts work together as a whole.

Whereas analysis sees the parts in isolation, synthesis views them as they interact. In informal usage, however, the notion of analysis encompasses both processes—that is, the study of both the parts and their relationships.

Analysis: Analysis is an essential thought process in a wide variety of situations. Anytime we examine something step by step, we analyze. Anytime we weigh the pros and cons of a decision or consider alternatives, we analyze. There is almost no problem solving without analysis, no reflection without analysis.

In the earlier story of the two Jewish students, the "parts" at each step in the argument are fairly obvious: something will either happen or it won't. However, analysis does not always yield a structure so easily. Wholes do not break into parts by themselves. Someone must choose how to divide them. And just as different people may slice a pie differently, people can analyze an idea differently. All analysis, however, will have a basis of analysis at each of various levels of analysis.

Levels of Analysis

Any part can itself be broken into parts. With the notion of analysis comes the notion of **levels of analysis**. Each level of subdivision is said to be "lower" than the previous one. To analyze on a lower level is to break any given part into component parts.

A diagram of a table of contents displays several levels of analysis:

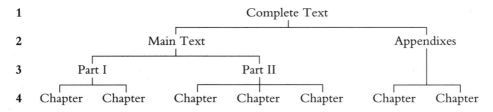

				Complete Text			
1							
2			Main Text				Appendixes
3		Part I			Part II		
4	Chapter	Chapter		Chapter	Chapter	Chapter	Chapter	Chapter

And this process can, of course, be carried further: to chapter sections and subsections, and even paragraphs and sentences. Similarly, jobs are commonly analyzed into two major divisions, but each level of subdivision yields still more parts at lower levels of analysis:

Animals, too, are classified into progressively lower and lower categories: kingdom, phylum, class, order, family, genus, and species, with various sublevels of each—possibly the greatest number of analytic levels in common usage.

The "parts" of analysis do not have to be physical parts. The parts may be steps in a process, factors in a decision, or participants in an encounter. Analytic parts can be formed any way one can think of dividing a topic for closer examination.

Bases of Analysis

Sorting a number of objects, we might divide them according to color, size, shape, or weight. We might focus on how they are used or what they are made of. The choice of "what goes with what" depends on, and defines, the **basis for analysis**.

· · · · · · · · · · · · · · · BASES OF ANALYSIS · · · · · · · · · · · · · · · ·

The following excerpt appears in Charles Hoffer's *A Concise Introduction to Music Listening*. How many different bases for analyzing musical instruments are mentioned? (*Hint*: There are at least three.)

There are hundreds of different instruments in the world, and they can be grouped in a variety of ways. One way is to discuss them according to the type of music they perform; this chapter is so organized.

Orchestral Instruments
The instruments of the symphony orchestra can be divided into "families" on the basis of similar design and principles of sound production. There are four families: strings, woodwinds, brasses, and percussions.

STRINGS   The strings are the backbone of the orchestra. They constitute about half its membership. The violin, the viola (vee-*o*-la), the cello (*chel*-lo; officially the violoncello), and the bass viol have essentially the same design. The main difference among them is one of size and consequently the general pitch level at which they play. The player produces tone by plucking the strings with the finger or, most often, by drawing a horsehair bow across the strings.[4]

· ·

Most topics can be analyzed from a variety of perspectives (bases of analysis). For example, the U.S. government can be analyzed on the basis of its branches (executive, legislative, judicial), its levels (federal, state, local), or its role in various aspects of our lives (environment, social services, public works). A sociologist may look at crime in terms of which groups steal, a psychologist in terms of people's reasons for stealing, a political scientist in terms of the effects of laws on stealing, and an anthropologist in terms of the cultural response to people who steal. A policy might be examined on the basis of its cost, its effectiveness, or its popular support—or on the basis of all three concerns.

ANALYSIS AND READING

Analysis is an important tool for understanding texts at all levels of investigation. One can hardly begin reading without analyzing. Consider the following phrase from the *Time* article in the Introduction:

. . . recruiters are catching . . .

Scanning these words, we instinctively recognize parts:

. . . recruiter / s   are   catch / ing . . .

The remainder of this chapter explores the many ways readers employ analysis—consciously or unconsciously—to understand written statements.

EXAMPLE: **Defining** *Society*

The following excerpt, from Rodney Stark's *Sociology*, an introductory college textbook, offers a useful example for examining the relationship between analysis and reading.

> Sociologists often use the terms *society* and *nation* interchangeably. But not all nations are societies, and not all societies are nations. A better definition of society is a group of people who are united by social relationships. Because a society often contains many such groups, the term must also refer to a group that is relatively self-sufficient and independent: A distinct social boundary should set off members of one society from all other persons and groups. Hence, most people will know which society they belong to. In addition, societies tend to occupy a definite physical location—even nomadic societies tend to travel a familiar route within a specific area. Finally, societies tend to have substantial periods of existence; they are not momentary arrangements.[5]

What understanding might we be responsible for upon reading this paragraph? If you were highlighting key ideas with a marker, what would you highlight? We will return to this passage to answer these and other questions throughout this chapter.

ANALYZING WORDS: ROOTS, PREFIXES, SUFFIXES

Spoken words can be analyzed on the basis of sound into units called **sylla-bles**. For example, the word *international* can be broken down into these syllables:

int / er / nash / en / l

int / er / nash / nel

Written words can also be analyzed into syllables to decide how to break the word at the end of a line:

inter / na / tion / al

(Notice that the syllables of the spoken and written words are not always the same.)

Written words can also be analyzed on the basis of meaning into three major parts: (1) a main section, the **root**; (2) a part at the beginning, the **prefix**; and (3) a part at the end, the **suffix**:

prefix-root-suffix

Using this third basis for analysis, the written word *international* is analyzed as follows:

prefix + root + suffix

inter + nation + al

To the root *nation* is added a prefix *inter-*, meaning "between," and a suffix *-al*, indicating an adjective. Putting the parts together, we have an adjective meaning "between nations."

Word analysis is important for two reasons. First, knowledge of roots, prefixes, and suffixes enables readers to decipher the meaning of complex or unfamiliar words by inference based on knowledge of similar words. Second, suffixes contain grammatical information that can aid in understanding. For example, suffixes distinguish between the verb *judge*, the noun *judgment*, and the adjective *judgmental*, as well as between the adjective *judicial*, the noun *judiciary*, and the adverb *judicious*. Only by recognizing these suffixes can readers make full sense of the words.

Word analysis is required in various places within the sample sociology passage. From the very first word, readers must analyze the words to make sense of them:

soci + ologist + s

(society) (one who studies) (plural) = people who study society

Anyone analyzing the word as *so-ciolog-ists* or *s-oci-olo-gists* would obviously have trouble understanding the meaning.

• • • • • • • • • • • • • • • • • **WORD ANALYSIS** • • • • • • • • • • • • • • • • • •

The same suffix can have different meanings in different contexts. What does the suffix *-es* indicate in the word *watches* in each of the following sentences?

1. He watches the game from the side lines.
2. They timed the game with their watches.

• •

• **WORD MEANING** •

Knowing a word means more than knowing its definition. It can include

- Knowing how to use that word in a sentence (its grammatical form and function)
- Knowing something about the concept for which the word stands
- Knowing the contexts in which the word is appropriate
- Knowing the level of social usage associated with the word
- Knowing how to pronounce the word
- Knowing connotations or associations of the word

Dictionary references supply many of these elements. An entry for the word *cop* might look like this:

cop /kop/ *slang n.* **1** police officer

This entry tells us the following: spelling (cop), pronunciation (kop), social usage (slang), grammatical form (noun), and the most common (1) definition (police officer).* The connotation as an unflattering term is not indicated, although it might be associated with the slang usage. (A separate entry would define the verb *cop*, as in *to cop a plea*.)

ANALYZING SENTENCES: GROUPING WORDS INTO MEANINGFUL UNITS

It would be erroneous to view reading as a process of recognizing each word one by one, one after another. Just as we do not read words letter by letter, we do not read sentences word by word. Our eyes scan the page a number of words at a time. The limitations of word-by-word reading become evident when we read

---

*Dictionaries vary in the order in which definitions for a given word are presented. Some place the most frequent usage first; others place the earliest usage first.

aloud. Only by emphasizing longer phrases can we convince someone that we have made sense of a passage.

Consider the following sentence:

Do not marry him because he's rich.

Should you marry him? The meaning of the sentence depends on how you analyze it:

Do not marry him   because he's rich.
Do not   marry him because he's rich.

The first sentence says not to marry him and gives a reason for not doing so. The second sentence says not to marry him for a certain reason, leaving open the possibility of marrying him for another reason.

Sentence analysis can be viewed either of two ways. In the traditional view, we can break the sentence into phrases, clusters, or grammatical constructions, each composed of a number of words. Alternatively, we can think of sentence analysis as a matter of grouping individual words into these larger units. Whether we think in terms of dividing or grouping, much of the effort in reading long sentences involves trying different analyses of the sentence to see which makes sense.

Consider the following sentence from the sample text:

A better definition of society is a group of people who are united by social relationships.

To understand the thought, we analyze the whole into parts:

A better definition of society
    is
        a group of people who are united by social relationships.

Our understanding is reflected in our analysis. Society is not defined as "a group of people" nor as "a group of people who are united." Rather, society is defined by the complete construction: "a group of people who are united by social

---

I would go as far as to say that no sentence is made up of words; a sentence is made up of constructions and it is the constructions that are made up of words, not the sentence. To treat a sentence as a string of words . . . is to overlook the most significant feature of the structure of the sentence.

• Robert L. Allen, ENGLISH GRAMMARS AND ENGLISH GRAMMAR[6] •

relationships." Only by recognizing the complete constructions do we include all of the qualifications of the original text. And only then do we recognize exactly what is being said.

The Relationship Between Parts of a Sentence

A number of the sentences in the sample text can be analyzed into two major parts. For example, in the following sentence, the second part offers a complementary observation. It expands on the initial idea by offering an additional but related observation:

> But not all nations are societies,
>> and not all societies are nations.

In the next sentence, the second part offers an example of the idea expressed in the first half to show that a seeming exception is actually consistent.

> In addition, societies tend to occupy a definite physical location
>> —even nomadic societies tend to travel a familiar route within a specific area.

And in the following sentence, the second half restates the idea of the first half in different words for additional clarity:

> Finally, societies tend to have substantial periods of existence;
>> they are not momentary arrangements.

In each case, to understand the meaning of the sentence, we must understand the relationship between the parts. And while each of these sentences can be broken into two major parts, the structure of the sentences is not really the same. Each sentence may have two parts, but the parts are related to each other differently. The concept of relationships between parts is examined more closely below in terms of the relationships between sentences.

Two Aspects of Sentence Awareness

Looking back on the previous discussion, notice that reading involves two forms of understanding. We are aware of the notion of society and what the term *society* might or might not refer to. We are, in other words, aware of what is being stated about the topic of discussion. We are also aware of the text itself as a written document. It is this second aspect of awareness that allows us to recognize how different parts of sentences are related.

This dual awareness suggests two ways in which we might talk about the text we have read. Not only can we repeat what the text *says* about the definition of the term *society*, we can also describe how the text goes about making its points, what the text *does* within that discussion. The importance of this distinction will become clearer when we recognize that critical reading is not so much a matter of repeating what we are told as of understanding how someone else pieces together thoughts to convey a particular view of the world.

Punctuation: The Writer's Analysis of a Sentence

Readers "read" punctuation as well as words. Punctuation reflects the writer's analysis of a sentence.

Capital letters and end punctuation—periods, question marks, and exclamation points—designate the beginning and end of individual sentences. Commas and semicolons separate items in a list or series. Commas also serve to isolate qualifications or other material at the beginning, middle, or end from a "root" idea within a sentence.* Note the use of commas in the following sentences:

> After the game was over, the team met at the bar for a beer.
>
> The book is about drinking, a social sickness of major importance.
>
> The game, a clever entertainment, intrigued the kids for hours.

The commas in these sentences function like brackets:

> [**After the game was over**] the team met at the bar for a beer.
>
> The book is about drinking [**a social sickness of major importance**].
>
> The game [**a clever entertainment**] intrigued the kids for hours.

With the material in brackets removed, only the root idea remains:

> . . . the team met at the bar for a beer.
>
> The book is about drinking . . .
>
> The game . . . intrigued the kids for hours.

The material within the brackets can offer important limitations on, conditions of, or reasons for the root idea. Other times, the additional material offers clarification, examples, or related ideas or information—as we saw in the previous examples of sentence analysis from the sample sociology text.

---

*The notion of a "root" idea within a sentence is intended to suggest something akin to the root or main part of a word. The term is used here to avoid more technical grammatical terminology.

Note that the main idea of a sentence and its root idea are not necessarily the same.

In the eyes of the jury, Harry had murdered his wife.

The overall thought of the sentence is not that Harry murdered his wife, but that the jury thought Harry had. Nevertheless, we understand the sentence by separating off the root idea:

Beginning material   **Root idea**

[In the eyes of the jury]   Harry had murdered his wife.

Here, as in many other cases, the bracketed material is crucial to the overall thought. And here, as elsewhere in reading, analysis is critical to making sense of the sentence as a whole.

The sample text on the definition of the term *society* uses a variety of punctuation marks to signal shifts in the thought besides periods, including commas (,), a colon (:), a semicolon (;), and dashes (—).

• LEVELS OF BRACKETING •

Written English uses a number of punctuation devices to indicate lower and lower levels of comment within a sentence. The lower the level, the more extraneous the comment is to the discussion at hand.

The comma is the most common means of bracketing. On a slightly lower level, added thoughts can be bracketed off by dashes:

> In addition, societies tend to occupy a definite physical location—even nomadic societies tend to travel a familiar route within a specific area.

Less important items, such as references to sources or slight digressions, are often enclosed in parentheses:

> The most controversial ratings periods for local stations are "sweeps" months—February, May and November. (Ratings are taken in July, too, but the numbers are not considered accurate because so many people are on vacation.)[7]

Square brackets are used to insert explanatory material into a quotation or to make other editorial comments.

> Four score and seven [87] years ago our fathers brought forth on this continent a new nation. . . .

Finally, material necessary only for reference can be inserted outside the flow of discussion in footnotes or endnotes.

Punctuation and Ambiguity

Ambiguity refers to a situation in which two or more equally legitimate analyses, and hence meanings, exist—as we saw with the sentence about marrying someone rich. Inserting a comma would force one of the interpretations:

Do not marry him, because he's rich.

This sentence is no longer ambiguous: it says not to marry him and gives a specific reason for that opinion.

Punctuation can resolve many potential problems of ambiguity. The importance of such punctuation can be appreciated by comparing the sentences in each of the following sets:

In the morning light, trucks were seen near the dump.
In the morning, light trucks were seen near the dump.

My gracious Auntie died.
My gracious, Auntie died.

The sergeant stopped ordering me to do push-ups.
The sergeant stopped, ordering me to do push-ups.

For each set the differences in meaning should be apparent.

When a change of punctuation would change the meaning, readers must assume that the meaning presented is the one intended and thus not change the punctuation—and hence the meaning—on their own. Once again, read this sentence:

Do not marry him because he's rich.

We would have to assume that because the addition of a comma forces one meaning, the absence of that comma implies the other meaning: that it may be okay to marry him for other reasons. When you cannot resolve potential ambiguity with punctuation in your own writing, you should rewrite the sentence.

ANALYZING PARAGRAPHS: STRUCTURE AND THE RELATIONSHIP OF ASSERTIONS

In the two topics of analysis considered thus far—words and sentences—we have focused on identifying parts, whether in terms of breaking the whole into smaller units (words into roots and affixes, sentences into sections) or grouping pieces into larger units (letters into syllables and words into larger constructions).

Paragraph analysis involves a slightly different approach. With paragraphs the parts are already established: Capital letters and end punctuation mark the beginning and end of sentences. Therefore, the issue is not really analysis, but synthesis. Just as making sense of sentences involves recognizing how the parts are related, making sense of paragraphs involves recognizing how sentences are related to one another.

Reading Ideas as Well as Words

The most basic way for sentences to be related is in terms of what they are talking about. For a paragraph to make sense, the remarks must be about some common topic. If the sentences seem disconnected, we might assume we have not "caught on," that we have somehow missed the point. Consider the following, from a textbook on politics:

> Making use of a coding system originally developed to score open-ended responses to a semiprojective test on the level of cognitive complexity, Tetlock has evaluated the complexity of various political documents, including letters, diaries and speeches. This measure of cognitive complexity includes both "differentiation" and "integration."[8]

What "measure of cognitive complexity"? To follow the train of thought from sentence to sentence, the reader must figure out precisely to what in the first sentence a "measure of cognitive complexity" refers. (The reference is to the coding system.) This passage is also a vivid reminder of the need for writers to make such references as clear as possible.

EXAMPLE: Economics Text

The following excerpt is from Paul A. Samuelson's *Economics*, a classic introductory college textbook. As you read the passage, you should have little trouble following the key ideas from sentence to sentence.

> **Strikes and Collective Bargaining**   Both sides realize that failure to reach agreement will mean a costly strike. It may sometimes happen that management refuses to go above $9.50 an hour while labor refuses to take less than $9.60. A "work stoppage" will result.
>
> Should we call this an "employees' strike" or an "employer's lockout"? Popularly, it will be referred to as a strike. But since each side knows it can end the work stoppage by agreeing to the other party's terms, we could call it either.[9]

In comprehending this passage you have actually engaged in a fairly sophisticated process of problem solving. The connections between the sentences are indicated in boldface below.

> **Strikes and Collective Bargaining [The head identifies the topic.]**   Both sides realize that failure to reach agreement will mean a costly strike. [**The initial**

sentence continues the discussion of the topic of strikes.] It may sometimes happen that management refuses to go above $9.50 an hour while labor refuses to take less than $9.60. [**"Management" and "labor" are identified as the sides in "both sides."**] A "work stoppage" will result. [**"Work stoppage" refers back to the idea of both sides refusing to agree on pay; "will result" echoes the notion that one event leads to another ("it may sometimes happen").**]

Should we call this an "employees' strike" or an "employer's lockout"? [**The pronoun "this" refers to "work stoppage" in the previous sentence.**] Popularly, it will be referred to as a strike. [**The pronoun "it" refers to the same topic as "this" did in the previous sentence.**] But since each side knows it can end the work stoppage by agreeing to the other party's terms, we could call it either. [**The discussion of (1) "work stoppage," (2) the problem of agreement on salary terms, and (3) what to call the events continues.**]

· · · · · · · · · · · · · CONNECTIONS BETWEEN IDEAS · · · · · · · · · · · · ·

How is the thought of these two sentences from Stark's *Sociology* connected?

> Control theory stresses human rationality. Whether people tend to deviate or conform depends on their calculations of the costs and benefits of deviance or conformity.[10]

· ·

Models of Sentence Relationships

The relationship among sentences within a paragraph can be examined in terms of different models of sentence interaction. Each model will contain various categories to describe specific relationships among sentences in a paragraph.

Three common models of paragraph structure are presented here. No single model is necessarily appropriate for any particular text. In fact, most analyses draw on a number of models simultaneously. (Many of the categories of one model are evident in another model under a different name.) Note also that the categories used to describe the relationship of sentences within a paragraph can also describe the relationship of paragraphs within a text as a whole.*

The role model

The first model is based on the roles sentences play in the development of a paragraph. Categories in such a role analysis might include the following:

- Raising an issue
- Shaping a discussion
- Discussing an issue

---

*Note: These models are discussed in greater depth, with further examples, in Appendixes C, D, and E.

- Offering support
- Emphasizing
- Concluding

Readers make sense of a passage by recognizing the role each sentence plays within it. Returning to the excerpt from Samuelson, we can identify the following roles:

> **Strikes and Collective Bargaining [raises issue]** Both sides realize that failure to reach agreement will mean a costly strike. **[discusses issue]** It may sometimes happen **[shapes discussion]** that management refuses to go above $9.50 an hour while labor refuses to take less than $9.60. A "work stoppage" will result. **[discusses]**
>
> Should we call this an "employees' strike" or an "employer's lockout"? **[question shapes discussion]** Popularly, it will be referred to as a strike. **[discusses]** But since each side knows it can end the work stoppage by agreeing to the other party's terms, we could call it either. **[concludes]**

> **Models:** Models are mental images that represent ways of looking at something. They focus attention on important features and provide useful terminology for discussion. The same topic can be discussed using different models to highlight different concerns.

The descriptive model

The second model of paragraph structure is based on descriptions of the remarks within each sentence. The resulting labels reflect traditional rhetorical categories of composition:

> **argument:** developing a conclusion based on evidence, reason, emotional appeal, or other persuasive devices

> **comparison/contrast:** examining two objects, ideas, events, or other topics to find either similarities or differences

> **definition:** indicating the meaning of a term or phrase; distinguishing one idea from another

> **description:** relating the characteristics or features of an event, process, place, and so on

> **narration:** telling a story or recounting events

As the categories suggest, this model focuses more on the kind of statement being made than on the actual relationship of one sentence to another:

Strikes and Collective Bargaining   Both sides realize that failure to reach agreement will mean a costly strike. **[description]** It may sometimes happen that management refuses to go above $9.50 an hour while labor refuses to take less than $9.60. **[comparison]** A "work stoppage" will result. **[narration]**

Should we call this an "employees' strike" or an "employer's lockout"? **[definition]** Popularly, it will be referred to as a strike. **[definition]** But since each side knows it can end the work stoppage by agreeing to the other party's terms, we could call it either. **[argument]**

The relationship model

The third model is based on conceptual relationships between sentences. This model has five major categories:

> **series:** a sequence of similar remarks; commonly used with description (a list of different characteristics) or narration (a series of events)

> **chronological order:** a special case of a series; a list in time order

> **general/specific:** general statements and specific examples or illustrations

> **comparison/contrast:** similarities or differences among objects, events, or ideas

> **logic:** assertion of a conclusion based on evidence and/or reasoning (reason/conclusion, cause/effect, conditional, analogy)

This model focuses on how the ideas in sentences are related:

Strikes and Collective Bargaining   Both sides realize that failure to reach agreement will mean a costly strike. **[from general to specific]** It may sometimes happen that management refuses to go above $9.50 an hour while labor refuses to take less than $9.60. **[second event in a series]** A "work stoppage" will result. **[chronology]**

Should we call this an "employees' strike" or an "employer's lockout"? Popularly, it will be referred to as a strike. **[series of labels]** But since each side knows it can end the work stoppage by agreeing to the other party's terms, we could call it either. **[reason/conclusion]**

Our purpose here is *not* to insist on the appropriateness or primacy of any one model. What really matters is not *how* a text is discussed, but *that* it is discussed at all—that readers go beyond repeating its assertions to examining features of the text itself. For the moment, you merely need to recognize the various ways of describing relationships among sentences within a paragraph, and, with that, a variety of ways of describing the ongoing discussion.

Signal Words and Phrases

Various terms and phrases often signal shifts in a text, and with that the relationship between specific parts of that text. The comments in the following article about the Gulf War, by William V. O'Brien, draw on all of the earlier models. Signal words and phrases are indicated in italics.

> *In my opinion,* [**raises an idea**] armed enemies who have not surrendered and who are capable of hostile actions are legitimate targets. *Even if* [**shapes the thought**] they are retreating they are subject to attack. *As the Riyadh [Saudi Arabia] briefing officer, Brigadier General Neale, explained,* [**persuades by quoting authority—support for argument**] a "retreat" is different from a "withdrawal." *Had Saddam Hussein announced* [**discusses—contrast argument**] that the Iraqi troops fleeing Kuwait City were being withdrawn to Iraq it might have been in order to permit them to do so unimpeded. [**discusses—argues**] *In fact, however,* [**discusses—contrasts**] those troops simply retreated, carrying their loot with them, *because* [**reason**] the U.S./coalition ground offensive had defeated them. *In these circumstances I consider that* [**conclusion**] the attacks on these retreating Iraqi along the highways back to Iraq were proportionate to the legitimate military objectives of destroying or incapacitating as much of the active armed forces as possible.[11]

Each phrase implies what is to follow. By recognizing these terms and phrases, attentive readers "read" both the structure of the argument and the argument about Iraqi soldiers itself.*

Signal words are also present in the sample sociology text; again, these words are set in italics:

> Sociologists often use the terms *society* and *nation* interchangeably. *But* [**contrast**] not all nations are societies, *and* [**series**] not all societies are nations. A better definition of society is a group of people who are united by social relationships. *Because* [**cause/effect**] a society often contains many such groups, the term must also refer to a group that is relatively self-sufficient and independent: A distinct social boundary should set off members of one society from all other persons and groups. *Hence,* [**cause/effect**] most people will know which society they belong to. *In addition,* [**series**] societies tend to occupy a definite physical location—even nomadic societies tend to travel a familiar route within a specific area. *Finally,* [**last item in a series**] societies tend to have substantial periods of existence; they are not momentary arrangements.

Signal words play the same role in more complex academic texts, such as Joseph Sheley's *Criminology*. Once again, signal words for the following text are in italics, and comments on the structure of the argument, drawing on all three models, are in boldface.

---

*The substance of this argument is examined in Appendix F, "Logic and Statistics."

Although [**sets up contrast**] crime statistics are sometimes reported in the news, most crime news consists of reports of particular crimes, *either* [**sets up series of items**] as they are occurring (as in the case of a bank robbery in progress) *or* shortly after they have occurred [**raises topic of crime and crime reporting**] (Graber, 1980; Fishman, 1981). [**source notes to persuade with suggestion of authority**] *Because* [**offers reason**] the "supply" of crimes is virtually unlimited, [**comma indicates end of reason, beginning of conclusion**] choices must be made as to which crimes to report. *As with* [**similarity**] any other kind of potential news material, the central criterion for choosing crime stories is "newsworthiness." [**shapes discussion by indicating main concern, describes how stories are chosen**] *In the case of crime,* [**specific example**] newsworthiness translates into seriousness*:* [**colon indicates example or further explanation to follow**] *the more* serious a crime, *the greater* the chance it will appear as a news story. [**further shaping of discussion of crime reporting**] The brutal homicide, *for example,* [**another example**] is *more likely* to be reported *than* [**comparison**] the nonviolent residential burglary. [**example that emphasizes point**] This standard is not in itself unreasonable, [**argues, justifies**] *but* [**contrast**] it is at odds with sociological reality. [**raises subtopic of appropriateness of reporting**] *Recall that,* [**reraises topic**] as a general rule, crimes occur in inverse proportion to their seriousness*:* [**colon again sets up further explanation**] *the more* serious the crime, *the less* [**comparison**] frequently it occurs (Erickson and Gibbs, 1979). [**information and references to persuade**] *Thus,* [**indicates reasoning**] *whereas* [**contrast**] thousands of homicides occur annually in the United States, millions of burglaries are committed. *Hence,* [**signal for conclusion**] by using seriousness as a criterion, the media are most likely to report precisely those crimes that are least likely to occur (Skogan and Maxfield, 1981; Sherizen, 1978; Sheley and Ashkins, 1981; Roshier, 1973).[12]

Certainly no reader would consciously make all of the observations or connections indicated here, yet most readers will recognize many of these terms and grasp the sentence relationships. And once you are conscious of this process, you possess a powerful tool for deciphering complex or confusing passages.

EXAMPLE: **Defining** *Society*

Returning to the sample sociology text, we can recognize a paragraph that defines what is meant by the term *society*. The paragraph indicates problems in how the term is sometimes used:

> Sociologists often use the terms *society* and *nation* interchangeably. But not all nations are societies, and not all societies are nations.

Then it offers its own interpretation:

> A better definition of society is . . .

• READING UP, DOWN, AND SIDEWAYS •

The reader's eyes may scan the page, but the reader's mind ranges up, down, and sideways, piecing together evidence, prior knowledge, and ideas to make sense of the overall presentation.

The paragraph offers a series of criteria ("in addition," "finally") that must be met to satisfy the sociologist's definition of a society. Ultimately, the paragraph offers four basic criteria:

a group
> of people who are united by social relationships
> that is relatively self-sufficient and independent
> that occupies a definite physical location
> that has a substantial period of existence

By recognizing the structure of the paragraph as a series of criteria, we realize that no single sentence within the paragraph gives a complete definition of society.

• READING: THOUGHT GUIDED BY SYMBOLS •

Reading, it has been said, is "thought guided by symbols."[13] This is simply another way of saying that we must recognize both words and the ideas for which they stand.

IMPLICATIONS

A text is read at various levels—as words, sentences, and paragraphs, and as a whole. Analysis is employed as a tool for understanding at each of these levels: (1) reading to break up words into prefixes, roots, and suffixes; (2) reading to break up sentences into meaningful chunks and bracketing off minor portions; and (3) reading to relate one sentence to another within paragraphs.

To these, in later chapters we will add the following goals of analysis: (4) reading to reflect on the real-world meaning of concepts and references and (5) reading to sense the significance or overall meaning of the discussion.* On

*In academic situations, we might add reading for test accountability—isolating and memorizing terms, concepts, and facts for which we might be held responsible.

many occasions, all of these goals can be accomplished simultaneously. With more difficult or unfamiliar material, however, a separate reading of the text may be required for each level of understanding.

The discussion has focused on the sequential development of a text, one word after another, one sentence after another, like links in a chain. This is, after all, our initial image of reading. Yet while our eyes may scan a text word by word and line by line, our minds move forward, backward, and sideways. In Section 2, analysis is applied to patterns of elements occurring through a text. There, as here, the process of analysis provides a framework for an active, problem-solving approach to reading.

EXERCISES/DISCUSSION

A. Analysis: Breaking into Parts

The "parts" of analysis can take various forms. Analyze each of the following according to the criteria indicated.

1. School courses are usually divided into categories in terms of academic disciplines or departments. Analyze your school's courses employing at least two levels of analysis.

2. Processes are analyzed one step after another. Analyze the process of setting the timer on a VCR. Does the concept of levels of analysis apply here?

3. What issues might you consider in an analysis of the possible benefits of a college education?

4. Description can be carried out from a variety of perspectives. A house might be described from the viewpoint of an architect, a builder, or an inhabitant. Each would divide the whole differently, focusing on different aspects or simply arranging the same concerns differently. Indicate the factors an environmentalist, a developer, and a tourist might consider when describing a lake.

B. Punctuation and Sentence Analysis 1

Punctuation provides a writer's analysis of the structure of a sentence. When punctuation is missing, readers must try various analyses until they discover one that makes sense. For each of the following, insert punctuation to clarify the meaning.

1. The boy hid the math book biology book and eraser from the teacher yesterday.

2. Last year [the school board] made $8,081 from the list which school officials say was used to cover clerical costs.

3. Clarissa Pinkola Estes has written a book of fairy tales for adults a collection of myths and stories that she uses to show how women's true natures have been suppressed and how they can recapture the true "wild" self that is theirs.[14]

4. Inspired by the long-standing custom by which each candidate for president selects his own running mate originally by agreement and now through his

party's nominating convention and attempting to retain some degree of "democratic procedure" the states ratified the Twenty-fifth Amendment in 1967. According to its provisions in the event of a vacancy in the vice-presidential office the president is empowered to nominate a vice-president who must then be confirmed by a majority of both houses of Congress.[15]

C. Punctuation and Sentence Analysis 2

During early negotiations the Constitutional Convention of 1787 agreed to include the following statement:

> The Legislature of the United States shall have the power to lay and collect taxes, duties, imposts and excises.

The sentence was later extended to indicate how this money was to be spent:

> The Legislature of the United States shall have the power to lay and collect taxes, duties, imposts and excises, to pay the debts and provide for the common defense and general welfare.

In its final version the statement read:

> The Legislature of the United States shall have the power to lay and collect taxes, duties, imposts and excises; to pay the debts and provide for the common defense and general welfare.

How do these last two versions differ in meaning? What can the Legislature do or not do in the final version that is different from the earlier version?

D. Pronouns

Support for the notion that we analyze sentences by grouping words into larger units is reflected in the observation that pronouns replace not individual nouns but complete *noun phrases*. Bracket the complete group of words that could logically be replaced by "it" in each of the following sentences.

1. The boy hid the math book.
2. The boy hid the math book from the teacher.
3. The boy hid the math book with a red cover from the teacher.
4. The boy hid the math book he had bought from the store on the corner.

E. Ambiguity

Indicate any possible ambiguity in the following sentences.

1. The man sought protection from the police.
2. The thief shot suddenly.
3. John and Mary went to the dance.
4. On Monday, Kuwait said it was planning to ask Britain and France to send forces to join 1,500 United States troops sent here to help protect Kuwait against any land assault by Iraq, a possibility that is dismissed by most foreign diplomats.[16]

F. Relationships Between Assertions

Using the categories of the relationship model, indicate how the sentences in each pair are related.

1. Delia danced. Jessica sang.

2. Delia danced. Jessica, however, sang.

3. In the morning Delia danced. In the evening, Jessica sang.

4. Jessica sang well. As a result, the show was a hit.

G. Following a Topic

Indicate how the topic moves from sentence to sentence in each of the following excerpts.

1. **(1)** The Reconstruction governments certainly contained corruption, but they were no more corrupt than their "lily-white" counterparts before or after the war. **(2)** Although black suffrage was essential for keeping these regimes in power, their electoral base, especially in the beginning, extended beyond the ex-slaves. **(3)** Many former Whigs, Southern Union men, and antisecessionists initially allied themselves with the new Republican governments. **(4)** Many whites in nonslaveholding regions who had always resented the rule of the planter elite voted for and participated in the Reconstruction governments. **(5)** These governments were in many ways reform governments. **(6)** But they spent comparatively little time trying to achieve social equality between whites and blacks. **(7)** Instead, they concentrated on such things as public education and eliminating the undemocratic features of the antebellum political system, by which the planter elite had maintained its dominion—things that benefitted poor whites as well as the freedmen. [Texts for Analysis 1C]

2. **(1)** Early in the nineteenth century, as many young men headed West (in those days, the "Wild West" was in western New York State and Ohio), many women in New England supported themselves in their homes by spinning wool into yarn. **(2)** This became so widespread that the term spinster soon ceased to mean female spinner and instead identified any unmarried woman over a certain age (Guttentag and Secord, 1983). **(3)** But as the proportion of males declined and the number of women needing work increased, new inventions made it possible for huge textile mills to spring up in New England—drawn there partly because of the supply of young women workers. **(4)** "New England textile factories from the start employed a vastly greater proportion of women than men" (Cott, 1977). **(5)** Thus began a trend that in the course of a century has drawn the majority of North American women from their homes to hold regular jobs.[17]

3. **(1)** Psychoanalysis, Sigmund Freud's method of treating psychological disorders, continues to exercise a strong influence on many psychologists. **(2)** Psychoanalysts assume that people have unconscious thoughts and motives as well as conscious ones. **(3)** The unconscious mind retains the memory of painful thoughts and experiences, often from early childhood, that the conscious mind ignores. **(4)** The unconscious may make itself felt in dreams, physical complaints, slips of the tongue, and actions that a person performs for no apparent reason.[18]

4. **(1)** Social psychiatrist Philip Tetlock employs a model that is similar to Rosenberg's, although its origins are quite different. **(2)** Making use of a coding system originally developed to score open-ended responses to a semiprojective test on the level of cognitive complexity (Schroder, Driver, & Steufert, 1967), Tetlock has evaluated the complexity of various political documents, including letters, diaries and speeches (Levi & Tetlock, 1980; Suedfeld & Tetlock, 1977; Tetlock, 1979, 1981a, 1981b). **(3)** This measure of cognitive complexity includes both "differentiation" and "integration." **(4)** Differentiation relates to the number of different aspects of an issue that an individual recognizes; integration measures whether an individual sees the differentiated characteristics as functioning independently (low integration), in simple patterns (moderate integration), or in complex patterns (high integration). **(5)** Tetlock (1983) thus makes the same distinctions that Rosenberg (1987) makes: Thinking that takes only a single perspective is judged to have a low level of cognitive complexity; thought that considers the possibility of two perspectives but that focuses on one is considered to be of moderate complexity; and thinking that sees interrelationships between multiple perspectives is judged high in complexity.[19]

H. Relationships Between Assertions

Using one or more of the models of the relationship of sentences within a paragraph, indicate the relationship between sentences in the excerpts in Exercise G.

I. Perspective and Bases of Analysis

Indicate the bases for analysis and the categories into which the whole is broken in the following excerpt.

A traditional means of classifying personal-service occupations is by the honor accorded them, with the liberal professions falling at one extreme and the humble trades and crafts at the other. This can be an obscuring distinction, separating by rank those who are similar in spirit. The division I want to employ places at one extreme those, such as ticket-takers or telephone operators, who perform a perfunctory technical service, and at the other those with an expertness that involves a rational, demonstrable competence that can be exercised as an end in itself and cannot reasonably be acquired by the person who is served. Perfunctory servers tend to have customers, "parties," or applicants; expert servers tend to have clients. Both types of servers are likely to have some independence from the persons they serve, but only experts are in a position to build that independence into a solemn and dignified role.[20]

J. Analysis (Parts) versus Analysis (Examination)

The term *analyze* is often used to suggest any careful examination, whether specific parts are examined or not. For each of the following excerpts, indicate whether the notion of analysis refers to breaking something into parts or to a more general process of investigation. Where parts are involved, indicate the parts that might be considered.

1. But it was sociologist Erving Goffman (1922–1982) who most effectively *analyzed* social interaction from the point of view that life really is a stage and that much of the time we are putting on performances for one another.[21]

2. If someone alleges that the rise in the number of violent crimes is caused by the increase in violence in TV programs, this seems like a rather simple idea with which we could either agree or disagree. When we begin to *analyze* the statement, however, we find that things become very complicated.[22]

3. When researchers *analyze* the collected data, they search for meaningful patterns or links between variables. When they have found these links, they use them to make decisions about whether to reject, accept, or modify their hypotheses.[23]

K. Texts for Analysis: Petition of the Inmates of Tombs City Prison

The petition of the inmates of Tombs City Prison [Texts for Analysis 7] analyzes conditions within the prison. List the bases of analysis that are employed.

L. Texts for Analysis: "Alarm Clocks Can Kill You. Have a Smoke."

"Alarm Clocks Can Kill You. Have A Smoke." [Texts for Analysis 14] examines articles in a number of women's magazines. What specifically does the essay analyze, and on what basis? Into what categories does the essay divide the whole? How many levels of analysis does the essay consider?

Prior Knowledge and Meaning— The Art of Controlled Inference

Obviously, we must bring a great deal of knowledge to the text, else we will be able to get nothing out of it, for we read with our minds. In fact, we always bring more to the text than we take away.

• W. Ross Winterowd, THE CULTURE AND POLITICS OF LITERACY[1] •

A reader's understanding is the result of inferences based on prior knowledge and experience.

The previous chapter examined ways readers use analysis to make sense of words, sentences, and paragraphs. This chapter is concerned with the ways readers use reason to make sense of the remarks in a text.

INFERENCE

The fictional detective Sherlock Holmes is famous for his uncanny skills of observation and reasoning. Here Sherlock Holmes describes his thought processes to his companion (and the narrator of the story), Dr. Watson:

> "I was then much surprised and interested on glancing down to observe that, though the boots which she was wearing were not unlike each other, they were really odd ones, the one having a slightly decorated toe-cap, and the other a plain one. One was buttoned only in the two lower buttons out of five, and the other at the first, third, and fifth. Now, when you see that a young lady, otherwise neatly dressed, has come away from home with odd boots, half buttoned, it is no great deduction to say that she came away in a hurry."
>
> "And what else?" I asked, keenly interested, as I always was, by my friend's incisive reasoning.
>
> "I noted, in passing, that she has written a note before leaving home, but after being fully dressed. You observed that her right glove was torn at the forefinger, but you did not apparently see that both glove and finger were stained with violet ink. She has written in a hurry, and dipped her pen too deep. It must have been this morning, or the mark would not remain clear upon the finger. . . ."[2]

From the evidence before him, Holmes inferred the woman's earlier actions.

Inference refers to a reasoning process by which one reaches a conclusion on the basis of some evidence. We regularly infer meaning. For example, when someone suggests we take an umbrella, we infer that they think it is going to rain. When we see someone wearing torn clothes, we infer that they are poor. In each case we find meaning in the evidence before us, and in each case the conclusion seems logical. However, inference is not foolproof. In neither case is the conclusion necessarily true, but rather merely consistent with the evidence at hand.

We draw inferences when we interpret movies, motives, or works of art. We draw inferences when we reason that an event must have had a certain cause or attribute reasons for someone's behavior. When someone leads us to draw an inference, we say that the person implied something. We can even speak of evidence implying a certain conclusion. Others imply; we infer. These are two sides of the same process.

INFERENCE AND PRIOR KNOWLEDGE

Inference relies on prior knowledge. Reading about an event, we create scenarios to explain peoples' behaviors, scenarios that reflect our own prior experience. Where we have no prior knowledge, we have no basis for inference. For example, anyone reading about a case of supposed police brutality will draw inferences about the officers' intentions and the appropriateness of their actions based not only on what they read but also on their knowledge of police practices and on their feelings of the effects of the police officers' actions—inferences that will determine their decision as to the guilt or innocence of the officers.

As this example suggests, the notion of prior knowledge encompasses more than factual knowledge. It also includes understanding based on experiences as well as assumptions about society and cultural values. It includes all the factors that we might be aware of when making a decision. Even ignorance functions as a form of prior knowledge—what we don't know influences understanding as powerfully as what we do.

Disagreements on political or social issues commonly have their roots in differences in what we construe as prior knowledge. An opinion on whether drugs should be legalized, for instance, might depend on one's definition of drugs, one's perception of the role government should play in shaping people's lives, one's understanding of the nature of drug addiction, one's expectation of how legalization might influence addiction levels and drug trafficking, and one's degree of faith in religious or law enforcement officials. And again, one's lack of prior knowledge of these issues will also color one's conclusion about legalizing drugs.

• • • • • • • • • • • • • • • **DRAWING INFERENCES** • • • • • • • • • • • • • • • •

List three inferences that might be drawn about Mary from the following:

Married at fifteen, Mary had her marriage annulled three weeks later.

What inference might be drawn when each of the following statements is added to the previous one?

1. She quit her first job when her boss made a pass at her.
2. She was convicted of shoplifting.
3. She was later elected to the Senate.
4. Her husband was arrested for sexual abuse.

Would all readers draw the same inferences?

• •

Assumptions

The notions of inference and prior knowledge are combined in the notion of assumptions. To reason, we must accept certain facts or assertions as self-evident or already proven. **Assumptions** are assertions of information or ideas that one takes for granted. An idea simply seems to follow naturally, or an inference is taken as obvious. Assumptions are sometimes spelled out, but other times they are left unsaid. Thus, readers often must infer assumptions to make sense of a text.

Assumptions are crucial in many forms of discussion. Even Supreme Court decisions can be based on assumptions. In 1896, for example, the Supreme Court heard *Plessy v. Ferguson,* a challenge to a Louisiana law requiring separate accommodations for white and "colored" railroad passengers. A majority of seven justices upheld the law by ruling that the Fourteenth Amendment to the Constitution, which guarantees "equal protection" under the law, did in fact allow racial separation in "separate but equal" accommodations. But then in 1954, in *Brown v. Board of Education of Topeka,* the Supreme Court ruled unanimously that separate facilities were inherently unequal. The words had not changed, nor had their meaning. What had changed was the assumption that separate facilities could, in fact, be equal.

Assumptions can be somewhat slippery, and even outright deceptive. Assumptions can masquerade as facts or appear to represent sound reasoning. Much thinking and writing may be based on assumptions, yet readers must be careful not to be sucked into accepting assumptions uncritically. Readers must consciously infer assumptions underlying a discussion and weigh their validity as carefully as any assertion within the text. They must examine what is *not* said—but is assumed—as carefully as what *is* said. In fact, much of the underlying meaning of a discussion can be found within the assumptions on which it is based.

EXAMPLE: **Academic Freedom**

To illustrate the role that assumptions play in the construction of meaning, consider this passage from John Gardner's essay "Decoding Your Professors."

> Academic freedom is a condition and a right most college faculty enjoy at the majority of private and state-sponsored institutions. Simply put, it is the freedom to pursue intellectual inquiry and research, or to raise questions that are legitimately related to scholarly interests and professions. The concept of academic freedom allows professors to raise controversial issues without risk of losing their jobs. It doesn't give them total immunity from pressure and reprisals, but it does allow them more latitude than your high school teacher had.[3]

Gardner's basic thesis seems fair enough, and yet it is based on assumptions. By describing academic freedom as a right to be enjoyed instead of simply as a practice of certain schools, the text assumes that raising scholarly questions is to be applauded, that college instructors should not be placed in jeopardy for voicing controversial views, and that that right can be properly limited. While this viewpoint is one generally shared within academia, in various circumstances each of these assumptions might be questioned.

• *ASSUME* VERSUS *INFER* VERSUS *DEDUCE* •

These three terms are often confused. To **assume** is to take for granted without analysis as though the assertion is obvious; it is a relatively passive form of thinking. One idea brings another to mind or simply seems to follow naturally. To **infer** is to reach a conclusion based on real, but not necessarily complete or compelling, evidence. To **deduce** is to draw a conclusion by reasoning with mathematical precision.

What meaning might we extract from the following simple sentence?

Jon graduated from Harvard.

- We might *assume* that, given its excellent reputation, Harvard was his first choice. However, we have no specific evidence to support the claim.
- We might *infer* that Jon is well educated on the basis of the reputation enjoyed by Harvard. However, it does not necessarily follow that everyone who went to Harvard is well educated.
- We might *deduce* that Jon must have spent some time in Cambridge, Massachusetts, because that is where Harvard is located.
- If we *assume* that everyone who has graduated from Harvard *is* well educated, we might *deduce* that Jon is well educated.

INFERENCE AND LANGUAGE

We often think language is fairly clear, that people say what they mean and that their remarks have specific meaning. Yet much human communication is inferred. When someone says, "Did ya'll lose yaw keys?" we infer that that person is from the South and that he or she has found some keys. When a sign says, "More parking in back," we infer that there is parking in front. Most readers would be surprised to realize the many little ways they regularly infer meaning with hardly a second thought.

EXAMPLE: **Assumptions and Perspective**

The following passage from Howard Kahane's *Logic and Contemporary Rhetoric* may seem straightforward, but in fact it makes several key assumptions. Can you spot them?

Americans are great sports fans. They love watching and hearing about football, baseball, basketball, and other physical games. But they aren't terribly interested in intellectual games such as chess, not to mention Go. The result is that the media provide much more information about relatively unimportant goings-on in sports than they do concerning a world-championship chess match; tons more is reported about Bo Jackson than Garri Kasparov—Garri who? (In the Soviet Union, chess greats such as world-champion Kasparov and ex-champion Anatoly Karpov are as famous as Joe Montana and Mike Tyson are in the United States.)[4]

Notice how Kahane distinguishes between "physical games" such as football and "intellectual games" such as chess, and uses the term "sports" only in reference to nonintellectual activities. The assumption is that games requiring intellect are, unavoidably, nonphysical. However, someone else might classify football and chess as games of strategy; baseball and chess as games with long, boring pauses; and basketball and soccer as games of constant activity. This assumption shapes the **perspective** brought to the discussion. The passage also assumes that the difference in coverage has to do with the popularity of the sport, not the nationality of its current stars. (Americans like Bo Jackson and Joe Montana are said to be popular here; Russians like Garri Kasparov and Anatoly Karpov are not.) Is this surprising?

Inferring Word Meaning from Context

Readers infer the meaning of unfamiliar words or phrases from the specific context. For example, how would you interpret the following?

The glurb assigned the students a glirb to read for homework.

From knowledge of the sentence structure and of the concepts implied by the surrounding words, we infer that "glurb" must mean "teacher," and "glirb" some type of written material. Normally, the words themselves might lead to an understanding. In this case, however, we infer the meaning of the words from an understanding of the ideas expressed by the accompanying words. Similarly, the Kahane passage refers to "intellectual games such as chess, not to mention Go." While we may not know what is involved in Go, we can certainly infer that it is offered as another example of an intellectual game.

•••••••• **INFERRING MEANING FROM THE CONTEXT** ••••••••

Indicate possible meanings for "gleeb" in the following sentences:

1. He gleebed the snow from the driveway.
2. The essays were written in different gleebs.
3. One is what one gleebs.

••

Inferring Word Meaning from a Set of Options

Many words have multiple meanings. For example, the word *ruler* might indicate a political leader or a device for drawing lines; the word *shop* might refer to a work room or to a business establishment. In any given instance, we must infer which meaning makes sense in the specific context.

> The water was *cold*.
>
> His response to the offer was *cold*.
>
> When the searchers turned left they were getting *cold*.
>
> Her sister had a *cold*.

Drawing on prior knowledge, we can infer the proper meaning of "cold" in each case from a variety of possibilities: a low temperature, unfriendly behavior, not close, or an illness. In much the same way, most readers do a double take when they read the following sentence, understanding the last word first one way, then another:

> Blackberries are red when they are green.

Only when the reader recognizes that "green" does not refer to a color, but is a synonym for "unripe," does the sentence make sense.[5] Without a problem-solving approach, a reader can make no sense of the sentence.

• LANGUAGE, PRIOR KNOWLEDGE, AND INFERENCE •

The link between language, prior knowledge and inference becomes apparent in the following sentences:

> The car skidded on the road because it was slippery.
>
> The car skidded on the road because it was speeding.
>
> The car skidded on the road because it was raining.

The meaning of each sentence is determined by deciding what the antecedent of "it" is—a decision based on prior knowledge of possible scenarios. No rule of grammar could, by itself, provide the answer. (Notice that you infer the antecedent only after having read the entire sentence.)

Inferring Meaning Within a Given Context

Sometimes, we may know the meaning of a word but still be unsure how to apply the word within the specific context. Once again, inference is called for. Recall the title of the passage in the Introduction on army recruiting:

A Graduation Gift from Uncle Sam

What is the "gift"? Readers must reflect on the ingredients necessary for a gift—who gives what to whom, for what occasion—to figure out what the term refers to as used here. While this might seem a simple act, it requires knowledge of the concept of a gift, the ability to draw inferences, and a problem-solving attitude.

Inferring Information

Readers often infer unstated information to make sense of a statement, as in the following:

> Henry Porter's book of poems, published in 1963, shows the influence of Margaret Fuller.

We infer that Porter knew, read, or was otherwise exposed to Fuller or her work prior to 1963. While this information is not stated in the sentence, it is implied. Without such an inference, the sentence would have no meaning: One cannot be influenced by someone without being exposed to them or their work. We cannot be sure that Fuller was a writer, but we might assume it for the moment—as a hypothesis to be tested by reading further. If the discussion later mentions Fuller's writing style, our hunch is confirmed. If it refers to Fuller's political activities, we revise our understanding of the earlier statement from one about Porter's writing style to one about her ideas.

In the previous passage on chess and American sports fans, reference to the chess player Garri Kasparov after a reference to a world-championship chess match implies that he is a participant in the match:

> The result is that the media provide much more information about relatively unimportant goings-on in sports than they do concerning a world-championship chess match; tons more is reported about Bo Jackson than Garri Kasparov . . .

And this inference is borne out by his subsequent identification as "world-champion Kasparov."

EXAMPLE: **"A Graduation Gift from Uncle Sam"**

The passage in the Introduction about armed-forces recruiters offers various examples of the processes just described:

> Armed-forces recruiters are *catching flak* for paying schools to get scouting information about students.

Readers unfamiliar with the term "catching flak" might still infer a meaning. Recognizing that the military does not normally pay schools, they might infer that "catching flak" suggests some form of trouble. If they already know "flak"

> You might think of the text as [a] set of instructions that you follow in order to achieve a given result. Some of these directions refer you "inward" to other instructions in the system, and some of them refer you "outward" to your knowledge of the world.
>
> • W. Ross Winterowd, THE CULTURE AND POLITICS OF LITERACY[6] •

refers to fragments of bursting anti-aircraft shells, they must decide whether the use of a military image in a discussion of military recruiters is meant as irony. Once again, we must "read" the ideas expressed, not just the words. Likewise, we may know immediately what "scouting" means with regard to athletics, but we might have to pause a second to figure out what armed-forces recruiters would be "scouting" for.

Let's look at one more sentence:

> The board was responding to complaints from parents, who consider the practice an invasion of student privacy.

"The board" can refer to a number of things, from a government agency to a piece of wood. "Practice" can refer to a repeated attempt to learn something or simply to a regular activity. Interestingly enough, the most common words tend to have the most meanings, making the skill of inferring meaning from the context all the more necessary.

• **READING: THE ART OF CONTROLLED INFERENCE** •

Inference provides the rules for going from what is "said" to what is "meant." It is in this vein that reading is sometimes characterized as "the art of controlled inference."

REFERENCE AND ASSOCIATION

Readers bring to a text a wealth of background knowledge on which to base inferences, as the following old joke demonstrates:

> Other than that, Mrs. Lincoln, how did you enjoy the play?

The meaning of the pronoun "that," and thus of the joke, depends on the listener's knowledge that President Abraham Lincoln was shot while watching a play. Without that shared knowledge, as well as the reader's ability to associate the name Mrs. Lincoln with President Abraham Lincoln once a play is referred to, the joke is meaningless.

References

Communication relies on shared knowledge. Writers rely on their reader/listener to recall information and ideas and to draw on that knowledge to infer unstated meanings. The simplest way for a writer to accomplish this is through the use of **references.** References require that the reader recall facts or ideas that are expressly alluded to. To illustrate, note how President Lincoln, in 1863, began the Gettysburg Address:

> Four score and seven years ago, our fathers brought forth on this continent . . .

Here, Lincoln counted on his listeners knowing that he was referring to colonial America's break from Great Britain in 1776.* Similarly, the sample text on Americans' interest in sports appeals to the reader's knowledge of Bo Jackson, Joe Montana, and Mike Tyson. While the context clearly implies that they are American sports stars, the full impact of the presentation is based on the reader's familiarity with the references. Indeed, a reader's understanding might change depending on whether the reference to Mike Tyson evokes the thought of a famous heavyweight boxer or of a notorious date-rapist.

Associations

The Gettysburg Address example highlights an additional aspect of references. A reference is often made to evoke the **associations** connected to it; that is, a writer raises one idea to remind us of another. Whereas references direct a reader's attention to a specific item, associations draw forth an image or idea from the reader in a more indirect way. If, for example, we say we are going to the Big Apple, we are making a direct reference to New York City. What one feels about New York City does not affect the reference. But if we say that a city has the civility of the Big Apple, we draw on the reader/listener's knowledge and feelings about New York City to make our point. Or consider a reference to Michael Jordan simply as a member of the 1993 championship Chicago Bulls basketball team:

> Michael was instrumental in the Bulls' winning their third championship in a row in 1993.

On another occasion, we might refer to Michael Jordan to evoke an association in the reader's mind of Jordan's grace in flight:

> Jeffrey jumped like Michael Jordan.

---

*In fact, Lincoln assumed that his audience knew that a score was equal to 20, that they could multiply and add "four score [4 times 20] and seven" and subtract (1863, the present year, minus 87 equals 1776), that they would recognize 1776 as the year of the Declaration of Independence, and, hence, that they would infer that he was talking about forefathers, not biological fathers.

References are generally neutral; associations commonly have emotional value attached. The following comments appeared in Richard Corliss's review of the movie *Star Trek IV: The Voyage Home:*

> Trekkies are the Moonies of pop culture. . . . To Trekkies it matters not that . . . [the film's] actors, outfitted in futuristic Dr. Dentons, read their portentous lines with nitwit solemnity.[7]

The mention of Moonies here is an example of association. The reader is expected to know that "Moonies" refers to members of the Unification Church, a religious sect led by the Reverend Sun Myung Moon whose members are often viewed as belonging to a mindless cult. While the term draws on a common cultural association, the meaning of the remark can vary according to one's view of the sect. And the mention of Dr. Dentons is a reference to a particular kind of clothing, a brand of one-piece pajamas; it carries no other associations, other than possibly the suggestion of immaturity, because Dr. Dentons are generally worn by small children.

Writers use associations to tap into latent feelings or ideas within the culture. They might suggest honesty by referring to President Lincoln as "Honest Abe" or deception with a reference to President Nixon as "Tricky Dick." Obviously, without shared knowledge and an ability to infer the proper association on the part of the reader, any intended meaning between writer and reader can never be realized.

Neutral Associations

Not all associations are loaded with emotional meaning. Associations may simply be whatever comes to mind when something is mentioned. For example, when we talk of someone "meeting their Waterloo" to indicate a personal downfall, we are not simply referring to the Belgian town, but also drawing on the knowledge that it was there the French Emperor Napoleon was defeated in 1815. The game of "saying the first thing that comes to mind" in response to a word draws on associations. The more informal the discussion, the greater the reliance on references and associations. In the interest of clarity, textbooks generally avoid references or associations unless they have already established the expected connections.

Cultural Understanding

References and associations function within specific cultural contexts. When we seek meaning from a group of words, we in effect "read" both the text and the world. And when readers do not share the same culture, confusion can result. For instance, a reference to the Little Bighorn River in Northern Wyoming, where Custer and his troops were massacred by Sioux and Cheyenne warriors at the Battle of Little Bighorn in 1876, obviously carries different associations for the

Army than for Native Americans. Many cultural associations draw on Greek and Roman mythology, the Bible, or contemporary political or cultural events.

•••••••••••••••• CULTURAL KNOWLEDGE ••••••••••••••••

1. Who is "Bird"?
2. Who is Larry Bird?
3. Who is Admiral Byrd?
4. What bird appears in the title of a ballet by Stravinsky?
5. What bird appears in a poem by Edgar Allen Poe?
6. What is "giving someone the bird"?
7. Name a giant yellow bird on television.

Which cultural or sociological groups are most likely to know the answer to each question?

••

Personal Associations

Ideally, two readers with the same cultural background will have similar associations, but in reality this is not always the case. While we may share cultural values, we remain individuals. Invariably, readers bring personal associations to bear on their understanding.

Personal associations generally are closely linked to prior experience, drawing on either active memory or the subconcious. All people have personal associations with, for example, thunder, the circus, or the smell of cinnamon. Whether positive or negative, personal associations can manifest themselves in our assumptions. If, for instance, we have had bad experiences after buying used cars, we might associate used cars with lemons and assume that only new cars are reliable.

Some personal associations were suggested in the sample interpretation of the passage on armed-forces recruiting:

> **Armed-forces** *images of the army, war* . . . **recruiters** *who try to grab youth . . . patriotism . . . "Be the best you can be"* . . . *glory* . . . **The city of Los Angeles** *oh . . . kooky California!*

Here, among other things, the reader associated Los Angeles with California and then reacted to that latter reference. Likewise, the reference to chess in the sample text on American sports fans might evoke associations of a slow, dull game or a fascinating, thought-provoking battle of wits depending on the reader's personal prior experiences.

Figurative Language

Some forms of association are sufficiently common that they have been classified as special forms of expression. For example, when we refer to someone having "a heart as big as Texas," we mean someone who is charitable, not someone who has

---

• COMMON FIGURES OF SPEECH •

metaphor: indirectly equating or comparing one thing with another that resembles it in some way:

> *She is a flower.*

simile: directly equating or comparing unlike objects by the use of *like* or *as:*

> *She is like a flower.*

personification: using a simile or metaphor to assign human qualities to an inanimate object or idea:

> *The pond beckoned the swimmers.*

synecdoche: naming a part to represent the whole or the whole to represent a part:

> *He bought a new set of wheels.*

simple imagery: creating a "word picture" to invoke a visual image:

> *They leap-frogged their way to fame.*

overstatement: exaggerating for emphasis:

> *The line reached to China.*

understatement: downplaying for emphasis:

> *Fixing the pipe should take only a second or two.*

---

an interior organ 275,415 square miles in size! Such expressions are referred to as **figurative language** or **figures of speech**. Figures of speech evoke an idea or suggest an image; they represent colorful ways of appealing to the imagination to convey meaning.

The following sentences suggest the wide range of possible figures of speech:

The course was a bear.

My brother sleeps like a bear in winter.

The coffeepot quietly burped that it was done.

The plane received confirmation from the tower.

The pilot had always wanted to own his own wings.

The Army's job is to prevent the flag from being bloodied.

Her image swam in his head.

I'd climb the highest mountain for you, swim the deepest sea.

None of these statements is to be taken literally. Rather, they all suggest ideas that go beyond the words themselves. In each case one image is substituted for another, on the assumption that readers will infer the intended meaning. In the same way, the sample text on sports assumes that the reader will recognize that "tons more is reported about Bo Jackson than Garri Kasparov" simply suggests a larger amount, not necessarily a comparison based on the actual weight of the reports.

Many fancy-sounding figures of speech are used in everyday conversation as a natural part of the language. Knowing the names of the different figures of speech is not as important as being sensitive to their existence. To recognize and understand figures of speech, readers must pay attention to the ideas being discussed, not just the words that are stated. Put simply, they must read with a little imagination!

IMPLICATIONS

Language is hardly the clear and simple tool we might otherwise have thought. Reading is an active, thinking process in which readers constantly draw on their prior knowledge and experience to infer meaning. The more readers bring to a text, the greater the likelihood they will be sensitive to references and associations. And, as noted in the previous chapter, readers must "read" ideas as well as words to make sense of the text.

EXERCISES/DISCUSSION

A. Inferring Missing Elements

Missing elements are often inferred from an existing pattern or sequence. Fill in the blanks.

1. 2, 4, 8, _____, 32
2. the b_____rd of education
3. You have the _____ to remain silent, . . .
4. square, circle, pentagon, _____
5. Box is to ring as _____ is to mat.

B. Inferring Explanations

Much inference involves asserting explanations for actions or events. What reasons might be offered to explain the following?

1. As you are driving, you see a police car with flashing lights directly behind you.
2. A winning candidate receives less than 50 percent of the total vote.
3. A movie gets good reviews but few people go to see it.

C. Inference: Cause and Effect

Much inference is based on the notion of cause and effect: From evidence of an effect, we infer a cause. What causes might be suggested for the following?

1. A lamp will not light.
2. All of the people with a certain disease know one another.
3. Certain states have a significantly higher death rate than others.

D. Inference: Assumptions

In everyday discussion we often do not spell out all of the reasoning underlying remarks. We assume information or ideas and leave our reader/listener to infer it.

example: It's going to rain. Take an umbrella.
assumption: You don't want to get wet and an umbrella will protect you from the rain.

Indicate the unstated assumption(s) underlying the following statements:

1. The president has proposed higher taxes. I think a fairer method of raising money must be found.
2. Whenever Stanley plays quarterback, the team loses. We need a new quarterback.
3. If you want to know what's going on in Washington, ask your senator or representative.

E. Multiple Meanings 1

Distinguish between the meanings of the term *fix* in each of the following.

1. fix a race
2. fix a car
3. fix a meal
4. fix a dye
5. fix a cat
6. fix a course
7. fix one's eyes on
8. get a fix
9. get out of a fix
10. get a fix on

F. Multiple Meanings 2

Distinguish between the meanings of *in* in the following sentence:

A man in a hurry took a package in brown paper from a woman in a doorway to give to a man in an overcoat.

G. Inferring Meaning

For each of the following excerpts, define the boldfaced words from the surrounding context. Use your knowledge of roots, prefixes, and suffixes to aid your decisions.

1. The **egalitarian** approach has brought many nontraditional and new students to America's college campuses. Cross (1980) defines *new students* as those who need help with basic skills, motivation, and guidance about how to make it in the educational system. They may be white or black, rich or poor, but they share the common experience of poor performance in school, and without special admissions programs they would not generally be considered college material.[8]

2. With the invention of plows and effective animal harnesses, agricultural productivity became so great that some people were freed from farming. At that point **agrarian societies** appeared, some of which became great empires and perhaps the first real human civilizations.[9]

3. There was a time when there were legal limits to this. Sort of. The National Bureau of Standards developed sizing standards for clothing in the early 1940s. They were voluntary, but virtually all manufacturers **hewed** to them. [Texts for Analysis 13]

4. They raise a serious issue. The use of a single word to name a group including people as disparate as Mexicans and Cubans **conflates** the cultures. And whatever conflates cultures destroys them. Nevertheless, there will have to be a name, for political power in a democratic society requires numbers, and only by **agglomeration** does the group become large enough to have an important voice in national politics. Agreement on one encompassing name is therefore vital. And possible, for any set that can be defined can be named. Which brings up another problem. [Texts for Analysis 10]

H. References and/or Associations

Explain any references, associations, or figures of speech in the following excerpts.

1. Believing what you read about preventive medicine in popular women's magazines can be hazardous to your health. [Texts for Analysis 14]

2. "It was before Spike, Mike and Bo, when a sports contract was worth more than a sneaker contract."[10]

3. Hank Williams, who was to country music what Elvis Presley was to rock and roll, died forty years ago—on New Year's Day, 1953, in the back seat of his baby-blue Cadillac, on the way to a concert in Canton, Ohio.[11]

4. Remember when only the Shadow knew? If you don't, you're not alone. Sometime between Looney Tunes and Nintendo, kids under 12 stopped listening to radio.[12]

5. For two hours in late January, the brass hats of the Pentagon cloistered themselves with President Clinton to try to explain to him why lifting the ban on alternative lifestyles in the military is not a terribly swift idea. Since the closest Clinton

has even come to people in uniform is quipping with the burger jockeys at McDonald's, the brass took on no enviable mission. [Texts for Analysis 3B]

I. Figurative Language

For each excerpt indicate the figure(s) of speech and its meaning.

1. Other publications raise red flags about salt; . . . [Texts for Analysis 14]

2. Clearly cigarette advertising revenue places a chill on free discussion of the dangers of smoking, . . . [Texts for Analysis 14]

3. . . . trade publishing has been the flagship institution, the one that carries the cargo of our heritage along the routes of the present to the ports of the future.[13]

4. Five score years ago, a great American, in whose symbolic shadow we stand today, signed the Emancipation Proclamation. This momentous decree came as a great beacon of light of hope to millions of Negro slaves who had been seared in the flames of withering injustice. It came as a joyous daybreak to end the long night of their captivity.

   But one hundred years later, the Negro still is not free. One hundred years later, the life of the Negro is still sadly crippled by the manacles of segregation and the chains of discrimination. One hundreds years later, the Negro lives on a lonely island of poverty in the midst of a vast ocean of material prosperity. . . .[14]

5. The fall of one after another corporate chief—Robert C. Stempel at General Motors, John F. Akers at I.B.M. and, a week ago, James D. Robinson 3d at American Express—has prompted many writers to muster a royal procession of metaphors. These men were monarchs or kings, we are told, holding sway over vast domains at imperial salaries until they were beheaded or toppled by coups.[15]

6. The physical condition of American cities and the absence of meaning in more and more lives come together at the barrel of a gun. If you were to select one thing that has changed most in cities since the 1960s, it would be fear. Fear covers the street like a sheet of ice. . . . For African-Americans in cities, violence isn't new. Mothers have sent their children to school through war zones for too many years. What is new is the fear among whites of random violence. No place in the city seems safe. Walking the streets seems to be a form of Russian roulette.[16]

7. Ants are so much like human beings as to be an embarrassment. They farm fungi, raise aphids as livestock, launch armies into wars, use chemical sprays to alarm and confuse enemies, capture slaves. The families of weaver ants engage in child labor, holding their larvae like shuttles to spin out the thread that sews the leaves together for their fungus gardens. They exchange information ceaselessly. They do everything but watch television.[17]

"I Know What It Says . . . But What Does It Mean?"— Inferring Meaning

. . . the reading material supplied by the author is like a blueprint for a building, and each reader constructs from the blueprint a structure that is, in its details, uniquely his own.

• Neil Postman and Charles Weingartner
LINGUISTICS: A REVOLUTION IN TEACHING[1] •

Readers construct meaning from evidence within a text. They test their understanding by imagining an author, audience, purpose, and context consistent with that interpretation.

We find meaning in works of art, music, and dance. We find meaning in the falling of the first leaf of fall and in a baby's smile. We find meaning in other people's behavior. From their gestures and actions, we infer motives and personality.

INFERRING MEANING

The process of inferring an underlying meaning is **interpretation**. Even though interpretation is a natural process, the interpretation of texts is often troublesome. Paintings, movies, and hand signals clearly convey meaning, but they do not state what they mean. Rather, we assign meaning to them. By contrast, language actually says something, but, paradoxically, the words themselves can hinder our interpretation of texts.

Readers are often reluctant to accept responsibility for inferring a meaning. They take a docile stand, trying to determine the writer's thoughts without imposing their own, hanging on to the statements of a text rather than evaluating the flow of ideas. They preface remarks with "I think," hesitant to assert their understanding as legitimate and defensible. (The problem is not as acute with fiction. We expect a fairy tale or short story to have an unstated moral.)

For some readers, the notion of interpreting a text takes on almost mystic qualities. For them, interpretation suggests somehow "reading between the lines," but that image implies seeing something that is *not* there rather than concentrating on what *is*. For others, interpretation involves "psyching out" the author, or what the author intended to convey. Here again, the focus is on something that is not

---

• THE ASSUMPTION OF MEANING •

Rightly or wrongly, we assume that any remark in print must have meaning—if only we can extract it. Consider these two sentences:

> The man ran in fog.
>
> Fog ran in the man.

Both make *grammatical* sense, but only the first one makes *common* sense. Still, we try to find meaning in the second sentence as well—possibly as a poetic description of mental confusion or physical disorientation.

there rather than on what is. We cannot literally read "between the lines." We need evidence. But we can reason about what a text does say, and in so doing find a deeper or "hidden" meaning. This chapter explores some general concerns. The notion of inference equations is developed in Chapter 8 as a format for interpreting a text as a whole.

EXAMPLE: **"Rules Are Made to Be Broken"**

There is a saying,

> Rules are made to be broken.

This sentence seems to make sense—it implies that it is all right to break rules. On reflection, however, the meaning seems a bit strange. Why make rules only to have them broken? What does this imply about the nature of rules? For that matter, what is meant by "rules"?

To answer these questions—to make better sense of the statement—we need to examine it one part at a time. Does the statement refer to all rules or just some rules? Note that it says "rules," not "some rules." Since it does not specify exceptions, we must, at least for the moment, assume it means all rules.

The statement says rules are "made" to be broken. From this, we can infer that we are not dealing with permission for criminals to break laws. Laws are, by definition, meant to be upheld, not broken. If laws were meant to be broken, there would be no such thing as criminals.

What kinds of rules might the statement be addressing? We have decided that it probably does not mean laws. What about rules of conduct or social norms? We would then have something like this:

> Social norms were meant to be broken.

The meaning of the statement is still not clear. When? Under what circumstances? How can rules be rules and people still be allowed, or even expected, to break them?

We might infer that, in certain conditions or situations, breaking rules is somehow permissible. According to this interpretation, no rule is absolute:

> All rules have exceptions.

This interpretation not only makes sense but seems to be consistent with the original statement.

A Diversity of Meanings

Once we recognize that understanding is influenced by prior knowledge, we must accept that people can draw different inferences from the same references and information. A text may, for different readers, have a diversity of meanings.

• INFERENCE AND AMBIGUITY •

There is a great deal of difference in believing something still, and believing it again.

• W. H. Auden •

Here, we are asked to understand and appreciate a difference between "believing something still" and "believing something again."

What do these two concepts refer to? Belief in "something still" might depend on deep conviction, unreflective belief, or lack of challenge. Belief "again" might depend on renewed conviction, proof by new evidence or reexamination, or simply recollection of an old idea. The text doesn't say so; we infer this.

What might the statement mean by posing such a difference? Does it suggest that one is preferable to the other? Some readers might interpret it to mean that ideas that have been reexamined are better than those that have not—that knowing why you believe something is important. Others might interpret it to mean that something that has withstood all challenges, thereby allowing continued belief, is preferable to something that one has, at some time, stopped believing. The two inferences are equally legitimate. Without further analysis or evidence, the aphorism appears meaningful but ambiguous—which is a reminder to us all as writers to spell out our meaning as completely and clearly as possible.

Our prior knowledge and experience can shape how we perceive a reference—or even determine whether we catch it at all. One's background can influence which elements one takes as significant and which are lost within the text. It can affect what one is looking for from the reading experience, whether entertainment or in-depth analysis. And background can shape the values with which one responds to the ideas within a text.

Other readers, for example, might propose other interpretations of the aphorism "Rules are made to be broken." One reader might see it as a call to live adventurously, to not be bound by traditions and social norms. Another might see it as a warning to not let other people control one's own life. Indeed, no evidence within the statement specifically prohibits these interpretations. (In most situations, the context would provide additional clues or information that might rule out some interpretations.) None of these views reflects any misreading nor stems from errors in understanding the grammar or vocabulary. Just as different psychiatrists will attach different significance to a dream, individual readers come away with unique interpretations.

Even readers with the same background may consciously approach a text in different ways. For instance, the Gettysburg Address can be read as a historical document, as an example of oratory excellence, or for the message it conveys about Americans and their image of America. Each perspective might stress different elements or place emphasis on different terms.

What analytic perspective is appropriate for any given text? It depends on both the reader and the setting. In a class on women's studies, a feminist reading of a text might be the most appropriate. In daily life, one reads according to one's personal needs and desires. The key element is self-awareness—the reader must be aware of any emphasis or bias he or she brings to the reading process so as not to overlook any major elements within the text.

Extending the Meaning

As noted previously, interpretation is the process of inferring an unstated or underlying meaning. Readers frequently infer meanings that are broader in scope than the text itself, meanings that are more abstract and far-reaching in their implications. If, for example, a text argues that the president's education policy for the elementary schools needs revising, some readers might accept the text to mean simply that. However, other readers will see it as a statement that the president is ineffective or that the U.S. educational system is in need of major repair. Such extensions of the meaning are often justified on the grounds that "this is what the text is really getting at."

In some cases, texts will specifically limit the scope of their remarks to prevent unwarranted inferences. Careful writers will spell out exactly what they do not mean—and say that they do not mean it! Thus, they limit the degree to which a reader can extend or restrict their argument. When no specific limitations are indicated by the text, readers are free to extend that meaning to all cases they see as similar.

EXAMPLE: "A Graduation Gift from Uncle Sam"

Let's return once again to the sample passage on army recruiting in Los Angeles high schools—specifically, this sentence:

> Last year [the school board] made $8,081 from the list, which school officials say was used to cover clerical costs.

Within the broader context, readers must decide whether the final clause ("which school officials say was used to cover clerical costs") serves to:

- Belittle the amount—it was really nothing
- Imply that the excuse offered by the officials is false—they only "say" it
- Provide additional information in passing

In the absence of further evidence within the text, one's interpretation might be determined solely by one's feelings about school officials. Someone who has experienced the repression of a military government might respond differently than someone raised in a democracy where civilians controlled the army. These differences would be translated into assumptions about the motives of each party and the ethics of their actions.

For some readers, the article is about a specific incident in Los Angeles. For others, Los Angeles is only an example; the article is really about military involvement with the schools on a national basis. These readers might be glad that the selling of names has stopped because they have a friend at the school and do not want to see him or her enlist. Or they might interpret the text as presenting an important victory for student rights. Other readers might view the text as a documentation of diminished respect for the armed forces. The parents who complained might see the article as a public announcement of their victory. Some board members might interpret the article as an exposé of their lack of independence. Finally, certain readers might think that the article claims that recruiters will be denied all access to the schools.

Two elements should be emphasized here. First, attentive readers seek evidence within the text on which to base an inference. This is accomplished by analysis of the text. Second, while bound by the evidence within the text, readers draw on their own imagination, resourcefulness, reasoning, and background to construct an interpretation.

As the preceding discussion suggests, while constrained by the evidence, each reader is author of his or her own interpretation. Section 2 provides a full description of the techniques and strategies of such analysis. The remainder of this chapter discusses other frameworks readers use to aid their investigation and understanding.

• **THE READER AS AUTHOR OF AN UNDERSTANDING** •

In the process of reading, readers become the author of their understanding of a text. Their understanding is their own creation, based on the evidence they find, the knowledge they bring to their reading, and the inferences they draw.

EXAMPLE: **American Sports and the Media**

What, then, is the sample paragraph in the previous chapter about? Is the ultimate meaning about sports in America (Americans prefer physical sports over intellectual games) or about the media (the press gives readers what they want). Or is the paragraph really about the media's influence on society—that the media plays to the lowest common denominator of American interests? Does the paragraph judge Americans? Answers to these questions depend on the reader's ability to find evidence within the text and to go beyond the specific wording to recognize broader themes.

MESSAGE, AUTHOR, AUDIENCE, PURPOSE, AND CONTEXT

Language as Social Communication

Computers can write grammatically correct sentences. More accurately, however, computers "generate" sentences—statements that, in and of themselves, have no purpose. Language is a social phenomenon involving five key elements: (1) the exchange of ideas (2) by someone (3) to someone (4) for some reason (5) in some situation:

(1)	Idea	(message)
(2)	By someone	(writer)
(3)	To someone	(audience)
(4)	For some reason	(purpose, motive)
(5)	In some situation	(context)

We must also distinguish between the *message* "sent" by the author and the *meaning* "received" by the reader, since they are not always the same.

All five elements of this communication exchange are closely related. For example, for each author, we imagine a suitable audience and purpose. And in each case, our understanding of the message reflects a social context.

Constructing Images to Form an Understanding

Understanding author, audience, purpose, and context are essential to deriving meaning from any communication. The problem is that, when reading a text, we have no direct knowledge of any of these elements, and no sure way of finding them out. Nevertheless, readers assume that authors knew what they were doing and that they achieved whatever purpose they had in mind. To find meaning in a text, then, readers construct images of the author, audience, purpose, and context. To a great extent, understanding is closely tied to an ability to construct a set of consistent images.

The Author—Real versus Imagined

Words do not just appear on the page. Someone put them there. We may or may not know the identity of the author, and knowledge about the author may suggest how that person *might* think. However, if we do our job as readers well, any such knowledge can only suggest clues as we search for evidence within a text.

Other than when we talk about the real-life person, any notion of the "author" is a construct on which we base explantions for what we have found in a text. To claim, for example, that the author of a text is a socialist is simply another way of saying that we find evidence of socialist thinking in the text. To explain that evidence, we imagine a person with those beliefs as author of the text. The danger is that, knowing the identity and beliefs of an author, we might impose those beliefs on the text without proper evidence. Just because an author has a reputation for racist remarks does not mean that the text before us has racist overtones. We must allow a previously racist person the opportunity to write an antiracist text, and vice versa.

In some cases, we are particularly concerned about the identity of the author. Indeed, the identity of the author can have a profound impact on the meaning or impact of a statement. A leading public figure expressed concern for black-on-black violence in America: "There is nothing more painful to me at this stage in my life than to walk down the street and hear footsteps and start thinking about robbery—then look around and see somebody white and feel relieved."[2] The impact of the statement arises from the fact that the speaker was black civil rights leader Jesse Jackson.

When we read personal mail or a political figure's policy statements, we read to learn the thoughts and feelings of the real-life author. In most circumstances, however, whether reading editorials, textbooks, or magazine articles, our concern is with understanding the article itself, rather than with speculating about the author. It's the content, not the creator, that's important. A good idea from a usually unreliable or unknown source is still a good idea!

· **AUTHOR** ·

Who might be the author of the following excerpt? Indicate the evidence for your inferences.

Resolved, that the speedy success of our cause depends upon the zealous and untiring efforts of both men and women, for the overthrow of the monopoly of the pulpit, and for the securing to women an equal participation with men in the various trades, professions, and commerce.[3]

· ·

Along with the notion of an author is the notion of the **tone** of a text. As the written equivalent of the intonation of a speaker's voice, tone refers less to the nature of the actual terms than to their cumulative effect on the reader. Thus, tone reflects the reader's emotional response to language usage. Tone indicates the feelings we sense from the choice of words. Tone describes an attitude or emotional state that can suggest seriousness or silliness, sincerity or condemnation.

Audience

Authors do not shout ideas from the rooftops, nor do they write in a vacuum. Communication is directed to a specific audience, whether a particular individual or a broad section of humanity. To convey ideas successfully, an author must

---

• WHAT DID THE AUTHOR MEAN BY THAT? •

Have you ever asked yourself this question:

> What did the author mean by that?

Ultimately you are *not* concerned with the author, but with the meaning. You are asking how a statement might make sense within the text—allowing that readers bring to bear all they know of the topic and the author in their effort to make sense of the remarks.

---

tailor a presentation to the intended audience. The text must reflect the audience's knowledge and the forms of persuasion that might move them.

Since the audience is an important participant in any communication, we try to make sense of a message by fitting it to an audience. Who might the following remarks be intended for?

> O.K., everyone take five!
>
> When the tax bill comes up in the House, it is imperative that it be defeated.
>
> Everybody has a right to happiness.

We might imagine the first example addressed to dancers or musicians in a rehearsal, the second directed to anyone who can influence the outcome of a particular tax bill (or who would be affected by it), and the third, near as we can tell, aimed at the world in general. Our decision is based on the terminology, information, or apparent message—but we still *imagine* the audience. We infer it from evidence within the text.

If we want to argue that a text is addressed to a particular audience, we must find evidence for that claim. Whether that is in fact the author's intended audience, only the author can know. As readers, we are less concerned with who in fact the author envisioned as the audience than with to whom the essay appears to be addressed on the basis of evidence within that text. As with the author, the notion of an audience is a construct readers employ in their effort to make sense of a text.

Readers often infer the intended audience of a text from evidence of where, or by whom, the text was published. Publication information can aid speculation about the author's desired audience for the text, but we must be careful not to infer too much from this information. Once again, we must seek corroborating evidence within the text itself. Just because a text appears in a feminist magazine does not necessarily mean that it expresses a feminist viewpoint. We must make allowance for both the essay and the magazine to express divergent views. Whatever our final decision, imagining the text addressed to a certain audience is an important part of an active, reflective problem-solving approach to reading.

Who might be the real-life intended audience for the following excerpt? Indicate the evidence for your inferences.

> In its simplest terms the animal rights position I uphold maintains that such diverse practices as the use of animals in science, sport and recreational hunting, the trapping of fur bearing animals for vanity products, and commercial animal agriculture are categorically wrong—wrong because these practices systematically violate the rights of the animals involved.[4]

· ·

Purpose, Motive, and Intended Meaning

Why does someone write a particular text? What might an author hope to convey? **Purpose** refers to what one hopes to achieve by doing something. **Motive** refers to what one hopes to gain.

All authors have a purpose for writing. It might be to inform, to persuade, to entertain; it might be to move the reader to take a certain action or to adopt a certain outlook. And all authors have motives. It might be to achieve fame and fortune, to win a promotion, or to share knowledge with others—or a combination of these.

Concern with purpose and motive are closely tied to the issue of intended meaning. If the author has done a good job, the intended meaning of the text should reflect the underlying purpose or motive for writing that text. Sometimes the author's purpose and audience are obvious, as with a love letter (amorous intent) or an argument for a raise (a desire for recognition and financial gain). But most writing is for a far more general audience, whether the public, a portion of the academic community, or some other group.

As with author and audience, the concepts of purpose and motive are, in practice, devices for explaining observations about material within the text. By imagining possible purposes or motives we attempt to explain the meaning of the text. Attributing intent is akin to saying that the remarks make sense to us, that we can imagine why someone might say something like that and what they might mean by it. We speculate on an author's purpose as a way of discovering potential meanings. We feel we have made sense of a comment when we can see how it is consistent with a reasonable motive or purpose.

In the article on army recruiters that appeared in the Introduction, we might initially assume that the purpose of the text is to inform the reader of events in Los Angeles high schools. As we read, we might wonder whether the text is attempting to convince us of the rightness of one side or another. If we infer that the purpose of the text is to make the parents' protest look silly, we might interpret the use of the military terms as satirizing these parents. Alternatively, we might infer that the purpose is to expose perceived army interference in public education. From this perspective, the donations to the schools would be seen as a payoff.

Ultimately, we can never truly know the author's real intentions. We thus speak of the text, and not of the author, attempting to make a case, for any justification will have to be found within the text itself. In much the same way, by convention texts are spoken of in the present tense: a text *argues* as opposed to *argued*.

• **PURPOSE** •

What might be the purpose of the following excerpt? Indicate the evidence for your inferences.

> The drug war can be beaten and the public health of the US can be improved if we are willing to substitute common sense for rhetoric, myth and blind persistence, and to put the war in the hands of the Surgeon General, not the Attorney General.[5]

• •

Context

In most cases, we read a text as though it had been written yesterday by someone who shares our understanding of the language and the world. In many cases, however, texts contain information or language that has changed over the years and rely on terms and ideas that evoke different meanings or associations from different audiences. A final factor in the interpretive process, then, is the notion of context. Previously, the notion of context was used in the sense of the surrounding text. Here, **context** refers not to physical location so much as to the historical, cultural, social, and/or philosophical framework of a text—the situation and setting inherent in the discussion.

An editorial proclaiming a candidate unelectable, for instance, can, after the election, seem particularly insightful or utterly out of touch with political reality depending on the results of the election. While we may praise or condemn the insightfulness of the editorial from a historical standpoint, our analysis of the text must be based not on hindsight, but on how the text summons its arguments on the basis of the facts as they were known at the time. In a similar vein, we must read particularly old documents with an understanding of the meaning words had

---

• **CONTEXT AND MEANING** •

In 1939, Dalton Trumbo wrote *Johnny Got His Gun*, a novel in which a soldier who had lost all of his limbs reflects on his life. Twenty years later, in a new Introduction, the author noted:

> *Johnny* held a different meaning for three different wars. Its present meaning is what each reader conceives it to be, and each reader is gloriously different from every other reader, and each is also changing.[6]

---

at the time. Obviously, when a Shakespearean play refers to someone as "gay," we cannot infer that he or she was a homosexual! We must be sensitive to standards of word usage at any given time and in any given setting—as with the choice of the term *colored*, *Negro*, *black*, or *Afro-American*—and not impose our own values on the text.

While it is important to understand a text within its own context, quite often we have only the text before us, and must simply read it within our own immediate context. Either way, all reading is done within *some* context, and all understanding reflects certain knowledge and concerns.

· **CONTEXT** ·

In what context might the following excerpt appear? Indicate the evidence for your inferences.

> In Mississippi and Washington the few make the decisions for the many. Mississippi Negroes are denied the vote; the voice of the thirty per cent of Americans now opposed to the undeclared war in Vietnam is not heeded and all Americans are denied access to facts concerning the true military and political situation. We must make it plain to the Administration that we will not be accomplices to a war that we did not declare.[7]

· ·

Putting the Elements of Communication Together

The elements of human communication discussed here—author, audience, purpose, motive, and context—are tools for interpretation. If reading is, as the Argentinean poet Jorge Luis Borges has suggested, "thinking with the mind of a stranger," we test our understanding by assuring ourselves that the text makes sense as an act of human communication on the part of the author.

To isolate the elements of communication, a reader might ask questions like these:

- • What might the author have meant by this?
- • Who might have a stake in the issue or outcome?
- • What special knowledge or background is assumed?
- • Who might be moved by such an appeal or presentation?
- • Where was the text published, and who reads such publications?
- • Under what circumstances might the discussion make sense?
- • What common perspectives influence people's thoughts about the topic?

While speculative, such questions help us assess what we have found and suggest elements we might look for to evaluate a particular interpretation.

"CORRECT" INTERPRETATIONS

Reading is based on the assumption that reasonably clear communication is possible if both the author and the reader do their jobs well. Given a text of reasonable difficulty, readers with similar ability and background will, for the most part, agree on what it says. Without such an assumption, both writer and reader would be wasting their time.

Only the author can know whether the reader's understanding meshes with the author's intentions. An author might intend to convey one meaning but provide evidence of another. Or a reader may not properly examine all of the evidence or make sloppy inferences and miss an otherwise obvious meaning. Readers may even discover meanings that the author never intended to convey but that truly reflect the author's unconscious thoughts or biases.

The Assumption of Competency

The analysis of texts proceeds on the assumption that each text is complete and consistent. Nothing has been left out, and nothing has been included without purpose. Every word, phrase, reference, and association matters.

This is, it should be stressed, only an assumption. Writers are not infallible. Like anyone else, they make mistakes, become confused, or get sloppy. But the assumption of the author's competence is essential to the reading process. Otherwise, readers would be free to challenge and change anything that did not initially make sense to them. We cannot simply assume a text is contradictory and reject certain remarks. We must try to understand everything in the text just as it is presented within that text. Interpretation has as its goal demonstrating the competency of the text.

Evaluating Interpretations

The goal of interpretation is not some mythical "correct" interpretation. Different readers, as we have seen, might interpret a text differently. We cannot, however, allow just any reading. Some standards apply. Above all, we require a careful,

---

• CRITERIA OF A GOOD INTERPRETATION: THE TWO C'S •

- Is your analysis *complete?* That is, have you covered all aspects of the text?
- Is your analysis *consistent?* That is, have you found consistency within the text?

---

thoughtful examination of the text, a reading that is as *complete* and *consistent* with the evidence as possible. One interpretation may be better than another not because it is "right," but because it is more consistent in its handling of the material within the text, because it brings a broader awareness to bear in drawing inferences from the text, or because it examines more possibilities.

Misreading

This chapter would not be complete if we did not also mention ways in which we *misread* a text. We can be distracted by noise, conflicting thoughts, bad lighting, or time constraints. We can allow our fixation on certain ideas to blind us to what is actually there. We can simply read sloppily and lazily. We can limit our search and understanding to a single main idea, thereby prohibiting any understanding of the nuances or complexity of a text. We can overlook the existence of exceptions, or otherwise take literally what is intended metaphorically.

Once the mechanics of analyzing sentences are taken care of, much of critical reading comes down to careful thinking. We can misread in all of the ways in which we misthink. We can be swayed by appeals to emotion, fear, or authority. We can refuse to accept ideas that conflict with our preconceived notions, or simply skip over material that is at first too challenging.

IMPLICATIONS

Reading is, as the section title indicates, an active, reflective, problem-solving activity in which readers invest texts with meaning by drawing inferences. Such interpretations are influenced not only by what readers believe might make sense—reading ideas as well as words—but by their understanding of the interactive nature of communication—how one person might attempt to convey ideas or feelings to another. In the end, a reader's understanding may not necessarily be the same as what the author might have intended, and a single text may be open to a variety of interpretations. Later chapters examine devices by which an author can prevent highly emotional or personal responses and techniques by which the reader can assure the greatest possible objectivity in drawing inferences.

EXERCISES/DISCUSSION

A. The Intentional Fallacy

Writing about fiction, the critic Northrop Frye argues:

> We have to avoid of course the blunder that is called the intentional fallacy in criticism. The question "What did the author mean by this?" is always illegitimate. First, we can never know; second, there is no reason to suppose that the

author knew; third, the question confuses imaginative with discursive writing. The legitimate form of the question is: "What does the text say?"[8]

In what ways can the quote be said to apply to **non**fictional writing as well?

B. Interpreting Aphorisms

Suggest interpretations of the following aphorisms:

1. The exception proves the rule.
2. The only thing necessary for the triumph of evil is for good men to do nothing. [Edmund Burke]
3. I would rather sit on a pumpkin, and have it all to myself, than to be crowded on a velvet cushion. [Henry David Thoreau]

C. Interpretation: "A Graduation Gift from Uncle Sam"

Responding to the article on army recruiting in the Introduction, different readers might come away with different interpretations:

1. That the army has been caught red-handed at an unethical practice
2. That Los Angeles parents have overreacted to a common practice
3. That the Board of Education keeps changing its mind, and doesn't know what to do
4. That the Los Angeles schools now have to find a way to make up for lost revenue

Are any of these interpretations justified? Give evidence to support your position.

D. Inferring Author, Audience, Purpose, and Context

What author, audience, purpose, and/or context would you associate with each of following excerpts? Indicate the basis for your inferences. (You can check your answer to many of the items against the bibliographic information in the Endnotes.)

1. $dx/dy = 2xy$

2. Stillwater Inn Dining Room

   1/2 mi nw on SR49; 1 blk e of jct US 59. 203 E. Broadway. Refined dining in converted home built in 1893. Antique pieces. Limited menu. A/C. Open 6pm–10pm; closed Mon, Tues & 12/25. Reserv advised wkends. MC, VI.[9]

3. Exercise 26: Shoulder Pull Prone. Lie on your stomach, pillow under hips. Pull your shoulder blades together and relax. This exercise can be helpful in combination with the "shrugging."[10]

4. RAIN—To collect rain water with the sail: Release a stay. Bring the sail top to the after part of the mast. Raise it on a slant, with men on each side. Allow the rain to clear away the salt, before you begin collecting water.[11]

5. It is not the purpose of this bibliography to idealize American Indian authors. Books by American Indians can be as slanted, self-serving, inaccurate, or as foolish as books by anyone else. Its purpose is to present American Indians *as they are*, through their writings, for all their human faults and for all their magnificence. Here are American Indians speaking for themselves, unmediated by non-Indians.[12]

6. Disconnect all loudspeaker systems in American schools—or at least reserve them, like the hotline between Moscow and Washington, for only the gravest emergencies.[13]

7. Much of our report is directed to the condition of those Americans who are also Negroes and to the social and economic environment in which they live—many in the black ghettos of our cities. But this nation is confronted with the issue of justice for all its people—white as well as black, rural as well as urban. In particular, we are concerned for those who have continued to keep faith with society in the preservation of public order—the people of Spanish surname, the American Indian and other minority groups to whom this country owes so much.[14]

8. Given any sentence in a natural language represented as a string of discrete entities, say morphemes or words, certainly almost all linguists are agreed that at least part of the structure of such a sentence can be represented in the form of a hierarchical categorization of these discrete elements.[15]

9. The future of the pro-family movement is bright. Exit polls in 1992 found that one out of every four voters was a self-identified evangelical. Their role will increase and their leadership will become more sophisticated and seasoned. But we must stay in this for the long haul, and we must return to our strength of grass roots organization if we hope to truly see "family friendly" public policy in America.[16]

E. Different Author, Different Meaning?

Every year after the Thanksgiving turkey has been devoured, I get frantic requests asking about the legality of giving handguns as Christmas presents. Most folks, after all, are like the rest of us; they don't really get around to shopping until the last minute. So when they run into problems purchasing handguns and transferring registrations, they don't have time to find legal solutions before the big day.

1. Who might you suppose is the author of this excerpt?
2. What difference in intent or purpose might you infer assuming
   a. the author is a comedian
   b. the author owns a gun shop
   c. the author is a police officer
3. Indicate the assumed audience in each of the above cases.

F. Real versus Imagined Authors and Contexts

For which of the Texts for Analysis later in this book do you imagine you would be most concerned with associating the thoughts expressed in the texts with the real-life authors? For which would the context be of particular interest?

G. Texts for Analysis: "One Size Fits, All the Way to Middle Age"

Readers might suggest that "One Size Fits All the Way to Middle Age" [Texts for Analysis 13] is:

1. An attack on the deception of commercial practices
2. A satire on women's vanity
3. A story of human gullibility
4. An example of women's changing self-perception as they age
5. A study in successful market research and marketing
6. An example of sexist behavior on the part of men
7. Evidence of fashion houses playing on women's insecurities

Cite evidence to support or oppose each of these interpretations.

"It's Not So Much What You Say, as How You Say It"— Responding to Texts

. . . a false ideal has taken [hold] of us, [namely], that to read is to say just what is upon the page, instead of to think.

• Edmund Burke Huey
THE PSYCHOLOGY AND PEDAGOGY OF READING[1] •

Texts can be discussed three ways: restatement, description, and interpretation. Each mode serves a different purpose, and each reflects a different understanding and image of the text.

Much of your time in school is spent discussing texts that you have read. In most cases, you are graded not only on how well you have understood the text, but on how well you convey your understanding. Different modes of discussion reflect different forms of understanding. Some may show only that you have understood the words; others reveal an awareness of an overall meaning. Understanding the text is not enough; you must communicate your understanding so that others can be sure of your grasp of the material.

This chapter distinguishes three ways of responding to a text, three ways of discussing what you have read: **restatement**, **description**, and **interpretation**. The immediate goal is not to teach you how to do all three, but simply to assure that you can distinguish between them.

One can, we should note, respond to a text in others ways. Readers can evaluate the truth of the remarks based on their prior knowledge and their faith in different sources. They can revise their prior thinking or relate what they have read to other texts or situations. Or they might simply express their own thoughts and feelings on the same topic as the text. While each of these modes of response is valid and worthwhile, all go beyond an initial understanding of the text and thus are beyond the scope of the current discussion.

THREE MODES OF RESPONDING TO TEXTS

The three modes of responding to texts reflect the previous discussion of analysis and inference. To recap:

- **Sentence analysis** (restatement)—involves grouping words to make sense of a sentence. The goal is to see what each sentence "says." With the sentence "Do not marry him because he's rich," we sought to understand whether it was asserting that we should marry him, and why we should or shouldn't. A reader might demonstrate an understanding of what is said by restating the idea in other words.

- **Paragraph analysis** (description)—involves recognizing how sentences work together to develop a discussion, or what each sentence "does" within the whole. We can now recognize when one sentence is an example of another, when one sentence is a description, another a reason, and so on. Thus, readers can demonstrate an understanding of the roles of the various sentences by describing the structure of the text.

- **Inferring an overall meaning** (interpretation)—involves detecting a meaning beyond what is stated. With the aphorism "Rules are made to be broken," we sought to understand what it meant. Readers demonstrate an understanding by offering an interpretation.

While the three modes of discussion seem to refer to activities on the sentence, paragraph, and text levels, respectively, any portion of text can be discussed at any level. We can restate the thought of a sentence, a paragraph, or a text as a whole; we can interpret the meaning of a sentence, a paragraph, or a text as a whole.

What a Text *Says*, *Does*, and *Means*

The terms describing the different modes of discussion—what a text *says*, *does*, or *means*—are used somewhat poetically, but the meaning should still be clear. By what a sentence "says" we mean the meaning of the original assertion as it would be understood by most native speakers of the language. By what a text "does" we mean how one part functions in relationship to others in the discussion as a whole. And by what a text "means" we are referring to each reader's own unique interpretation, not to some mythical final or "correct" meaning.

• THREE MODES OF DISCUSSION •

Restatement: talking about what a text says is, for the most part, a question of understanding the language. You prove your understanding by restating in your own words what is said about the original topic.

Description: talking about what a text does is a matter of describing the nature of the remarks within it. To do this, you have to describe the text, not talk about the topic.

Interpretation: talking about what a text means is a matter of asserting an overall meaning based on your analysis of the way in which topics are presented within the text.

EXAMPLE: **Philo of Alexandria**

Consider the following passage by Harry Austryn Wolfson describing Philo Judaeus, a Jewish philosopher of Alexandria, Egypt, who lived from the first century B.C. to the first century A.D.:

Philo, professionally, was not a teacher of philosophy. He was a preacher, a preacher on biblical topics who dispensed his philosophic thoughts in the form of sermons. And because he was not professionally a teacher of philosophy, some modern students of his works say that he was not a philosopher.[2]

How might we discuss this passage? Following an initial reading of the passage, we might restate it in this way:

Since Philo was a preacher who expressed philosophic thoughts as sermons, not a teacher of philosophy, some people say he wasn't really a philosopher.

Here, the message conveyed by the original sentence is simply repeated.

Next, we might describe what the passage is saying:

The excerpt discusses what Philo did and the fact that some insist on classifying him on the basis of his actions rather than his thoughts.

This description of the original statement makes no claims as to how to classify Philo—that's the job of the original text. The description has only to state what is going on within the discussion, what the text "does."

Finally, we might interpret the passage's overall meaning based on our prior description of what the text does and says:

By pointing out that some students classify Philo on the basis of his actions rather than his thoughts, the text suggests that Philo has been misclassified.

Here, our concern is with inferring some broader meaning.

• PUTTING IT IN YOUR OWN WORDS •

To select alternative wording for a restatement, you must understand the material you are restating. This responsibility is most critical when the meaning is not immediately clear. Consider this statement:

All men are created equal.

You might restate it in a variety of ways:

Everyone is the same.

All people have the same rights.

No one is born better than another.

The ability to "put something in your own words" is often a significant test of understanding.

Restatement is also an important tool for retaining ideas; by actively forcing yourself to restate ideas you increase your grasp of them.

In some ways, each mode reflects an increasing level of analysis, with each preceding mode supporting the next. Having observed the meaning of a sentence (what it says), one recognizes what role that sentence plays within the discussion (what the text does) and how such remarks might contribute to an overall meaning. The reader infers an interpretation reflecting how and why the text does what it does. In practice, the division into three levels of analysis is not necessarily as clean-cut. With relatively simple texts, we may respond on all three levels simultaneously. With more complicated texts, however, we may proceed in more linear fashion from one level to the next before achieving full understanding.

EXAMPLE: **"Mary Had a Little Lamb"**

While nursery rhymes may appear simple, they generally convey a deeper meaning to the attentive reader. For that reason, they are useful for demonstrating the different modes of reading. For example:

> Mary had a little lamb,
> Its fleece was white as snow,
> And everywhere that Mary went
> The lamb was sure to go.

A typical response to this text might take the following forms:

> A girl named Mary had a little white lamb that followed her everywhere. [**restatement**]
>
> This is a nursery rhyme about a girl named Mary and her lamb. [**description**]
>
> The idea of innocent devotion is presented through the story of an animal's constant companionship with its mistress. [**interpretation**]

Note that while all three statements "talk about" the nursery rhyme, each sentence is actually about something different.

•••••• DISTINGUISHING AMONG THE RESPONSE MODES ••••••

Which response mode is evident in each of the following sentences? (Notice that you do not need the original text to answer.)

1. Birds descended from dinosaurs.
2. Professor Mandrake's article claims that dinosaurs evolved into the birds of today.
3. By discussing a possible relationship between birds and dinosaurs, the article suggests that other animals may have evolved from very different species as well.

• •

RESTATEMENT: WHAT A TEXT SAYS

Restatement provides a useful means of conveying facts that you have read, but things become more complicated when we move from facts to ideas. Presenting someone else's ideas as your own constitutes plagiarism, one of the most serious of academic offenses. Writers must have some means of separating their thoughts from those of their sources, some way to avoid taking credit for someone else's ideas. Some safety from plagiarism is found in the two forms of restatement that mention the original author—direct and indirect quotation—but we still need some other means of discussing works that we have read. In addition, restatement does not provide an opportunity for readers to add their own insights and inferences.

While a decidedly limited mode of response, restatement is nevertheless appropriate in many contexts. In class and on examinations, teachers accept repetition as proof that you have at least read—if not necessarily understood—the text. Where a text defines concepts, states definitions, or explains a theory, you will probably be expected to simply repeat what the text says. Where the text is taken to be authoritative or your repetition clearly is just that, a repetition of someone else's remarks, repetition can be a valid mode of response. This is especially true with science texts, since most authors will agree on the basic information and its analysis.

DESCRIPTION: WHAT A TEXT DOES

The following excerpt appears on the back cover of a travel book, *Walker's Britain*:

> Walking is the very best way to get the very best out of Britain's countryside and here's the book that every walker needs—the complete guide to walking in Britain . . . and it's small enough for almost any anorak pocket.[3]

Most readers will understand this excerpt in two ways. On the one hand, they will understand what the statement asserts about the book, what the statements says—that the book is a convenient and useful tool for enjoying the English countryside on foot. At the same time, readers will recognize it to be an advertising blurb claiming supposed virtues of the book. This latter understanding describes the nature of the remark—what the statement does. The terminology and concepts of the models of sentences discussed in Chapter 1—the role, descriptive, or relationship model—can be used for descriptive purposes.

• FORMS OF RESTATEMENT •

A restatement can take various forms. For example, for the following sentence by the economist Milton Friedman, you have several options.

> Legalizing drugs would simultaneously reduce the amount of crime and raise the quality of law enforcement.[4]

direct repetition: repeating the original, word for word, as your own:

> Legalizing drugs would simultaneously reduce the amount of crime and raise the quality of law enforcement.

paraphrasing: restating the original as your own in different words:

> Making drugs legal would both cut down on crime and improve police efficiency.

condensing: restating the original as your own in shorter form:

> Legalizing drugs would reduce crime and improve policing.

direct quotation: attributing the remarks to the original speaker, exactly as originally stated, within quotations:

> Milton Friedman said that "legalizing drugs would simultaneously reduce the amount of crime and raise the quality of law enforcement."

indirect quotation: restating the remarks and attributing them to the original speaker:

> Milton Friedman claims that making drugs legal would both cut down on crime and improve police efficiency.

In each case the basic thought is repeated. The comments contain no attempt to either describe or interpret the remarks in the original text.

For some, the distinction between restatement and description may be easier to grasp in terms of spoken rather than written remarks. With vociferous salespeople, aggressive pick-up artists, or raving politicians, where the performance is exaggerated or overwhelms the message, we have far less trouble recognizing the performance as well as the meaning—what someone is doing as well as what they say. Readers must learn to recognize that, like speeches, texts can argue, describe, plead, whine, and so on.

By describing the nature of the remarks, you not only show that you have read the text but also demonstrate a further understanding of what is being said. And by discussing how the text works, instead of repeating what it says, you distance yourself from the ideas, thereby protecting yourself from possible plagiarism and avoiding the repetition of ideas with which you might disagree. In general, if you merely repeat the topic of the text, you are restating. If you talk about the text, you are describing it.

INTERPRETATION: WHAT A TEXT MEANS

A description indicates how a text uses evidence and arguments; an interpretation indicates what you make of that evidence and the arguments. You defend your inference of an underlying meaning by offering a description of what the text does as evidence. The remainder of this book examines techniques for pursuing and presenting an interpretation.

• ACHIEVING UNDERSTANDING •

According to an old adage, we achieve an understanding of something when we can explain it to someone else. In reading, we understand a text when we can restate the assertions in our own words, describe the structure of the discussion, and recognize underlying values or perspectives.

IMAGES OF THE TEXT

The three forms of response arise from different ways of approaching a text. With each mode, we expect to find something different within a text. Thus, we can think of each mode as stemming from its own image of a text—what a text is and what one can hope to take from it.

With restatement, the assertions within the text are assumed to be factual and authoritative. Reading, then, involves memorizing the assertions within the text. It is as though the text is an open window on reality through which one can gaze to acquire all relevant knowledge.

With description, the text is seen as constructing a discussion based on certain evidence to reach a particular conclusion. The image here might be one of a photograph conveying a select portion of reality. This view assumes the evidence presented is accurate, but since the text represents only a selection of the available evidence, one is wary of accepting the final conclusions. Rather than simply repeating the assertions as their own, readers describe how the discussion is constructed. Validity can be evaluated later. The task at hand is to see how the presentation is made.

With interpretation, the text is viewed much as someone might think of a painting, as the creation of an individual depicting reality a certain way. The text is seen as a portrayal of the topic, with the various elements of the text contributing to a unified picture. In this view, one can think of the various aspects of a text as conspiring to persuade the reader to think in a certain way. This is not to assume evil intent, distortion, or falsification, but merely to point out that all aspects of the text contribute to shape the reader's perceptions and understanding. Discussion focuses on asserting an overall or underlying meaning to the presentation as a whole and offering support for that interpretation.

• IMAGES OF AND PURPOSES IN READING •

Response Mode	Image of the Text	Purpose in Reading
restatement	undistorted window on reality	to learn facts and authoritative opinion
description	photograph of selected evidence	to discover one of several possible understandings
interpretation	subjective portrayal	to understand one individual's views

---

IMPLICATIONS

The three modes of discussion reflect different images of the text and, with that, different ways of reading texts. Students must be able to distinguish between them not only to decide what it is they wish to acomplish but also to recognize what they have actually done when their work is completed.

The important thing is not to discuss a text one way or another, but to accomplish what you intended. This is easy to verify. Examine the topic of your most general comments. Are you talking about the same topic as the text (restating), the text as a written document (description), or the meaning of the text (interpretation)? Remember, interpretation does not require that all of the sentences address the overall meaning. Other remarks may support those assertions by describing the text.

EXERCISES/DISCUSSION

A. Restatement, Description, Interpretation

Select a nursery rhyme, a short news article, and a song lyric. Give a restatement, description, and interpretation of each.

B. Personal Frameworks for Restatement

While a restatement essentially repeats the original thought, it still reflects your understanding. This can present dangers. Care must be taken not to infer too much from a statement or to shift its emphasis. Care must also be taken to recognize the significance of all portions of a remark, not just some aspects of it.

Imagine that someone concerned with the crops exported by various countries comes across the following sentence:

The bulk of Colombia's exports can be traced to Americans' addiction to caffeine.

They might restate the assertion this way:

Coffee is Colombia's primary export product.

Someone else might approach the sentence with a focus on the significance of coffee in different cultures and restate the assertion differently:

Coffee has significance as a crop for both Colombians and Americans.

And someone else, concerned with Americans' addictions, might restate the remark as follows:

Americans' addiction to coffee is so great that it can support a country's economy.

Which, if any, of these restatements is illegitimate?

C. Appropriate Levels of Response

Indicate the mode of reading and discussion that might be most appropriate for the following:

1. Memorizing facts
2. Uncovering bias
3. Looking up statistics
4. Learning definitions
5. Finding out why someone believes something
6. Understanding what someone believes

CRITICAL READING
OF A TEXT AS A WHOLE

Methods of teaching that stress "the facts," and set up the teacher or textbook as the sole and indisputable authority on the "Truth" of facts, do not prepare the student for life in a world where he must choose in some meaningful way between conflicting bodies of "fact" and conflicting versions of the "Truth" given by different "authorities."

• Neil Postman and Charles Weingartner
LINGUISTICS: A REVOLUTION IN TEACHING[1] •

The Text as Portrayal—
Choices

If it was published in True, *it must be true.*

• Traditional aphorism •

Critical reading begins with the realization that all writing involves choices. Critical reading involves recognizing how those choices shape a text.

THE SUBJECTIVITY OF TEXTS

Over half a century ago, Chinese leader Mao Tsetung took to task those who believed "whatever is written in a book is right. . . . We need books," he argued, "but we must overcome book worship."[2]

Today, many readers still find something almost sacred about the written word. They believe ideas "spelled out in black and white." While they question the spoken remarks of a stranger, they believe similar remarks appearing on the page. Such faith in the written word is often buttressed by the belief that the process of publication filters out inaccurate statements and by the notion that texts are objective. Journalists and academic authors remove their feelings and prejudices from their works, presenting only "the facts of the matter"—or so we've been told.

EXAMPLE: **Earvin "Magic" Johnson**

On November 7, 1991, Earvin "Magic" Johnson retired from professional basketball after having tested positive for HIV, the virus responsible for AIDS. One newspaper reported the event this way:

> INGLEWOOD, Calif.—Earvin "Magic" Johnson, one of the most popular and accomplished players in basketball history, announced Thursday that he has the virus that causes AIDS and is retiring immediately from the Los Angeles Lakers.
>
> "It can happen to anybody—even me, Magic Johnson," Johnson said at a news conference at the Great Western Forum, where he played with the Lakers for 12 seasons.
>
> He said he learned Wednesday that he was infected with human immuno-deficiency virus, which can lead to AIDS, a disease of the immune system for which there is no known cure. . . .[3]

Johnson devoted himself to AIDS education and served on the President's Commission on AIDS. A year later, he returned to basketball to lead the United States "Dream Team" to a gold medal in the Olympics. In the fall of 1992, he rejoined the Los Angeles Lakers, only to retire again.

For different commentators, this last event signified different things. For one observer, Johnson's second retirement focused concern on the team's future:

Lakers Regrouping Again Without Magic

Los Angeles—Even with Magic Johnson in the lineup, this was to be a transitional season for the Los Angeles Lakers. . . .

All of this changed, however, when Johnson announced Monday morning that he was retiring again, 361 days after first ending his playing career because he had tested positive for the virus that causes AIDS. Several controversies surrounding his comeback were cited as reasons why Johnson again stepped aside.

And now, for the second straight year, the Lakers are in an early season state of shock. Suddenly the transition looks a lot more difficult.[4]

Others viewed Johnson's retirement in terms of the AIDS crisis:

It is a situation that has baffled and horrified AIDS health-care providers for years: Blacks are among the fastest-growing number of reported AIDS cases locally and nationally, yet they lag far behind in their response to the epidemic.

Now Magic Johnson has the AIDS virus.

Many AIDS activists and health-care workers are hoping that Johnson's fame and outspoken admission about his condition brings the same awareness to minority communities that [white actor] Rock Hudson's death in 1985 from the virus brought to many whites and others.[5]

One writer saw the event as a human drama:

For the past month, what had once been a wonderful tale showed all the signs of going sour. All through his Olympic summer, Johnson had been hailed as some kind of medical pioneer, an AIDS victim capable of playing the most grueling game. Where many once saw horror, they now saw hope.

But all that had been sickly predicated on acceptance by mainstream America: So long as Johnson contracted the disease through straight sex, he was still a viable commercial property, still a network commodity. Then came the recent weird rumblings about a player saying Johnson had gotten the disease through homosexual contact—and that Magic believed the whispers came from his former best friend, Piston's guard Isiah Thomas.

That kind of speculation—and the certainty that it would never end—drove Johnson out.

Sports is a black-and-white world, with clear winners and defined endings. Heroes with diseases die young. There are no books about stars who look great but have slow death coursing through them, no inspiring stories about losing bits of hair and skin. Johnson's mistake came from believing that all he had to do was play well again.[6]

And, as time passed, members of the Denver Disease Control Service and University of Colorado Health Science Center saw the event from their own perspective:

On November 7, 1991, world-renowned professional basketball star Earvin "Magic" Johnson announced that he was infected with the human immunodeficiency virus (HIV). The publicity associated with this event was extraordinary and resulted in an unprecedented increase in awareness of acquired immunodeficiency syndrome (AIDS). At the Denver Public Health Department, we noted an immediate increase in persons seeking HIV counseling and testing. . . . In the 20 working days following the announcement, the number of clients at our HIV counseling and testing site increased 203% over the same period in 1990, and 151% over the 20 days preceding the announcement. . . .[7]

These commentaries are more expressions of personal opinion than objective news reporting. They go beyond the facts of the retirement—Johnson's statements and the fact that he retired—to discuss implications and present personal interpretations. The writers select those facts they view as important, shaping their discussion to mold readers' perceptions of the event. Each text reflects its individual author's knowledge, outlook, purpose, and concerns. Each presentation is, in other words, inherently subjective in nature—a single, unique perspective on the matter.

Subjectivity and Academic Texts

Subjectivity is not limited to journalism. Subjectivity is as much a concern with academic texts. At one time, many considered Charles Beard's *A Basic History of the United States* the authoritative text in its field. Students wanting to "know" American history read Beard. At some point in each student's career, however, came the realization that Beard's history of the United States offered just that— not *"the* history of the United States," but *"Beard's* history of the United States." Beard, himself, was quite aware of the subjectivity of his own work:

> Every student of history knows that his colleagues have been influenced in their selection and ordering of materials by their biases, prejudices, beliefs, affections, general upbringing, and experience. . . . Every written history—of a village, town, county, state, nation, race, group, class, idea or the wide world—is a selection and arrangement of facts, of recorded fragments of past actuality. And the selection and arrangement of facts—a combined and complex intellectual operation—is an act of choice, conviction, and interpretation respecting values, is an act of thought. Facts, multitudinous and beyond calculation, are known, but they do not select themselves or force themselves automatically into any fixed scheme of arrangement in the mind of the historian. They are selected and ordered by him as he thinks.[8]

Like many other texts, Beard's offered but one of many credible accounts and interpretations.

Commentators have long recognized the difficulties in achieving objectivity. "When sociologists 'do sociology,' they do not come to their subject matter cold, their minds a blank," note the authors of *Contemporary Sociological Theory*. "They approach their subject from a certain angle, with certain assumptions; they emphasize particular research methods; and they have particular types of questions they want answered."[9] Perhaps the strongest statement on objectivity appears in the glossary of Earl Babbie's classic text, *The Practice of Social Research*:

objectivity   Doesn't exist. See *intersubjectivity*.[10]

The Text as Portrayal

Rather than expecting every text—or *any* text—to provide "the truth, the whole truth, and nothing but the truth," critical readers focus on the facts as presented. They treat each text not so much as a window offering an unobstructed view of reality, but as one person's portrayal of the truth. The author's choice of words, images, and ideas are seen to shape the reader's perceptions. Texts are viewed not as objects of worship, but as expressions of one person's understanding—not as objective truth, but as the subjective understanding of a unique individual.

CHOICES: THE KEY TO CRITICAL READING

Critical reading begins with the realization that all writing involves choices.

The first choice an author must make is what to write about. This choice is more significant than it might seem. Information, it has been said, is power. Choosing to write about a topic gives that topic importance, and even urgency.

• CHOICE AND THE TELEVISION CAMERA •

The notion of choice is essential in any communication medium. A television camera may appear to represent an objective, all-seeing eye, but, as S. I. Hayakawa notes, summarizing Edith Efron's *The News Twisters*:

> . . . the events selected for coverage by television are a matter of choice; the facts isolated are a matter of choice; the participants involved are a matter of choice; the authorities and experts cited are a matter of choice; and even this is not where selectivity stops. It continues throughout the period in which the reporter sits down at the typewriter. He selects a vocabulary; he selects connotations, implications, associations, dramatic structure, organization. Emotional, intellectual, moral and political stresses—all these are a matter of choice.[11]

Once again, the issue is content, language, and structure. Commentator Linda Ellerbee, noting that "we are all raised to believe that the camera doesn't lie," observes that "in fact nothing lies so easily as the camera. Every time you point a camera at something, you're pointing it away from something."[12]

Once a topic is chosen, additional choices shape the presentation. Writers may write for a variety of purposes and compose texts in a variety of ways. But, one way or another, they must make decisions about the following:

- **Content**—what information and ideas to assert as either true or false
- **Language**—what words and phrases to use to express thoughts
- **Structure**—how to present ideas and information

Each decision helps shape the thought of the text. Different choices alter the presentation and thus the meaning.

The choices discussed here need not be made in isolation from one another or in the order suggested. Indeed, authors may hardly give them a second thought while writing a text. But the additional time and thought devoted to editing will probably focus on these very concerns. Other than for correcting spelling and grammar, revision involves refining choices about what to say (content), how to say it (language), and how to relate the remarks (structure).

IMPLICATIONS

All texts are, inherently, subjective. While authors may strive for fairness and honesty, they must, in a variety of ways, select what to include and what to leave out, what to say and what not to, how to reason and what to reason about. All of the statements may themselves be factual, but the presentation as a whole remains subjective. This realization should not diminish our appreciation for the value of texts; it merely requires that we see texts in the proper perspective—as expressions of belief by fellow human beings. In doing so, we still value facts over lies or unsupported claims and demand high standards of reasoning and candor. But we no longer read to memorize someone else's conclusions as the only, or the final, thoughts on a topic.

One can accept the view that the historical record is fragmentary and incomplete, that recovery of the past is partial and difficult, and that historians will never finally agree in their interpretations, and yet can still believe intelligibly and not naively in an objective truth about the past that can be observed and empirically verified. Historians may never see and represent that truth wholly and finally, but some of them will come closer than others, be more nearly complete, more objective, more honest, in their written history, and we will know it, and have known it, when we see it. That knowledge is the best antidote to the destructive skepticism that is troubling us today.

• George Wood, "NOVEL HISTORY"[13] •

The chapters that follow examine how choices of content, language, and structure affect the overall meaning of a text. From an understanding of "how texts work," we can discover tactics for analyzing texts and for inferring an overall meaning.

EXERCISES/DISCUSSION

A. What Took Place versus What Happened

Authors will see facts differently and draw different conclusions. Novelist Toni Morrison distinguishes between "what took place," or the facts that all might agree on, and "what happened," or our understanding of an event after thought and reflection.[14] To what extent do the articles on Magic Johnson's retirement agree on "what took place"? On what "facts of the case" do they all agree?

B. Choices and Meaning

There is a children's game that asks each player to list (1) a color, (2) an animal, (3) a place, and (4) an action. Each player then inserts his or her choices into this sentence:

The boy with ____(1)____ eyes took his pet ____(2)____ to ____(3)____ to ____(4)____ .

The following sentences indicate the variety of possible versions:

The boy with blue eyes took his pet dog to school to read.

The boy with black eyes took his pet hippopotamus to Disneyland to fly.

The boy with green eyes took his pet snake to the moon to sleep.

The sentences may make sense, seem poetic, or be nonsense. Either way, the choices control the outcome.

In a somewhat similar fashion, we might imagine a news reporter confronted with the following information about a candidate:

He worked his way up from poverty.

He once stole an election by stuffing ballot boxes.

He has taken political risks to support minority rights.

He married his childhood sweetheart.

He has an ego as large as his state.

Select pairs of sentences from this list and indicate how each pair portrays the candidate differently.

C. Choice of Content: "A Graduation Gift from Uncle Sam"

Make the following changes in the news article from Chapter 1 on military recruiting and explain how they would alter the overall meaning.

1. Relocate the event to Peoria
2. Make the payments $25 per name
3. Have the School Board question the policy while the parents request its continuance
4. Have the Pentagon say that this was a one-time occurrence
5. Have the Pentagon announce that this was a trial program to be used elsewhere

D. Choice of Content: "Mary Had an Alligator"

What specific differences can you note in these two nursery rhymes, and how do those differences affect their meaning?

Mary had a little lamb,
Its fleece was white as snow,
And everywhere that Mary went
The lamb was sure to go.

Mary had an alligator,
Its teeth were sharp and yellowed,
And everywhere that Mary went
The alligator followed.

E. Personal Portraits

Write three separate paragraphs portraying yourself differently by using different examples or illustrations. All of the information in each paragraph should be true.

F. Choice of Language

Fill in the blanks in the following sentence by selecting one word or phrase from each column:
The ___(1)___ ___(2)___ the ___(3)___ .

(1)	(2)	(3)
policeman	ran after	supposed culprit
cop	chased after	alleged criminal
pig	pursued	fleeing man
law enforcement officer	stalked	

How does the meaning of the sentence change when you select different terms? Indicate the overall meaning for three possibilities.

G. Choice of Structure

Consider the following sequence of remarks:

John got a medical degree.

John decided to become a clown.

John was a failure.

How is John portrayed in the sequence of remarks above? How does the meaning change if the sentences are rearranged? Indicate as many meaningful arrangements as you can, and state the image of John that is portrayed by each arrangement.

H. Interpretation: Michael Jordan's Retirement

"I've reached the pinnacle. I don't have anything else to prove."

With these words, Michael Jordan announced his retirement from professional basketball in October 1993. This statement and his retirement were viewed in a different light by different observers. How might one interpret Jordan's statement based on each of the following quotes.

1. It is not only arrogance for a man to leave on top but bad form as well, like a big winner leaving the [gambling] table early. [Bernie Lincicome, Knight-Ridder/Tribune News Service]

2. For all the money and the glory, his life has seemed dreadful. [George Vecsey, *The New York Times*]

3. Acrobatic body control, 3-point shooting range, pinpoint passing ability, tenacious defensive skills, tremendous desire—Jordan had it all. And it was thrilling to watch. [Clifton Brown, *The New York Times*]

4. Basketball without Jordan is like ballet without [legendary Russian ballerina] Maya Plisetskaya. [Romanian television, Bucharest]

5. You know how sometimes people have a gift and you don't get to say thank you? We didn't get to say thank you. [Allen McCoy, fan]

6. Just as death turned out to be a career move for Marilyn Monroe, James Dean and Elvis Presley, so too, could Michael Jordan's spectacular career as a celebrity endorser continue with his sudden end of his spectacular career as a basketball player. [Stuart Elliott, *The New York Times*]

7. The Windy City is gasping for Air [Jordan], and the condition is certain to worsen. [*Austin American-Statesman*]

8. Michael Jordan tried to close the door on his NBA basketball career Wednesday, but thank heaven he left the door just slightly ajar. [John Maher, *Austin American-Statesman*]

9. I used to think that Michael Jordan was the Babe Ruth of basketball. I have now come to believe that Babe Ruth was the Michael Jordan of baseball. [Jerry Reinsdorf, owner, Chicago Bulls]

10. Las Vegas betting odds on the Bulls winning a fourth championship dropped from 2-1 to 25-1.

11. The league is always going to have great players and popular players. . . . There will be other special players who will come along. [LaSalle Thompson, Indiana Pacers]

12. Life is bigger than basketball. [James Worthy, Los Angeles Lakers]

13. Michael Jordan's retirement will not end an investigation into his alleged off-court activities. [David Stern, Commissioner, National Basketball Association]

I. Quotations for Discussion

1. [From an advertisement for the International Edition of the *Herald Tribune*]

   INTERNATIONAL/HERALD TRIBUNE
   No local bias, no national slant,
   no partisan viewpoint.[15]

2. We sophisticates apply several grains of salt when we read in a checkout line the latest report of Hitler being discovered in his hideaway in the Andes alive and well (at the age of 102), or of the woman in Idaho who gave birth to a sheep. But the capacity for discrimination between truth and sheer invention seems to desert us when we read similar nonsense enshrined between hard covers.[16]

3. Journalism is simply finding the best available version of the truth. The truth can get messy, but we aim for it. When we stop aiming for the truth, we have ceased being the people we tell ourselves we are.[17]

4. The techniques of the new journalism had more in common with the making of documentary films than with the writing of novels. The writer seeks to make an image, not a work of art. He begins with an attitude of mind and a mass of random observations—notes on the weather; tones of voice; landscapes; fragments of conversation; bits and pieces of historical incident; descriptions of scene; impressions of character. These materials correspond to the film maker's unedited film or the raw information received every week by the news-magazines. In order to impose a form on the chaos of his notes the writer decides on a premise and a point of view. He then can arrange the materials into a coherent design, as if he were fitting small stones into the pavement of a mosaic.[18]

5. In general, the participants [scholars from across the country] agreed that, even if in their heart of hearts scholars have always known themselves to be human beings with prejudices and axes to grind, most of them have continued to present their work as if it were completely rational, objective, and "scientific."

   But, in fact, the participants further agreed, elements of rhetoric (point of view, say, or techniques of persuasion) are so thoroughly ingrained in scholarly research as to affect every step of the enterprise—how sources are used, how data are interpreted, how findings are communicated.[19]

6. When we seek to know the facts, the questions which we ask, and therefore the answers which we obtain, are prompted by our system of values. Our picture of the facts of our environment is molded by our values, i.e., by the categories through which we approach the facts; and this picture is one of the most important facts which we have to take into account. Values enter into our facts and are an essential part of them. Our values are an essential part of our equipment as human beings.[20]

7. While we can use euphemisms that the search [in a trial] is for truth, attorneys know that it is persuasion, not truth, that is the job of the attorney. . . . To bring a case to trial is, for the attorney, the effort to present a picture and to attempt to convince the [jury] to adopt the client's position as the truth instead of the picture that the advocate of the other side will attempt to create.[21]

"A Rose Is a Rose Is a Rose" . . . or Is It?— What Examples Are Examples Of

---

Sometimes a cigar is only a cigar.

• Attributed to Sigmund Freud •

Critical reading focuses not on the examples, but on what the examples are examples *of*.

THE CONTENT OF A TEXT

Ask any ten lawyers the same question, the saying goes, and you will get ten different opinions. While the comment is intended as a joke at the expense of lawyers, it does have a basis in truth. The law may be the same for all, but opinions about a specific case can differ widely. Why is this so?

What, versus How, People Think

Most disagreements do not result from misunderstandings or ignorance. Nor do patterns of reasoning change from person to person, even though lapses in reasoning—logical fallacies—are fairly common. Logic is the same for all. And yet people still reach different conclusions. Contrary to what we might think, the source of disagreement lies more in *what* people think than in *how* they think.

Conclusions are more a reflection of initial beliefs than of the reasoning by which they were reached. When legislators argue whether to fund a bill, they do not really challenge one another's reasoning ability—other than maybe to trade insults. The debate revolves around conflicting assumptions about the role government should play and differing statements of what the relevant facts really are. If we know someone's views on government's proper role and the relevant facts, we can predict their position with reasonable accuracy.

・・・・・・・・・・・・・・・ **DOMESTIC PARTNER LAWS** ・・・・・・・・・・・・・・・

A number of cities have enacted "domestic partner" laws extending health benefits to the unmarried companions of city workers, regardless of gender. City councilpersons considering such a law might view this as equivalent to:

- Granting approval of sinful actions
- Promoting equality of economic opportunity
- Enacting a low-priority increase in expenditures
- Acknowledging support for committed relationships

How would a councilperson who supported each viewpoint probably vote on the law?

・・

Content: All That Is True or False

One of the first choices an author must make relates to content. Here, the notion of content refers to the building blocks upon which a text is constructed. Just as prior knowledge is not limited to factual knowledge alone (see the section "Inference and Prior Knowledge" in Chapter 2), content refers to more than simply facts. **Content** includes the claims, assumptions, ideas, values, principles, portrayals, quotations, statistics, and other assertions of belief or fact on which a text is based. The content is all that an author takes to be true or false on the way to reaching a conclusion—wherever it may appear within a text.

EXAMPLE: *Roe v. Wade*

The choice of content is most apparent when we compare opposing views of two or more authors confronting the same topic. In the landmark 1973 abortion case, *Roe v. Wade*, Supreme Court Justices Harry A. Blackmun and Byron R. White issued opposing decisions. In the following excerpts from these contrasting opinions, notice in particular the women's circumstances that each considers.

> The detriment that the state should impose upon the pregnant woman by denying this choice [of getting an abortion] altogether is apparent. Specific and direct harm medically diagnosable even in early pregnancy may be involved. Maternity, or additional offspring, may force upon the woman a distressful life and future. Psychological harm may be imminent. Mental and physical health may be taxed by child care.
>
> There is also the distress, for all concerned, associated with the unwanted child, and there is the problem of bringing a child into a family already unable, psychologically and otherwise, to care for it. [Justice Harry A. Blackmun]

> At the heart of the controversy in these cases are those recurring pregnancies that pose no danger whatsoever to the life or health of the mother but are nevertheless unwanted for any one or more of a variety of reasons—convenience, family planning, economics, dislike of children, the embarrassment of illegitimacy, etc.
>
> The common claim before us is that for any one of such reasons, or for no reason at all, and without asserting or claiming any threat of life or health, any woman is entitled to an abortion at her request if she is able to find a medical adviser willing to undertake the procedure. [Justice Byron R. White]

For Justice Blackmun, those seeking abortion would otherwise be subject to potential medical harm, "a distressful life and future" or "psychological harm," and their "mental and physical health may be taxed." Women seeking abortions are portrayed as vulnerable to future adversity they cannot otherwise avoid. For Justice White, the "heart of the controversy" lies with cases in which there is "no danger whatsoever." An abortion is requested for reasons of convenience and preference, such as family planning, economics, or dislike of children. Women seeking abortions are portrayed as irresponsible and/or selfish, and in no danger.

The opinions reflect two distinct starting points: each justice takes different information to be fact. The portrayals of women who might seek abortions are the essential content on which the justices base their decisions. Whether the justices actually consider different women or merely describe the same women differently, we cannot be certain. But given that they seem to be talking about different women in different situations, it is no wonder that they reach different conclusions.

EXAMPLE: **The Scholastic Aptitude Test**

The following excerpts, the first from a psychology and the second from a sociology textbook, discuss the Scholastic Aptitude Test (SAT) familiar to all college-bound students. How does each portray the test?

> Although most people do not regard the Scholastic Aptitude Test (SAT) as an intelligence test, it serves the same function: It predicts performance in college. . . . The SAT offers a way to compare students who have attended different high schools and taken different courses. As a predictor of college success, the SAT by itself is even less satisfactory than high school grades by themselves. When combined with high school grades, however, SAT scores significantly improve the prediction of college success.[1]

> Many studies in the United States and elsewhere have suggested declines in student achievement in recent years (Peaker, 1971). But the major focus of interest and anxiety has been the long downward slide in the average scores of American high school seniors on the Scholastic Aptitude Test (SAT). Each year many high school students planning to enter college take the SAT because many of the better colleges and universities give great weight to the exam scores in deciding whom to admit. Throughout the 1950s, the national average of the SAT rose, and those who took the exam in 1963 set an all-time high. But then scores began to drop. Every year the average was lower. . . . In the late 1970s a national commission was convened to determine why the scores were falling. It concluded that part of the decline was due to a change in who took the exam; in earlier periods only better students tended to take the exam. But much of the decline was regarded as reflecting real changes in the educational achievements of Americans.[2]

Both passages discuss the SAT test, but the content is different. The first takes as a fact that the SAT functions much as an intelligence test; the second starts from the assumption that the SAT can be examined as an indicator of academic achievement. The authors have different starting points and different assumptions as to the nature of the test, and these differences lead to different assertions about the significance of the test. The first excerpt evaluates the usefulness of the SAT for predicting academic success; the second draws on data of declining SAT scores as evidence for the claim of a decline in educational achievement in America.

EVIDENCE AND CONCLUSIONS

For a text to portray a person as just, miserly, intelligent, demented, or charming, it must do more than simply claim it. Some evidence to justify that generalization must be presented. "When I come across a generalization or a general statement in history unsupported by illustration," historian Barbara Tuchman has observed, "I am instantly on guard; my reaction is, 'Show me.' If a historian writes that it was raining heavily on the day war was declared, that is a detail corroborating a statement, let us say, that the day was gloomy. But if he writes merely that it was a gloomy day without mentioning the rain, I want to know what is his evidence; what made it gloomy. Or if he writes, 'The population was in a belligerent mood,' or 'It was a period of great anxiety,' he is indulging in general statements which carry no conviction to me if they are not illustrated by some evidence."[3] The evidence—the examples that provide the basis for the generalizations—constitutes the initial content from which a conclusion is drawn. Prove it, more often than not, means "Show me!"

The impact of the content on our ultimate understanding cannot be overemphasized. Consider what happens if a text labels someone as moral but offers an example of that person behaving in a decidedly immoral manner:

> The candidate is a just and honorable man. He beats his wife and lies to children.

The example contradicts the claim (conclusion). In all such cases, the example wins. We disregard the claim and draw our own conclusion from the evidence: the candidate is not just and honorable, he's wicked! If we do not simply reject the passage for being contradictory, we must interpret the claim that he is just and honorable as sarcasm. But in no case will we disregard the evidence and accept the conclusion as offered.

RECOGNIZING WHAT EXAMPLES ARE EXAMPLES OF

A conclusion is convincing only when supported by accompanying evidence or examples. Yet no author expects the reader to remember the actual examples. Like the individual frames of a movie, the examples are meaningful only insofar as they contribute to the whole. *Any* example pointing to the desired generalization will do.

In an attempt to portray a person as moral, for example, the specific behavior can vary as long as whatever is chosen is *an example of* moral behavior. The meaning of a fairy tale, for instance, does not lie in the specific events of the story, but in the underlying meaning. It matters little whether Cinderella has two stepsisters or three, whether she loses her slipper or her glove, or whether she meets a prince at a ball or a count at a fox hunt. As long as virtue triumphs, the story works! *Any* similar events would do.

Examples may vary in strength, urgency, or clarity. Particularly graphic examples can even remain in our mind as symbols of an idea. For instance, in a petition of grievances, the inmates of Rahway Prison in New Jersey described the prison as "a place where the diet is so bad that various blood banks have refused to accept donations from inmates."[4] Their grasp of biology may have been weak, but there was little doubt what they meant—that they were being stripped of human dignity by being fed unhealthy food.

In the end, meaning is generated not by the specific details but by the *idea* conveyed by those details. Weak or strong, the examples or illustrations are there to play a role. They matter only insofar as they are examples of the desired idea.

EXAMPLE: **E. B. White's Democracy**

During World War II, the following editorial by E. B. White appeared in *The New Yorker* magazine:

July 3, 1944

We received a letter from the Writers' War Board the other day asking for a statement on "The Meaning of Democracy." It presumably is our duty to comply with such a request, and it is certainly our pleasure.

Surely the Board knows what democracy is. It is the line that forms on the right. It is the don't in Don't Shove. It is the hole in the stuffed shirt through which the sawdust slowly trickles; it is the dent in the high hat. Democracy is the recurrent suspicion that more than half of the people are right more than half of the time. It is the feeling of privacy in the voting booths, the feeling of communion in the libraries, the feeling of vitality everywhere. Democracy is the score at the beginning of the ninth. It is an idea which hasn't been disproved yet, a song the words of which have not gone bad. It's the mustard on the hot dog and the cream in the rationed coffee. Democracy is a request from a War Board, in the middle of a morning in the middle of a war, to know what democracy is.[5]

• WHAT IS IT AN EXAMPLE OF? •

The question "What is this an example of?" often amounts to "How might this be explained?"

During the Reconstruction era, 97 percent of the criminal defendants in Warren County, Mississippi, were white, and yet two-thirds of the residents of the county were black.[6] How might this be explained?

The editorial defines democracy through a series of examples. Like all authors, White assumed readers would look beyond the specific examples to infer an overall meaning. The examples are not to be taken literally; they stand for broader concepts. The meaning of the text depends on what those examples are understood to be *examples of.* To understand the thought, we must classify the examples.

Precision in Classification

When we **classify**, we determine the nature of something—what kind of thing it is, what group it belongs to. **Labels** are names for those groups of things. Labeling "what examples are examples of" must be done with care lest we find ourselves discussing ideas for which there is simply no evidence in the text. Our labels must indicate precisely what we mean—no more and no less.

Labels must be *broad* enough to cover all of the items under consideration yet *narrow* enough to exclude other items that do not fit the pattern or category. Consider this series of items:

John, Henry, Frank, Michael, Hubert

The label "names" is too broad because that category would also include female names, last names, and even street and pet names. The label "male first (or middle) names" offers a better fit. Now consider another series:

John, Henry, Frank, Helen

Here, the label "male names" is too narrow because that label excludes "Helen," presumably a female name. A more appropriate label might simply be "people's first names."

Classifying collies as "animals" is probably too broad. The classification does not indicate what kind of animal, and hence does not distinguish between collies and peacocks or dolphins or worms (unless, of course, we simply wanted to distinguish between collies and nonanimals, such as rocks). Similarly, to classify collies as "large, blond, long-haired dogs" may be too narrow since not all collies are blond.

• • • • • • • • • • • • • • • • • • • CLASSIFICATION • • • • • • • • • • • • • • • • •

Classify the items in each series:

1. Jose, Margaret, Sean, Jaime, Angelo, Mark, Angel
2. Albuquerque, Los Angeles, San Francisco, Albany, San Diego, Santa Fe
3. frying pans, kettles, spatulas, sieves, ladles, sauce pans
4. urge, force, intimidate, offer incentive, persuade, pressure, influence, request, motivate, encourage, appeal to
5. Martin Luther King, Jr., Thomas Jefferson, Yasser Arafat, Malcolm X, Gandhi, Jesse Jackson, Cesar Chavez, Geronimo

• •

EXAMPLE: **E. B. White's Democracy Revisited**

E. B. White's editorial describes democracy through a series of examples. But what are those examples examples of? Overall, the examples are from everyday life, rather than politics and government. From this we infer that the text is portraying democracy as a way of life, rather than as a formal philosophy.

Examining the examples further, we see that they suggest various qualities. For instance, "the don't in Don't Shove" might suggest civility or respect. "It is the line that forms on the right" suggests orderliness. However, governments can be orderly without being democratic, and it is democracy that is being described. We can distinguish between a line that forms on the right and one that forms on the left, but that distinction does not seem to get us anywhere. We might finally label the example as an example of "fairness" or "equal opportunity."

What about "Democracy is the score at the beginning of the ninth"? We must find some relationship between democracy (a system of government) and the score at a particular time (a situation in a baseball game). What is special about the score at the top of the ninth inning? Perhaps that, even then, the game is not over—opportunity still exists. The important thing, then, is not the score, but that the score can change. This realization suggests classifying the example as an example of "continued opportunity for all."

Classification can, obviously, get fairly tricky. It can require looking at an example from various perspectives. And it can require the same creative, problem-solving attitude discussed previously in this book.

• • • • • • • • • • • • • • • • **EXAMPLE OF WHAT?** • • • • • • • • • • • • • • • •

> Democracy is a request from a War Board, in the middle of a morning in the middle of a war, to know what democracy is.

What might this final example in the E. B. White editorial be an example of?

• •

Calculations

Measurements and numbers function in much the same way as other content. Just as we can ask what examples are examples of, we can ask what numbers are examples of. In many cases, it is necessary to do some calculation to discover the significance of those numbers. How might you respond to the following:

> Save $500 on your next new car!

Five hundred dollars might sound like a large sum of money. But does it really represent a big savings? For a $10,000 car, it amounts to 5 percent ($500/10,000 = .05 = 5\%$), or 5 cents on each dollar, which may be less than the sales tax that would be added to the original price in many locations. As another example, recall the sample passage on army recruiting in high schools, which indicated that the Army paid 3 cents per student and that the schools received $8,081. Calculate how many students that would cover ($8,081/$.03 = 269,367—about a quarter of a million juniors and seniors). This should give you a sense of how many students were involved and thus whether $8,081 is an example of a sizable or a small amount.

PERSONAL INTERPRETATIONS OF EXAMPLES

"A rose is a rose is a rose." Or so Gertrude Stein claimed. But is it? Is a rose given to a prom date the same as a rose given to someone allergic to flowers? Is the rose on a pillow the same as a rose on a coffin or in a flamenco dancer's teeth? The rose may be the same, but its significance changes. In each case, it becomes an example of something different. Indeed, almost any example can represent different things to different people.

Some of the most striking examples of differences in interpretation occur with people from different cultures. Several years ago, in Salt Lake City, Utah, an immigrant from the South Pacific island of Tonga was arrested for killing a Shetland pony he had bought for his son's birthday. "'We don't ride horses, we eat them,' he explained."[7] What was an example of a pet to the American seller was an example of food to the Tongan.

One does not have to go to such cross-cultural extremes to find different perceptions. When the columnist Anna Quindlen wrote an editorial entitled "Life in the 30's," she was referring to her age. "Some readers," she later realized, "thought it referred to the [1930s] Depression and some thought it referred to the Murray Hill section of Manhattan . . . [and] readers who were over 40 felt disin-

---

• SOMETIMES THINGS ARE NOT WHAT THEY SEEM •

Interpreting what an example is an example of can yield surprising insights. In 1991, researchers examining women's injuries discovered that women ages 25–34 fell as often as women age 65 and older. Increasing age did not explain the incidence of falling—it was not "a difference that made a difference"—and yet common sense suggested it should. Younger women, one might think, would be steadier on their feet.

Examining the data more carefully, the researchers noted that the majority of falls by younger women were reported to have occurred on stairs within the home. How might this be explained? The researcher concluded: "Although the extent of unrecognized violence within our study group cannot be estimated, the observed peak in falls for young adult women . . . may reflect an under-reporting of domestic violence."[8] For older women, falls were an example of accidents due to loss of balance; for younger women, falls were evidence of domestic violence.

---

vited from the audience, which is the last thing any writer wants."[9] Each reader read the example differently, and each found different meaning in the title.

Controlling Meaning Through Patterns

Classification, it appears, can be based on guesswork and a reader's personal biases. Left uncontrolled, such a situation would make effective communication extremely difficult.

Fortunately, no example stands alone within a text. Rather, all evidence appears within a broader context, and each text limits any single example by placing it in a larger pattern. The key issue thus becomes not what the example is an example of, but what the example is an example of *within the particular text*. (You will recall that the earlier classification of names was based on classifying items within a pattern of items.)

To illustrate, consider the construction of a highway through a national park. For some people, this might be an example of the destruction of our natural heritage; for others, it might be an example of a benefit to the local economy, convenience for tourists, opportunities for the unemployed, or even the need to revise road maps.

Suppose we pair the initial example with an example of providing information booths along major highways:

- Building a highway through a national park
- Providing information booths along major highways

} have in common making touring easier

Or we might pair the initial example with an example of allowing more logging on public land:

- Building a highway through a national park
- Allowing more logging on public land

} have in common increased use of public land

What happens if we add a third example?

- Building a highway through a national park
- Allowing more logging on public land
- No longer protecting endangered species

} have in common attacking the environment

To make up for the lack of input from a face-to-face encounter, writers build patterns of examples to "lock in" a particular interpretation. Rather than classifying single examples, readers find common characteristics within those patterns of examples. The more examples one groups together, the more limited the options for classifying the examples, and hence the more precise the classification. Critical reading, then, involves identifying patterns of examples occurring throughout a text and classifying how those patterns portray the evidence.

EXAMPLE: *Playboy* **Magazine**

The following is an excerpt from a textbook on contemporary media. Notice how an initial image of *Playboy* is reshaped as a pattern of evidence evolves.

> Hugh Hefner launched *Playboy* in 1953 to shock America's postwar readers with a nude Marilyn Monroe. The nudity in *Playboy* challenged the limits of magazine respectability, but the magazine also challenged social conventions. Was nudity acceptable in a general circulation magazine?
>
> A different kind of shock had come one year earlier when *Mad* magazine began. *Mad* was directed at a young audience, and it mocked traditional social and political values. Like *Playboy*, *Mad* sought to extend the boundaries of magazine journalism.
>
> *Playboy*'s success led to a number of imitators, including *Penthouse* and, later, *Playgirl*. *Mad* magazine and *Playboy* and its imitators typify how, beginning in the 1950s, magazine publishing sought new audiences in an environment that was becoming more crowded with other types of media.[10]

The initial image might be of a shocking magazine. When the notion of challenging social conventions is added to that of challenging respectability, the initial analysis seems to be substantiated. But when *Playboy* is compared favorably to *Mad*, the image begins to change. Condemnation yields to an image of "extend[ing] the boundaries of magazine journalism"—a seemingly favorable reading of the prior challenge to the establishment. When *Playboy* is then identified as the initiator of a trend, it is as a trailblazer in its field, not as a contemptible publication.

Going back to the earlier examples, the notion of shocking readers and challenging the limits of respectability must be seen—*within the pattern of evidence*—as positive actions from a commercial standpoint within the history of magazine publishing. The excerpt makes no judgment on moral, ethical, or aesthetic grounds about the magazine or its publication.

IMPLICATIONS

Unsure whether evidence in a text is complete and accurate, readers must instead turn their attention to how the existing evidence portrays the subject. Their concern shifts from what the examples are to what the examples *are exam-*

ples of. To limit personal associations, classification is based on patterns of examples rather than individual examples.

The next chapter examines strategies for recognizing patterns of content within a text. Chapter 8 offers a strategy for inferring additional meaning from the ways in which these patterns are interrelated.

EXERCISES/DISCUSSION

A. What Is the Example an Example Of?

What was Magic Johnson's retirement "an example of" as portrayed in each of the news articles in Chapter 5?

B. Classification

Classify the following sets of items:

1. short stories, term papers, love poems, essays
2. television, radio, telephone, telegraph
3. cigar, church, cymbal, cough
4. Democrats, Conservatives, Socialists, Republicans
5. "Nice guys finish last," "Do unto others before they do unto you," "It's not how you play the game, but whether you win"

C. Classifying Examples: "Harper's Index"

Each issue of *Harper's Magazine* includes a page of statistical facts known as "Harper's Index." The following are from one such index. What might these facts be examples of?

1. Chances that a black child will be born to a single mother: 2 in 3
2. Chances that an American's credit card record contains errors: 1 in 2.
3. Average number of hot dogs Americans eat in July: 1,000,000,000.[11]

D. Classifying Patterns of Evidence

Critical reading requires an ability to suspend judgment on the significance of individual remarks until they have been considered within the full context. An essay on a city contains the following statement:

While designed to hold 500 students, the high school presently holds 763.

What might this statement be an example of when paired with each of the following examples?

1. New textbooks have not been ordered for five years.
2. There are 43 students in each class.

3. The leaks in the roof of the city hall have not been repaired for eight months.

4. New road construction is three years behind schedule.

5. Seven new industries have built offices in the city in the past year, and 15 percent more houses were built this year than last.

E. Assumptions as Content

Assumptions function as a form of content. What assumptions are made about the behavior of gays in the articles on gays in the military [Texts for Analysis 3A–3D]?

F. Classifying Patterns of Evidence: The Changing Status of Women

The following excerpt speaks of "the changing status of women." What examples are offered and what, exactly, is the status portrayed? By classifying the changes, you determine the nature of the "most dramatic of the social upheavals of the second half of the 20th century" referred to in the first sentence.

> The changing status of women has been one of the most dramatic of the social upheavals of the second half of the 20th century. Women are entering the labor force earlier and remaining at work for more years, even if they have young children. More women are divorced and heading their own households. More women are going to college, obtaining professional and advanced degrees, and seeking careers in law, medicine, and business. There are more women active in politics at every level of government. Women artists, writers, and musicians are gaining significant recognition, far more than achieved in any previous era. Women are even finding an increased place in the armed services. And more women are living longer than have ever done so before.[12]

G. Description and Values

Values enter into our descriptions and definitions. In some cultures, cannibalism is classified as a sin; in others, it might be a form of war, a social ritual of manhood, or even a form of food gathering. For each of the following examples, indicate various possible classifications of the activity and the values inherent in each description.

1. A doctor aiding the death of a terminally ill patient

2. The state paying for food for homeless people

3. One student helping another complete a writing assignment

H. Texts for Analysis: "Alarm Clocks Can Kill You. Have a Smoke."

This essay [Texts for Analysis 14] cites actions that magazines suggest are either good or bad for the reader's health. From the standpoint of the essay, what are these examples really examples of?

"Know That We Have Divided into Three Our Kingdom"*— Identifying Analytic Parts

. . . good detectives and good readers are good interpreters. A good detective gathers all the clues, explains how the clues fit together to make a pattern and so discovers the criminal. The good interpreter of texts works in much the same way.

• Thomas E. Porter, Charles Kneupper, and Harry Reeder
THE LITERATE MIND: READING, WRITING, CRITICAL THINKING[1] •

King Lear, 1.1.37–38

No example stands alone. Critical readers identify patterns of elements recurring throughout the text.

Chapter 5 argued that choices of content shape the portrayal of a topic within a text. Chapter 6 showed the need to classify patterns of content rather than focus on isolated examples. This chapter offers techniques for isolating patterns of content, while Chapter 8 presents a strategy for inferring meaning from the relationships between these patterns.

RECOGNIZING PATTERNS OF CONTENT

Overview: Identifying the Lay of the Land

Always start an analysis with an initial scan of the text to discover the topics covered and the length of the discussion. This overview allows you to test any expectations you might have based on the title, the author, or the source of the text, and to distinguish between major concerns and digressions.

Once you have obtained an overview, you are ready to identify major patterns of content within the text. Each major pattern can then be examined at lower levels of analysis.

Identifying Patterns Throughout a Text

Texts are normally read from beginning to end, one paragraph after another, one sentence after another:

A–B–C–D–E

We might imagine this as similar to lining up a random handful of coins one after another. Pattern recognition, on the other hand, focuses on elements recurring throughout the text:

A–B–A–C–B–A–C

Our image changes from one of lining up coins to sorting them according to their value. When we find a coin with a different value, we start a new pile. Some patterns may still occur sequentially:

A–A–A–B–B–B–C

However, the emphasis is on locating elements that occur at various places throughout the text.

After an initial reading, start your analysis by marking references, topics, or terms that seem essential to the discussion. Begin with topics or references that reappear throughout the text, then sift through the text again for similar references. Be alert for both similar and dissimilar elements. Where does the discussion seem to shift focus or direction? If some feature of a text catches your attention, it is probably significant.

When searching for patterns of content, actively involve yourself in the process. Mark potential patterns with circles and boxes and triangles or with different colored pens. (To fully analyze an essay in a library book, make a photocopy.) Mark tentative labels in the margin. Each pattern you recognize should suggest others. Ultimately, most of the text should be covered in no more than five major patterns or divisions. (See Appendix A, "Outlining.") Whatever the number of parts and however many examples you find for each, the goal is to identify patterns of content throughout the discussion.

EXAMPLE: **The Ku Klux Klan**

The following is an excerpt from Texts for Analysis 1A:

> As the year 1870 drew to a close, conditions in South Carolina became more and more terrible. Crimes among the negroes—murder, burglary, and house burning—were frequent. The negro militia grew more insolent each day, encouraged as they were by the "Carpet Bag" government with United States troops at its back.
>
> This dreadful condition of affairs forced the white people of the State to organize secretly for their own protection. They formed small bands called Ku Klux Klans whose purpose was to frighten the negroes from their evil doing. The Ku-Klux met only at night. They dressed in long white robes and caps. They were always mounted, and the very sight of these ghostly riders galloping by in the night was usually enough to terrify the superstitious negroes. Many of the best men in South Carolina belonged to the Ku Klux Klan.
>
> The negroes in the town of Union were the first to suffer punishment at the hands of the Klan. In January 1871, a one-armed Confederate soldier was cruelly beaten and then murdered by a company of 40 negro militiamen. The Klan forced the militia to disarm and put in jail thirteen of the negroes believed to have taken part in the murder. The negroes in Union became so threatening that the Klan visited the jail and shot the murderers except three who escaped.
>
> Wherever the negro militiamen became intolerable, the Klan set itself to work to frighten or punish them. Seeing the determination of the white people to take justice into their own hands, Governor Scott finally disbanded the negro militia in the counties where they were giving the most trouble. The Ku Klux Klan then stopped its work.

This passage offers a narrative of the rise of the Ku Klux Klan in South Carolina. It describes events involving the Ku Klux Klan and the black population—admittedly, offering assertions that are neither "politically correct" nor historically defensible. Here, as with all analysis and interpretation, the initial concern is not to evaluate the correctness of the text, but to understand that text—to recognize how it reaches certain conclusions by portraying evidence in a certain way. To refute this or any other text, we must first fully grasp its meaning and how that meaning is achieved.

We can base our initial analysis on an examination of the examples describing the actions of each group. Here the actions of the whites are printed in boldface, the actions of the blacks in italics.

> As the year 1870 drew to a close, conditions in South Carolina became more and more terrible. *Crimes among the negroes—murder, burglary, and house burning—were frequent. The negro militia grew more insolent each day*, encouraged as they were by the "Carpet Bag" government with United States troops at its back.
>
> *This dreadful condition of affairs* **forced the white people of the State to organize secretly for their own protection. They formed small bands called Ku Klux Klans whose purpose was to frighten the negroes from their evil doing. The Ku-Klux met only at night. They dressed in long white robes and caps. They were always mounted,** and *the very sight of these ghostly riders galloping by in the night was usually enough to terrify the superstitious negroes.* **Many of the best men in South Carolina belonged to the Ku Klux Klan.**
>
> **The negroes in the town of Union were the first to suffer punishment at the hands of the Klan.** *In January 1871, a one-armed Confederate soldier was cruelly beaten and then murdered by a company of 40 negro militiamen.* **The Klan forced the militia to disarm and put in jail thirteen of the negroes believed to have taken part in the murder.** *The negroes in Union became so threatening* **that the Klan visited the jail and shot the murderers except three who escaped.**
>
> *Whenever the negro militiamen became intolerable,* **the Klan set itself to work to frighten or punish them.** Seeing **the determination of the white people to take justice into their own hands,** Governor Scott finally disbanded the negro militia in the counties *where they were giving the most trouble.* **The Ku Klux Klan then stopped its work.**

The Negroes are portrayed as engaging in criminal activities, being subject to irrational behavior, and continually challenging the social order. The evil of their actions is epitomized with examples of a beating and a murder.

In contrast, the whites are portrayed as acting only when provoked, acting reluctantly and only in self-defense, and attempting to restore law and order. The Klan is portrayed as arising from a specific need and being terminated when that need no longer existed. Notice that the text indicates that the Klan, in response to the earlier murder, jailed only some of the suspects (a restrained and seemingly lawful action), and then, only when provoked, executed only those labeled actual murderers (in contrast to the indiscriminate violence of the Negroes).

The following chapter examines how patterns of content such as these can be reinforced through the choice of specific terms and phrases.

At this point, we can describe the text as discussing the rise of the Ku Klux Klan in South Carolina. The actions of the blacks are portrayed as the behavior of criminals and trouble-makers; the actions of the whites are portrayed as necessary responses by well-meaning people who hesitate to be violent.

•••••••••••••••• **PATTERNS OF EXAMPLES** ••••••••••••••••

Each of the news articles on the assassination of Malcolm X [Texts for Analysis 2A–2C] describes the actions of various groups or individuals. Read through one of the articles, marking the different participants with different-colored highlighters or different styles of underlining. Classify how the actions of each group are portrayed.

•••

Identifying Differences That Make a Difference

Pattern identification depends on isolating "differences that make a difference" while overlooking superficial variations in the presentation. Differences that you feel are not important to the overall meaning should be deemphasized or examined at a lower level of analysis. In sorting coins by their value, for instance, the difference between Indian head and Lincoln pennies would not make a difference. The difference between a dime and a nickel would. Reading a discussion of a war, we would concentrate on the goals or tactics of the opposing armies, not the color of their uniforms.

In an article on the need for increased funding to clean the environment, we might find references to toxic dump sites in need of cleanup in Houston, New Orleans, and Newark. In this case, differences between the specific cities probably do not matter. Evidence from other cities with toxic dumps would do just as well. What matters is that there are examples of toxic dumps in need of cleanup. On the other hand, in an article on where to locate a toxic dump, the differences between the cities would assume greater importance.

Refining an Analysis

As you search, you will define patterns by what you include or exclude and by how you label each pattern in your mind. Only by recognizing some similarity would you group things together in the first place. This process will send you back through the text in search of additional evidence that will further define each pattern of elements.

For an analysis of a text to be complete, it must include the complete text. Having found major patterns, look for content that has not as yet been grouped into a pattern. If a particular example does not fit into one pattern, see if it might fit into others, or consider broadening a heading. If you find yourself fragmenting the text into many patterns with some elements still unaccounted for, look for broader headings at a higher level of analysis.

• PATTERN RECOGNITION AND CLASSIFICATION •

Classification and pattern recognition go hand in hand. To identify patterns, you look for things that are alike in some way. It is not enough simply to feel that things "go together." You must specify how or why. What do they have in common?

If someone were to claim that the following sequence forms a pattern, we might be somewhat skeptical.

shorts, triangle, onions

But when you recognize that these items are all asociated with the island of Bermuda (Bermuda triangle, Bermuda shorts, Bermuda onions), the sequence suddenly makes sense as a pattern.

PREDICTING THE PARTS OF AN ANALYSIS

Pattern recognition has been described so far as similar to sorting coins. As you work through a text, you recognize which qualities are important and which are irrelevant. The process of pattern recognition need not, however, be so haphazard. When sorting coins, we can predict beforehand which piles we will need: pennies, nickels, dimes, quarters, and so on. When classifying teachers, we are aware of possible categories: tough or easy graders, clear or confusing lecturers, and so on. In similar fashion, aspects of a text such as the type of discussion or the topic can suggest bases for analysis.

Patterns Based on the Nature of the Text

The descriptive model presented in Chapter 1 distinguished texts according to various types: argument, comparison, definition, description, and narration. Different text types contain different kinds of information or remarks. For example, narrations portray events, generally involving different people or time periods, and indicate actions or behaviors. Arguments contain reasons and conclusions, and often evaluate opposing positions.

The ingredients of each text type can suggest bases for analysis. A search for patterns of content in a narration, for instance, might focus on events in different time periods or the actions of different participants. A search for patterns in an argument might focus on how different positions are portrayed. In each case, the nature of the discussion suggests possible analytic divisions. Using a bit of common sense, we can extend this approach to other text types. We can expect, for instance, that a petition (a form of argument) will contain a section describing a situation and a section listing demands or that a proposal (another form of argument) will suggest a need and a potential solution.

Applying this approach to the article on army recruiters, we recognize that the text narrates events in Los Angeles. An initial analysis of the article might focus on how the various participants—the Army, the parents, and the School Board—are portrayed. (See the analysis of this article in Chapter 13.)

· · · · · · · · · **WHAT WOULD ONE HAVE TO INCLUDE?** · · · · · · · · · ·

Abraham Lincoln's Gettysburg Address was delivered at the dedication of a cemetery. What might a reader expect to find in such a speech?

· ·

Patterns Based on Ingredients of a Particular Topic

Every topic has certain concerns that must be covered. In discussing environmental pollution one must, obviously, discuss the environment and pollution—specifically, some aspect of the environment that is affected by some specific pollutant. Any such discussion would probably include assertions about the current level of damage and the possibilities for avoiding further damage. By anticipating these issues and concerns, readers can also anticipate potential patterns of content within such a text.

For example, a text on raising taxes might be expected to examine the following:

- Why additional money is necessary or desired
- What potential sources of additional funding might be
- What possible shifts in spending might occur
- How the public feels about tax increases
- How taxes would be assessed

Note how one's analysis of this text might be guided by prior knowledge of this or similar topics. And, once again, an understanding is based on reflecting on the *ideas* within the discussion, not simply the words.

In order to persuade, you need evidence, as well as logic and a well-constructed argument. An important first step in writing a paper is to determine what kind of data you need to prove your point.

• Ronald Walters and T. H. Kern
"HOW TO ESCHEW WEASEL WORDS . . ."[2] •

• • • • • • • • • • WHAT WOULD IT TAKE TO SHOW . . . ? • • • • • • • • • •

Suppose a writer wants to argue that admitting women to previously all-male military schools will not result in a decline in the quality of the program. What kind of evidence or arguments would be necessary to support this point?

• •

EXAMPLE: "Alarm Clocks Can Kill You. Have a Smoke."

Scanning this article [Texts for Analysis 14], we find two major patterns of content, one following the other:

- Descriptions of the nature of health advice in certain magazines (paragraphs 4–7)
- Descriptions of the magazines' policies toward cigarettes (paragraphs 8–10)

These two patterns, boldfaced for emphasis, are suggested in the first paragraph:

> Believing what you read about preventive medicine in popular women's magazines can be hazardous to your health. A review of the July, August and September issues of 10 such publications reveals not only that the **health "advice" is a distortion of scientific reality**, but that the **disinformation about health is sponsored— through advertising**—by the manufacturer of the leading cause of death.

That accounts for paragraphs 4–10. What about the other paragraphs? To the two major patterns of content we can add another:

- A section on the real medical hazards (paragraphs 2–3)

In addition, the first major pattern, the nature of the health advice in the magazines, is split on a lower level into a discussion of what the magazines claim is hazardous (paragraphs 4–5) and what they claim is beneficial (paragraphs 6–7). Finally, we have a conclusion (paragraph 11).

IMPLICATIONS

Initially, patterns of content within a text may be recognized by identifying the nature of the discussion or the nature of the topic, or by noting recurring references within the discussion. Whichever way, pattern recognition usually requires a number of readings. Initial observations are tested and refined as further evidence is sought for each pattern.

Patterns of content should be described and classified. It is not enough simply to note that a certain topic is portrayed with certain examples; you must also classify the nature of those examples and thus the nature of the portrayal—what the examples are an example of. Differences that are not important to the overall meaning must be deemphasized or examined at a lower level of analysis. Ultimately, the depth of the critical insight will depend on isolating "differences that make a difference" while overlooking superficial variations. The strength of the final interpretation rests on this continuous process of examination and discovery, reflection and reexamination.

EXERCISES/DISCUSSION

A. Divisions Based on the Type of Text and the Topic

Into what major divisions might you expect to be able to analyze the following?

1. An account of a soccer game

2. An evaluation of a proposal to limit automobile exhaust in the atmosphere

3. An argument for allowing men to compete for the title of campus queen at Homecoming

4. A discussion of the proper way to address professors

5. A plea to provide more housing for the homeless

B. Classifying Patterns of Evidence: Thomas Love Peacock on Science

Classify the characteristics attributed to science in this excerpt by Thomas Love Peacock (1785–1866). How many patterns do you find?

> Science is one thing and wisdom is another. Science is an edged tool with which men play like children and cut their own fingers. If you look at the results which science has brought in its train, you will find them to consist almost wholly in elements of mischief. See how much belongs to the word Explosion alone, of which the ancients knew nothing. Explosions of powder-mills and powder-magazines; of coal-gas in mines and houses; of high-pressure engines in ships and boats and factories. See the complications and refinements of modes of destruction, in revolvers and rifles and shells and rockets and cannon. See collisions and wrecks and every mode of disaster by land and by sea, resulting chiefly from the insanity for speed, in those who for the most part have nothing to do at the end of the race, which they run as if they were so many Mercuries speeding with messages from Jupiter. Look at our scientific drainage, which turns refuse into poison. Look at the subsoil of London, whenever it is turned up to the air, converted by gas leakage into one mass of pestilent blackness, in which no vegetation can flourish and above which, with the rapid growth of the ever-growing nuisance, no living thing will breathe with impunity. Look at our scientific machinery, which has destroyed domestic manufacture, which has substituted rottenness for strength in the thing made, and physical degradation in crowded towns for healthy and comfortable country life in the makers. The day would fail, if I

should attempt to enumerate the evils which science has inflicted on mankind. I almost think it is the ultimate destiny of science to exterminate the human race.[3]

C. Classifying Patterns of Evidence: Amerigo Vespucci on the New World

Classify the characteristics attributed to life in the New World in this letter by Amerigo Vespucci (1415–1512):

> The manner of their living is very barbarous, because they do not eat at fixed times, but as often as they please. And it matters little to them that they should be seized with a desire to eat at midnight rather than by day, for at all times they eat. And their eating is done upon the ground, without tablecloth, or any other cloth, because they hold their food in earthen basins which they make or in half gourds. They sleep in certain nets made of cotton, very big, and hung in the air. And although this their way of sleeping may appear uncomfortable, I say that it is a soft way to sleep; [because it was very frequently our lot to sleep] in them, and we slept better in them than in quilts. They are people neat and clean of person, owing to the constant washing they practice. When, begging your pardon, they evacuate the bowels, they do everything to avoid being seen; and just as in this they are clean and modest, the more dirty and shameless are they in making water [both men and women]. Because, even while talking to us, they let fly such filth, without turning around or showing shame, that in this they have no modesty. They do not practice marriage amongst themselves. Each one takes all the wives he pleases; and when he desires to repudiate them, he does repudiate them without it being considered a wrong on his part or a disgrace to the woman; for in this the woman has as much liberty as the man.[4]

D. Identifying Patterns: The Gettysburg Address

Identify as many examples as you can of the following patterns in the Gettysburg Address [Texts for Analysis 5]:

1. References to the future
2. References to the present location
3. Life-death imagery
4. Terms of equality
5. Notions of dedication
6. Terms of high moral action
7. Pronouns
8. Contrasts

E. Identifying Patterns: Charts

The following chart provides information on the cost, average SAT scores, and percentage of students accepted for a number of colleges.[5] What patterns can you detect? What assumptions might you expect to document? Are those predictions supported by the evidence?

College	Tuition ($)*	Average SAT Scores	Acceptance Rate (%)
Alaska Pacific Univ.	6,200	925	55
Bowdoin	16,070	1300	27
Florida State Univ.	1,491	1097	61
Hope College	10,022	1040	86
Univ. of California (Davis)	2,463	1088	66
Univ. of Texas (Austin)	916	1095	67
Williams College	16,635	1335	28
Wright State Univ.	2,649	850	94

F. Classifying Patterns of Evidence: Robert Lynd on American Values

Americans' daily lives are governed by assumptions that are rooted in a value system. In many cases, the assumptions are contradictory, and a conflict of values is apparent. Robert S. Lynd has offered an extended series of such contrasting beliefs, such as:

Poverty is deplorable and should be abolished.

But: There never has been enough to go around, and the Bible tells us that "The poor you have always with you."

Such "contrasting rules of the game," Lynd argues, are "one of the most characteristic aspects of our American culture."[6]

The uncritical reader can simply read Lynd's list of beliefs as statements of contradictory values. To the critical reader, however, the notion that it is peculiarly American to live by contradictory rules deserves more thought. Do the contrasting pairs offer consistently different systems of beliefs—and, if so, what is the underlying nature of those systems of belief?

Lynd presents the contradictory beliefs as pairs. In the following list, the pairs have been split up. Your task is to identify the six pairs of conflicting statements, and in so doing to identify the aspect of the culture described by each pair (the example above is about poverty). Then, split the pairs you identified into two lists of contrasting rules and characterize the overall outlook of each philosophy.

1. The thing that distinguishes man from beast is the fact that he is rational; and therefore man can be trusted, if let alone, to guide his conduct wisely.

2. Business is our most important institution; and since national welfare depends on it, other institutions must conform to its needs.

3. The old, tried fundamentals are best; and it is a mistake for busybodies to try to change things too fast or to upset the fundamentals.

*Tuition figures for Florida State University and the universities of California and Texas are for in-state students; out-of-state tuition is higher.

4. Some people are brighter than others; and, as every practical politician and businessman knows, you can't afford simply to sit back and wait for people to make up their minds.

5. Life would not be tolerable if we did not believe in progress and know that things are getting better. We should, therefore, welcome new things.

6. The family is our basic institution and the sacred core of our national life.

7. The kind of person you are is more important than how successful you are.

8. A man owes it to himself and his family to make as much money as he can.

9. Business is business, and a businessman would be a fool if he didn't cover his hand.

10. Religion and "the finer things in life" are our ultimate values and the things all of us are really working for.

11. Everyone should try to be successful.

12. Honesty is the best policy.

G. Texts for Analysis: Senator Danforth on the National Endowment for the Arts

Indicate major patterns of content and label the nature of the examples in Senator John Danforth's speech on the National Endowment for the Arts [Texts for Analysis 9]. Do not worry about an overall idea for the moment; concentrate solely on finding patterns of content throughout the text.

H. Texts for Analysis: "Running Out of Time"

The article "I'm 38, and Running Out of Time" [Texts for Analysis 12] indicates various reactions the author received in response to her plight. Classify the major patterns of response.

Inferring Meaning from Relationships— Inference Equations

Every thought tends to connect something with something else, to establish a relationship between things.

• Lev Semenovich Vygotsky
THOUGHT AND LANGUAGE[1] •

From specific parts, in specific relationships, we infer meaning.

Analysis of a text begins with the recognition of patterns of content. The goal, however, is not simply to<None> identify how different aspects of the content are portrayed. Each aspect of the text is portrayed that way, we assume, to convey an overall meaning. The ultimate goal is to determine that meaning.

INFERRING MEANING FROM THE RELATIONSHIPS OF PARTS

What must one show to argue that a text conveys a particular meaning? Imagine a description of an arrest that portrays the suspected criminal as savage and the police as restrained. The description would seem to suggest proper behavior by law enforcement officers:

savage and restrained police ⟶ proper behavior by law
criminal enforcement officers

But if both police and suspect are portrayed as acting brutally, the message is not immediately clear:

savage criminal and brutal police ⟶ ?

Which action came first? Was one the cause of the other? Were the police provoked, or were the officers out of control? What, in other words, is the relationship between the parts? We must go beyond **analysis**, or dividing into parts, to **synthesis**, or recognizing how parts are related to one another.

The Relationship of Parts

The way in which things are related affects their meaning in various situations. The following group of unrelated words, for instance, has no meaning:

book the new the on table is school

Only when the words are related to one another in a particular order do we recognize meaning. Arranged differently, the words take on different meaning:

The new book is on the school table.

The school book is on the new table.

The new school book is on the table.

The book is on the new school table.

The book on the school table is new.

The meaning depends on the relationships between the parts. Change the relationships, and the meaning changes. Specific parts, in a certain relationship, convey a particular meaning.

Consider the meaning of the following sentences:

1. They went to the beach *although* it rained.
2. They went to the beach *and* it rained.
3. They went to the beach *before* it rained.

The three sentences present the same action and the same weather conditions—the same "parts"—but the sentences express different thoughts. As in the previous examples, the meaning in each case is controlled by the relationship between the ideas—whether contrast ("although"), a series of similar remarks ("and"), or chronological order ("before"). These examples demonstrate what we shall call the **inference equation model**.

• THE INFERENCE EQUATION MODEL •

According to this model, specific parts, in a certain relationship, convey a particular meaning. By recognizing the nature of and the relationship among the parts, readers infer meaning that reflects their prior knowledge and understanding.

The Inference Equation Model

The inference equation model offers, in effect, a "grammar" of meaning. The first step is concerned with analysis—the recognition of parts. The second step is concerned with synthesis—the recognition of how parts are related. The final step calls on the reader's powers of inference. We can diagram this equation as in the earlier examples:

part	**relationship**	**part**	⟶	**inferred meaning**
savage	and	restrained		proper behavior by law
criminal		police		enforcement officers

While this model may appear new or novel, the idea underlying it should be quite familiar. It is simply a formal way of articulating common thought patterns.

The Relationships of Inference Equations

The relationships encountered in inference equations are the same as in the relationship model of paragraph structure:

> **series:** a list of items similar in some way, and sometimes arranged in a particular order (big to little, most to least important, and so on):
>
> *and, also, in addition, then, another, finally, moreover, besides, next, first, furthermore, many, some, other, several, lastly, as well as*

> **chronological (time):** one thing occurring before or after another:
>
> *then, after, before, soon, immediately, at that time, until, when, during, later, next, prior*

> **general/specific:** one event offered as an example of another:
>
> *in general, for example, overall*

> **comparison/contrast:** one thing shown to be similar to, or different than, another:
>
> similarity: *like, both, similarly, in the same way, comparatively, equally*
>
> difference: *yet, except, but, although, or, rather, on the contrary, however, in contrast, even though, otherwise, not, in spite of, whereas*

> **reason/conclusion:** one thing portrayed as a reason for, or conclusion of, another:
>
> *because, if, since*

> **cause/effect:** one thing portrayed as a cause or effect of another:
>
> *thus, hence, therefore, then, consequently, so, after all*

> **conditional:** one event or argument portrayed as a condition for another:
>
> *if, then*

For further discussion of these categories, see Chapter 1 and Appendix E, "The Relationship Model."

EXAMPLE: **Going to the Beach**

Classifying the content of the sentences about going to the beach, we recognize a relationship between something pleasurable (going to the beach) and bad conditions for such an action (rain). Drawing on the prior description of the relationships involved, we can diagram each sentence and then infer meaning as follows:

1. Doing something pleasurable   contrasted with   bad conditions for that action   ⟶   determination

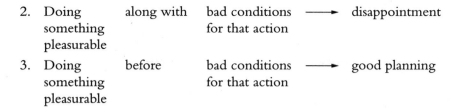

2. Doing something pleasurable | along with | bad conditions for that action ⟶ disappointment

3. Doing something pleasurable | before | bad conditions for that action ⟶ good planning

Phrased slightly differently, the sentences are about:

1. An overwhelming desire to be at the beach
2. A disappointing experience
3. Successful or lucky planning

Shifts in Meaning

Important shifts in meaning result from any change in an inference equation. The difference between a felony and a misdemeanor, for instance, is in the nature of the action. Suppose someone commits an illegal act. The inference equation would look like this:

person   cause of   illegal act ⟶ guilty

The extent of that person's guilt is determined by the nature of the illegal act:

person   cause of   misdemeanor ⟶ guilty of *minor* crime
person   cause of   felony ⟶ guilty of *major* crime

Here the relationship "cause of" amounts to "is shown to have committed."

Other times, the critical difference will lie in the relationship. Using the same example, showing the person to be innocent of the action obviously eliminates guilt:

person   not cause of   illegal act ⟶ innocent

Return to the description of an arrest at the beginning of this chapter. If the police actions are presented as *caused by* the suspect's violence, we have justification for the police actions:

suspect brutality   cause of   police brutality ⟶ justifiable police violence

The police were brutal *because* the suspect was brutal. But if the police actions are portrayed as the *cause of* the suspect's brutal actions, we have abuse of power and an understandable reaction:

| police | cause of | suspect | $\longrightarrow$ | justifiable |
| brutality | | brutality | | suspect violence |

The suspect *reacted* brutally *to* the police brutality. Each of these equations is based on a cause/effect relationship.

To indicate an inappropriate action, we document:

| behavior | inconsistent with | a standard of social behavior | $\longrightarrow$ | inappropriate behavior |

The relationship is one of contrast.

To show an honest action, we demonstrate:

| behavior | consistent with | a standard of ethical action | $\longrightarrow$ | honesty |

The relationship is one of comparison (similarity).

To show the need for a particular policy, we show:

| a problem | and | some reason to believe that a certain action will solve that problem | $\longrightarrow$ | support for that policy |

In each case, the meaning depends on showing certain ingredients in a specific relationship. Additional examples of inference equations appear at the end of this chapter.

APPLYING THE INFERENCE EQUATION MODEL

EXAMPLE: The Ku Klux Klan

To read critically, you must recognize terms and phrases that indicate how different elements of content are related. In the following passage [Texts for Analysis 1A], signal words appear in boldface.

As the year 1870 drew to a close, conditions in South Carolina **became** more and more terrible . . . this dreadful condition of affairs **forced** . . . **In January** 1871, a one-armed Confederate soldier **was** cruelly beaten **and then** murdered. . . . The Klan . . . put in jail thirteen of the negroes believed to have taken part in the murder. The negroes in Union **became so threatening that** the Klan visited the jail. . . . **Whenever** the negro militiamen became intolerable, the Klan set itself to work. . . . Seeing the determination of the white people . . . Governor Scott **final-ly** disbanded the negro militia. . . . The Ku Klux Klan **then** stopped its work.

The text contains words and phrases indicating chronological order ("became," "In January," "finally"), and cause and effect ("forced," "whenever") in a discussion contrasting the actions of two groups.

Throughout the excerpt, the activities of the two groups are contrasted and presented in a cause/effect relationship. From each equation we infer an unstated meaning:

evidence of evil action	as cause of	evidence of actions to suppress	⟶	justified retaliation
evidence of rash, evil behavior	contrasted with	evidence of controlled, good acts	⟶	moral superiority of the latter

We can interpret an unstated meaning as follows:

By portraying the Klan's actions as controlled and provoked and the black's actions as evil and unprovoked, the excerpt justifies any brutality by the Klan, laying all blame on the blacks.

These overall assertions can then be backed up with a more detailed description of the patterns of evidence:

The text consistently contrasts the actions and motivations of the blacks and the Klan. [**description**] Blacks are portrayed as trouble-makers, whites as law-abiding people provoked into action. [**further description**] This portrayal is highlighted in the example of the black militia beating a defenseless white soldier to death for no apparent reason. [**description at a lower level of analysis**] By contrasting the groups in this way, the excerpt justifies the Klan's actions, portraying them as reluctantly violent and even restrained in their actions. [**interpretation**]

The more we analyze this text, the clearer it becomes how skillfully the text justifies the actions of the Klan through its portrayals of events. As with all critical reading, this process of analysis in no way implies acceptance of the text as accurate or justified. The goal is to understand what the text's message is and how this message is conveyed. The better we do that job, the better equipped we are to criticize the ideas later.

EXAMPLE: **Charles Drew Biographies**

The following paragraphs are excerpted from minibiographies of Dr. Charles Drew, a black doctor who, as a leader in the effort to store blood and as director of the Red Cross, developed the first blood banks.

Text 1

For a long time, the Army and Navy refused to accept blood from black people. Even after it started to accept "colored" blood, the Army told the Red Cross to separate the donated blood of black people from that of whites. Charles Drew explained that there was no such thing as "black" and "white" blood. Blood was blood. But no one listened. This made Charles Drew very sad and angry. He resigned from the Red Cross.[2]

Text 2

Due to the success of his program [to collect, store and ship blood for transfusions in England], Drew was appointed as Red Cross director of a nationwide project to collect blood for the U.S. military. The project was going well until the armed forces told the Red Cross that it did not want any "colored" blood. Such a racist policy made no sense from any scientific or medical point of view. In an angry editorial, the Chicago *Defender* said

No Negro blood accepted but—

When the terrible blitz raids of London . . . killed and wounded thousands . . . it was an American Negro surgeon [who organized and sent] U.S. blood plasma overseas

No Negro blood accepted but—

When the Japanese bombed Pearl Harbor and maimed hundreds of American soldiers and sailors, it was blood collected by a Negro surgeon that saved their lives.

Because of this kind of protest, the military agreed to accept "colored" blood but insisted that it be kept separate from blood donated by whites. To Dr. Drew this directive was completely unacceptable, and he resigned from the blood program.[3]

In the first text, Dr. Drew resigns out of frustration, "very sad and angry." In the second text, he resigns on principle in response to the Red Cross's "unacceptable" position. In each case, his resignation is presented as a response to the actions of others. But by portraying the manner of his resignation differently, the texts imply very different assessments of his character.

The two presentations rely on different inference equations:

Text 1: resignation   due to   frustration $\longrightarrow$ quitter

Text 2: resignation   due to   principle $\longrightarrow$ courageous behavior

USES OF THE INFERENCE EQUATION MODEL

Using Inference Equations to Write Effectively

Inference equations suggest an approach to effective writing. Writers must first identify the concepts they wish to convey. By analyzing those concepts according to the inference equation model, they can select the ingredients necessary to communicate their message.

To indicate a gift, for instance, one must show who gave what to whom and for what reason. Each of these elements is necessary to fulfill the idea of "gift" and to distinguish a gift from a bribe or bartering. To suggest exploitation, it is not enough to show that one group has something that another group does not; this would be an equation for inequality, but not necessarily exploitation. The first group must be shown to benefit in power, property, or prestige at the expense of the other. If writers provide the proper patterns of evidence and appropriate words to signal the desired relationship, readers with similar backgrounds will, presumably, complete the equation. Editing involves refining the elements of the inference equation to ensure the desired interpretation.

Using Inference Equations to Test an Interpretation

Just as writers can use the inference equation model to ensure the presence of the ingredients necessary to convey an idea, readers can use the same model to check the inferences they draw from texts. To test an interpretation, readers ask:

- What elements would have to be present to support that interpretation?
- Are they present in that manner?

Using Inference Equations as a Format for Discussion

The inference equation model is also a powerful tool for presenting an interpretation. The model offers a format for discussing inferences:

By relating certain concepts in certain ways,
    the text suggests certain ideas.

By contrasting Cinderella's modest behavior with the greed and ambition of her sisters,
    the fairy tale teaches the lesson that virtue is ultimately rewarded.

A certain concept is conveyed
    by presenting certain evidence in a certain way.

E. B. White's essay suggests that democracy is more a way of life than a political philosophy
    by portraying democracy through examples of everyday experiences that suggest opportunity and civility.

The above responses both assert new meaning and indicate the evidence on which the inferences are based. Looking back on the commentary on the Klan excerpt, we can see that this is what we have done:

By portraying the Klan's actions as controlled and provoked and the blacks' actions as evil and unprovoked,
    the excerpt justifies any brutality by the Klan, laying all blame on the blacks.

The same model used for analyzing a text is used for presenting the interpretation based on that analysis.

IMPLICATIONS

Inference equations draw together the notions of analysis and inference. While the model may appear novel, it is really nothing more than a formula for common sense, a formal way of talking about what we mean by certain ideas and how we reason in everyday life.

The real power of the inference equation model lies in the fact that it can be applied to both reading and writing, to both the analysis of texts and the discussion of one's interpretation, to both defending an interpretation and testing that that meaning is really there. The following two chapters extend the use of the model to include evidence of language usage and persuasive devices.

• SAMPLE INFERENCE EQUATIONS •

belief in an idea	contrasted with	evidence of truth of a contrary idea	⟶ evidence of mistaken belief
holding one view	followed by	holding an opposite view	⟶ changing one's mind
action	compared to	standard of behavior	⟶ judgment of behavior
action	contrasted with	law to the contrary	⟶ illegal behavior
ignorance	followed by	knowledge	⟶ learning
potential event	cause of	unwanted consequences	⟶ threat of danger
asserted belief	contrasted with	absence of information	⟶ speculation

These examples are just that, examples of the myriad of thought units that might be constructed to describe the countless concepts and ideas by which we communicate with one another.

EXERCISES/DISCUSSION

A. Ingredients of Concepts

What would one have to show to indicate the following concepts?

1. Deception
2. An irresponsible action
3. An unnecessary action
4. An honest action
5. Disrespect

B. Drawing Inferences from Inference Equations 1

Indicate the meaning suggested by the following:

1. A good deed and good intent
2. A good deed resulting in a bad outcome
3. A good outcome resulting from a bad deed

C. Drawing Inferences from Inference Equations 2

What meaning might be conveyed by showing that a politician voted for a bill favoring a constituent in each of the following cases?

1. Following the receipt of a campaign contribution
2. Because of the receipt of a campaign contribution
3. As a condition for the receipt of a campaign contribution

D. Completing Inference Equations

Complete the inference equations:

1. evidence of   and   evidence of ⟶ _____
   fewer eagles   increased
                                pesticide use

2. evidence of   caused   _____ ⟶ need to ban
   fewer eagles   by   a certain
                                                 pesticide

3. increase in   _____   evidence of ⟶ uncertainty
   number of   increased
   eagles   pesticide use

E. Patterns of Content and Their Relationships

Indicate how meaning is derived from patterns of content and their relationships in the following excerpt:

> At no time in the first years of the war did Lincoln say it was being waged to abolish slavery; the purpose of the war was to preserve the Union, not to destroy the institutions of the Southern States. Though he consistently argued for a plan of compensated emancipation, he opposed with equal consistency the efforts of some of his generals to use local emancipation as a war weapon against the Confederacy. But as month after month went by and casualties rose, Northern anti-slavery men began to demand that emancipation be espoused as a war aim. They insisted that slavery was the real cause of the war, and that to win the war and reconstitute the Union without destroying slavery would only be asking for further trouble with "The slave owner." The most notable assertion of this point of view was Horace Greeley's "Prayer of Twenty Millions," an open letter to Lincoln dated August 19, 1862. Lincoln's answer was another instance of his capacity for memorably succinct expression: he was fighting only to save the Union; if he did anything about slavery he would do it only because it contributed to this end. But even while this interchange was going on, Lincoln was, in fact, changing his mind about the value of emancipation to the Union cause. Exactly a month after his answer to Greeley, he issued a proclamation giving notice that on January 1, 1863, he would declare free the slaves in those states still rebelling. On the day designated, he issued the Emancipation Proclamation. Since the Proclamation did not free slaves under Union jurisdiction, but only those under Confederate jurisdiction whom the Union could not actually liberate, it was much criticized as having no force. But by committing the Union to emancipation, it made emancipation inevitable, and paved the way for the Thirteenth Amendment.[4]

"Freedom Fighters" or "Terrorists"?— The Choice of Language

Words are the tools for the job of saying what you want to say.

• Bergen Evans
THE WORD–A–DAY VOCABULARY BUILDER[1] •

Language separates men from other animals. It also reduces them to the level of animals—as in calling Jews "vermin" or policemen "pigs."

• Thomas Szasz, THE SECOND SIN[2] •

Choices of language complement choices of content to shape how a topic is portrayed.

Authors must choose not only *what* to say but *how* to say it. Much of the work of writing is a matter of choosing appropriate words to convey the desired thoughts. (The use of language for persuasive purposes is considered separately in Chapter 10).

DENOTATION AND CONNOTATION

Two kinds of meaning are involved in the selection of words: denotation and connotation.

Denotation is what a word specifies—that is, the dictionary meaning.

Connotation refers to the emotional overtones and associations that accompany the use of a specific word. For example, *rap* denotes a style of musical performance involving rhythmic expression. The same term can connote anything from insightful social commentary to racist expletives, depending on the listener. *Family* denotes biological relatives, but it can also connote closeness or warmth. *Cop*, *policeman*, and *law enforcement officer* denote the same person, but each term connotes different ideas, different emotional and intellectual associations. *Jalopy* denotes an old car; *roadster* connotes an old car.

• CONNOTATION AND WORD USAGE •

Commenting on why the term *suicide* is not applied to cases involving the terminally ill, a widely respected text on biomedical ethics offers one of the more involuted phrasings on the subject: "Terms in their ordinary meaning often contain evaluative accretions from social attitudes that render them difficult to analyze."[3] Or, in other words, words come to have connotations that can affect their usage.

The Variability of Connotations

Some connotations are fairly universal, others decidedly personal. The term *yacht* has a connotation of wealth for most people, including the rich. (The dictionary definition simply indicates a small sailing vessel used for cruising or racing.) The connotation of the term *liberal* as a tax-and-spend social do-gooder, on the other hand, is limited to the political Right.

Connotations are in constant flux: as values change, connotations change. (Denotations also change, but much more slowly.) In February 1993, for instance, the New York Zoological Society decided that the term *zoo* was degrading since it had acquired the connotation of a place marked by confusion and disorder. The world-famous Bronx Zoo was renamed the more fashionable "International Wildlife Conservation Park." The zoo remained the same; only the name changed. As if to vindicate the change, a reporter noted that a New York taxi driver, on being asked to take a passenger to the Central Park Zoo, observed, "Which zoo? The whole city's a zoo."[4]

Connotation versus Association

We should distinguish between the associations one has with a concept and the connotations evoked by specific words. A response to the mention of fresh-baked bread, for example, is to the concept or the thing itself, not to the term. Any similar terms referring to fresh-baked bread would produce the same thoughts or reactions. The notion that eggplant is unappetizing is sufficiently widespread that even people who like eggplant will make the connection. Again, however, this reflects a cultural association with the vegetable, not a response to the word. A distinction between a menu listing for *hamburger* and one for *chopped steak patty* is one of connotation.

The difference between association and connotation is real and important, and yet in many instances, the boundary between associations and connotation is blurry. Readers often respond to both the concept and the term. A reference to *the physically challenged*, for example, draws on both the reader's associations with those with physical limitations and the connotation of dignity that would be absent with a phrase such as *the disabled*. In the end, readers should be more concerned with recognizing all aspects of meaning than with determining whether they result from association or connotation.

•••••••••••• **DENOTATION AND CONNOTATION** ••••••••••••

Words with inappropriate connotations can, at times, seem almost poetic. More often, however, such terms are simply wrong. Indicate any inappropriate terms in the following. Why are they inappropriate? What terms would work better?

> Prodding more tobacco into his pipe, the antique gentleman glanced over to the youngest of his litter and orated: "When you have finished pruning the grass, please get me my slippers."

••

The Elusiveness of Neutrality

If we choose our words carefully, we are told, we can avoid unwanted connotations. We can be objective and describe things "simply as they are." This may be possible in some situations, but many times there is no "neutral ground." Any word choice from a variety of options represents a conscious decision to portray a topic one way instead of another.

EXAMPLE: Freedom Fighters

In December 1990, Richard Harwood, ombudsman for *The Washington Post*, offered the following observations.

> In Israel recently, an Egyptian ambushed military and civilian cars and buses, killing four people and wounding 26. Was he a "terrorist"? A "freedom fighter"? A "fanatic"? He may have been all three. He may have been insane. The Israeli police don't know. Jackson Diehl, *The Washington Post*'s correspondent in Jerusalem, didn't know. So he described the man as a "gunman," an "Egyptian," an "assailant."
>
> That was unsatisfactory to some readers. They hung a label on *The Post*—"anti-Israel"—for failing to label the gunman a "terrorist." I'm sympathetic to those critics, because we are often not as rational and disinterested as Diehl in labeling the subjects of our stories. Instead, it is frequently the case that the labels we use are more descriptive of our own states of mind—expressions of approval and disapproval—than descriptions of the individuals or acts we hang them on.[5]

The choice between "fanatic," "freedom fighter" and "terrorist" is one of denotation. While the terms may have various overtones, they indicate different types of people: someone with an uncommonly strong, and even irrational, commitment to an idea or cause; someone taking up arms, actually or figuratively, to combat oppression; and someone inflicting indiscriminate violence. To most people, ambushing civilians amounts to terrorism; denying that label seems to deny the horror of the action. Whether one views a gunman as a freedom fighter depends on whether one believes him to be the oppressed or the oppressor. Finally, labeling the person a "gunman" rather than "fanatic" avoids the suggestion of extreme adherence to a political cause that might justify, or condemn, the

---

The choice of rhetoric is a central problem for the historian of slavery in America. In what tone, with what language, should he depict the South's "peculiar institution"? If he portrays life under slavery as an unending sequence of horrors and brutalities, his tone becomes so shrill that he loses credibility. If he gives too much emphasis to the sunshine amidst the shadows, he sounds like a proslavery apologist.

• David Herbert Donald, review of
BLACK ODYSSEY by Nathan Irvin Huggins[6] •

action. Any choice of the four terms reflects a political position, a favoring of one political view over another.

For our purposes, it is Harwood's final observation that has the greatest significance: by analyzing the choice of terms, we can discover the mind-set underlying the discussion.

THE EFFECT OF CHOICES OF LANGUAGE

Choices of language and content go together. Heroic actions will be portrayed in heroic terms. Evidence of deceit will be couched in terms suggesting deception. At times, patterns of one may be more obvious than the other. Together or alone, however, patterns of content and of language offer evidence of the underlying values in a text.

EXAMPLE: **Chief of Staff Sununu**

The easiest way to see the effect of specific language is to change the terms and observe the resulting shifts in meaning. Writing a few weeks after the opening of an international conference on acid rain, and during Operation Desert Storm, columnist Jim Fain observed:

> Almost unnoticed among the war excitement, the U.S. managed to stonewall the rest of the industrial world's efforts to curb greenhouse gas emission [gases such as carbon dioxide that collect in the atmosphere and cause the temperature of the earth to increase].
>
> It was a virtuoso performance by one stubborn, arrogant man—White House Chief of Staff John Sununu. The ultimate blame rests, of course, on President Bush. He licensed Sununu to throw all that White House weight around. But Bush doesn't much care about this issue except as it affects his ratings. Left to his druthers, he'd just as soon be an environmentalist.
>
> Sununu is downright pigheaded on the subject. He preens on his IQ and familiarity with science. From these eminences, he has concluded that greenhouse warming is a myth and developed his own computer model to show that the other models don't know what they're talking about.[7]

Consider an alternative version (alternate words are indicated in boldface):

> Almost unnoticed among the war excitement, the U.S. managed to **delay** the rest of the industrial world's efforts to **ease** greenhouse gas emission.
>
> It was a **skillful** performance by one **determined, self-assured** man—White House Chief of Staff John Sununu. The ultimate **responsibility** rests, of course, on President Bush. He **allowed** Sununu to throw all that White House weight around. But Bush doesn't much care about this issue except as it affects his ratings. Left to his druthers, **he would** just as soon be an environmentalist.

Sununu is downright **determined** on the subject. He **prides himself** on his IQ and familiarity with science. From these **abilities**, he has concluded that greenhouse warming is a myth and developed his own computer model to show that the other models **do not** know what they're talking about.

The original condemns; the latter version does not. And yet the new terms are seemingly synonyms of the old:

Original	Alternate
stone wall	delay
curb	ease
virtuoso	skillful
stubborn	determined
arrogant	self-assured
blame	responsibility
licensed	allowed
he'd	he would
pigheaded	determined
preens	prides himself
eminences	abilities
don't	do not

Distinct language patterns shape the tone and thus the message in each passage. Classifying the terms in the left-hand column, we note uncomplimentary terms that build an image of an overblown ego and a lack of consideration for others. Classifying the terms in the right-hand column, we note more formal and flattering terms that suggest an independent-minded, self-confident nature. In the second version, much of the venom is gone. Instead of pigheadedness we have simple determination. For the most part, the content has not been changed. The same actions are indicated; the denotations are the same. And yet the differences in connotation radically shift how the actions are portrayed.

EXAMPLE: *Silent Spring*

Rachel Carson's *Silent Spring* is often cited as the work that brought environmental pollution to public attention. In this excerpt from her book, notice the way in which man's effect on the environment is portrayed.

> The most alarming of all man's assaults upon the environment is the contamination of air, earth, rivers, and sea with dangerous and even lethal materials. This pollution is for the most part irrecoverable; the chain of evil it initiates not only in the world

that must support life but in living tissues is for the most part irreversible. In this now universal contamination of the environment, chemicals are the sinister and little-recognized partners of radiation in changing the nature of the world—the very nature of its life.[8]

As the boldfaced terms from the original passage show, the sense of an active, malevolent force is overwhelming:

The most **alarming** of all man's **assaults** upon the environment is the **contamination** of air, earth, rivers, and sea with **dangerous** and even **lethal** materials. This **pollution** is for the most part **irrecoverable**; the **chain of evil** it initiates not only in the world that must support life but in living tissues is for the most part **irreversible**. In this now **universal contamination** of the environment, chemicals are the **sinister** and little-recognized **partners of radiation** in changing the nature of the world—the very nature of its life.

Whether this is an accurate portrayal of the role of pesticides in environmental degradation is not the question here. Our immediate goal is not to evaluate the truthfulness of the text, but to recognize the patterns of language and content by which the text portrays things. Having done so, we have no doubt about how the text portrays the situation.

At times, a pattern of condemning labels can be carried too far, creating more smoke than fire. The following is from Alabama Governor George Wallace's July 4th speech responding to the 1964 Civil Rights Bill:

A left-wing monster has risen up in this nation. It has invaded the government. It has invaded the news media. It has invaded the leadership of many of our churches. It has invaded every phase and aspect of life of freedom-loving people.

It consists of many and various and powerful interests, but it has combined into one massive drive and is held together by the cohesive power of the emotion, setting

---

There is a joke among newspapermen that if a woman is pretty, she is called "beautiful"; if she is plain, she is called "attractive"; and if she is hideous, she is called "vivacious." Half the joke is the exaggeration; the other half is that this is no exaggeration at all. In describing a woman involved in a murder or a robbery or a divorce case, the same technique is generally applied to every aspect of her appearance. If she is tall, she is "statuesque." If she is short, the word is "petite." Thin women are "slender," while fat ones are "curvaceous." Physical appearance is not so important in a man, and the emphasis shifts to financial appearance. "Socially prominent" is a popular description of any man who is murdered by his wife. Bookies and gigolos may be identified as "sportsmen." And one connoisseur has defined "socialite" as "a tabloid term meaning human being."

• Otto Friedrich, "A VIVACIOUS BLONDE WAS FATALLY SHOT TODAY OR HOW TO READ A TABLOID"[9] •

forth civil rights as supreme to all. But, in reality, it is a drive to destroy the rights of private property, to destroy the freedom and liberty of you and me.[10]

The speech offers a pattern of language portraying a malignant force out of control ("left-wing monster . . . invaded . . . massive drive . . . destroy") demolishing cherished American institutions and values ("government . . . the news media . . . churches . . . freedom-loving people . . . private property . . . freedom and liberty"). What actually has happened remains unclear.

ANALYZING PATTERNS OF LANGUAGE USAGE

Texts contain evidence of their thinking in the selection of words. While we may debate whether the words within a text accurately portray the topic as we know it, we must assume that those words accurately portray how the author wishes that topic to be viewed.

Describing Patterns of Language Usage

The first step in assessing the language of a text is to describe patterns of that usage—that is, to identify what kinds of terms are used and what they are applied to. Readers can assure the greatest objectivity in their descriptions by classifying broad patterns throughout the text. Patterns of content are generally reflected in patterns of language. Evidence to be accepted is presented in favorable terms, evidence to be rejected in unfavorable terms.

Drawing Inferences from Patterns of Language Usage

Having identified patterns of terms, the next step is to draw inferences from that evidence. How does such language usage contribute to the meaning of the text? Why might the author have selected this wording? While this last question is phrased in terms of intent or purpose, it focuses attention on the nature of the language and its effects on the discussion. To better appreciate the implications of specific word usage, recall how the alternate terms in the Sununu passage radically altered the overall meaning.

Any interpretation of a text should indicate both the inferences drawn and the evidence on which they are based. How, then, should we interpret the Sununu passage? Having condemned President Bush's efforts to limit acid rain, the article extends that condemnation to Bush's choice of assistants by portraying his chief of staff, Sununu, in uncomplimentary terms that emphasize an oversized ego and a lack of consideration for others. At this point, readers may wish to assess the degree to which the article is an attack on Bush, Sununu, or the policy on acid rain.

To interpret figurative language, we must identify the associations suggested by the specific image and indicate how that meaning contributes to the overall thought. For example, if someone is said to "run like a deer," we might observe that a sense of speed and grace is conveyed by comparing the person to a deer. We might then observe that portraying them as swift and graceful in this way suggests unusual athletic prowess.

Note the structure of the earlier comments. The comments have the form:

A particular tone is achieved
   by referring to a certain topic in a certain way.

or

A certain meaning is conveyed
   by terms that portray a certain topic in certain ways.

It is not enough to say that a certain tone exists; you must indicate the basis for the remark. Similarly, having shown that the language portrays a topic a certain way, you want to extend the observation to include the inferences you draw from that state of affairs.

EXAMPLE: **The Assassination of Malcolm X**

In the newspaper reports of the assassination (murder? killing? demise?) of Malcolm X [Texts for Analysis 2A–2C], language patterns emphasize the content. For example, the sympathetic account of the *Post* stresses the sneaky action of the killers by referring to them with the conspiratorial term "lead-off" men and describing their action with the slang phrase "made their move" (in contrast to the openness and forthrightness of Malcolm X and his followers). By contrast, the unsympathetic account in *Newsweek* labels the followers' response as "bedlam" and as "howling in pursuit," terms implying a lack of control and, hence, irrationality and disrespect.

When we couch behavior in the language of religion, we legitimize it; when we couch it in the language of psychiatry, we illegitimize it.

We say that Catholics who do not eat meat on Fridays and Jews who do not eat pork at all are devoutly religious; we do not say that Catholics suffer from recurrent attacks of meat phobia, or that Jews are afflicted with a fixed phobia of pork.

• Thomas Szasz, THE SECOND SIN[11] •

Malcolm X was, himself, familiar with how the choice of terms can shape one's thought. Discussing the Detroit riots (disturbances? uprising? demonstrations?) of 1964, he observed, in a classic example of critical reading and interpretation:

> If you noticed, [the press] referred to the rioters as vandals, hoodlums, thieves, and they skillfully took the burden off the [larger] society for its failure to correct these negative conditions in the black community. They took the burden completely off the society and put it right on the community by using the press to make it appear that the looting and all of this was proof that the whole act was nothing but vandals and robbers and thieves, who weren't really interested in anything other than that which was negative.[12]

The language usage may appear as the choice of nouns (protester versus rioter versus hoodlum) or the use of adjectives (beating versus savage beating). Either way, choices of language go hand-in-hand with choices of content.

• INTERPRETATION AND PATTERNS OF LANGUAGE •

In any given instance, readers might prefer one term or phrase to another. That is not the issue. The task of interpretation is to observe the choices within the text and to relate them to the remainder of the discussion.

IMPLICATIONS

Choices of language complement choices of content. Together, these two elements control how topics are portrayed. For the most part, terms are chosen to emphasize specific qualities, to make favorable things look better and unfavorable things worse, or to praise or damn by invoking positive or negative connotations. Language patterns provide further evidence of the underlying outlook of a text.

Readers have a responsibility to recognize not only the connotations that are common within the culture but also these connotations that are, or are not, appropriate within a given discussion. As we saw with content, a degree of control can be found by focusing not on individual terms, but on patterns of terms and their common characteristics.

EXERCISES/DISCUSSION

A. Interpreting Examples

A striking but by no means isolated example of the selection/presentation of evidence occurred in a discussion of the 1974 Boston school busing dispute in *The*

Boston Globe (October 10, 1974). Referring to an injured white, the article stated: "He suffered face cuts when a rock was thrown through the windshield." Referring to an injured black, it stated: "She told police she was hit by rocks thrown by white youths." How do these examples differ? What implications might be drawn from the difference? Is this a difference in content or language—or both?

B. Sexist Terms

Sexist terms are receiving increasing attention and condemnation. To be politically correct, for example, a farmer and his wife should be referred to as a "farm couple" to place husband and wife on equal footing. Rewrite the following terms in nonsexist language:

1. the fair sex
2. the men debated while the women chattered
3. Congressman
4. the common man

C. Denotation and Connotation

Connotations of common terms and phrases are often most evident when those terms are compared to others. Distinguish between the meanings and overtones of the following:

1. murder, execute, kill, exterminate, assassinate, rub out
2. quickly, suddenly, hurriedly, in a flash, all of a sudden
3. claim, argue, assert, proclaim, state, remark, observe
4. bribe, contribution, gift, gratuity, tip, honorarium

D. Social Usage

Different terms are appropriate in different social settings. A term appropriate in street conversation, for example, may be colloquial in informal speech and slangy in formal settings. Fill in the blanks and add a few more examples.

Colloquial	Informal	Formal
bread	_____	money
_____	car	automobile
tub	boat	_____

E. Choosing Terms

Just as authors must choose their words carefully, readers must select precise terms when commenting on a text. Under what conditions can we say that an article *claims* that a particular chemical is dangerous to our health? Under what conditions can we say an article *argues* the same point? Or *proves* the point?

F. Patterns of Language

Identify patterns of language within the following excerpts, and indicate their effect.

1.   The ritual anointment of Bill Clinton as the Democratic presidential candidate, so rudely interrupted by charges of infidelity and draft evasion, has resumed with lavish pomp. Scarcely had the Florida exit polls been processed on Super Tuesday than the popes of politics and punditry laid on their hands. You knew it *had* to be a defining moment when Dan Rather opened his barrel of Southern metaphors and produced such crackers as, "Bill Clinton roared through the South like a big wheel through the cotton fields."[13]

2.   While confined here in the Birmingham city jail, I came across your recent statement calling my present activities "unwise and untimely." Seldom do I pause to answer criticism of my work and ideas. If I sought to answer all the criticisms that cross my desk, my secretaries would have little time for anything other than such correspondence in the course of the day, and I would have no time for constructive work. But since I feel you are men of genuine good will and that your criticisms are sincerely set forth, I want to try to answer your statement in what I hope will be patient and reasonable terms.[14]

G. Texts for Analysis: Buckley on Abortion

How are the views signaled by choice of language in William F. Buckley, Jr.'s essay on abortion [Texts for Analysis 11]?

H. Texts for Analysis: "Sex Work"?

Much has been written on the political implications of terminology ("garbage men" versus "sanitation engineers," "housewives" versus "homemakers"). In the Senate Judiciary Committee hearings to confirm Ruth Bader Ginsburg as a justice of the Supreme Court, Dennis DeConcini asked why she used the term "gender discrimination" instead of the more common term "sex discrimination" in her work on discrimination suits affecting women. Ginsburg responded that in the 1970s her secretary complained of constantly typing "sex, sex, sex . . . " and suggested that for the lawyers she was addressing—all men—gender distinctions were not the first thing that came to mind.[15]

How many different terms for prostitutes are used in the Letter to the Editor by Tracy Quan [Texts for Analysis 16], and how are they used differently in the text?

I. Texts for Analysis: "Latino, Sí!"

What reasons does Earl Shorris give for his concern about the selection of a name [Texts for Analysis 10]?

J. Texts for Analysis: Medical Progress

Classify language patterns in "An Open Letter to the Press About a Real Threat to Medical Progress" [Texts for Analysis 8]. Indicate how they shape or contribute to the overall meaning of the text.

"Authoritative Sources Said . . ."— Invoking Belief and Acceptance

"Everyone lives by selling something," Robert Louis Stevenson wrote. *The* effective writer *"sells" his ideas; his reader says, consciously or unconsciously, "I'll* buy *that."*

• D. G. Kehl
"THE ELECTRIC CARROT: THE RHETORIC OF ADVERTISEMENT
AND THE ART OF PERSUASION"[1] •

Authors attempt to sway readers through a variety of devices that appeal more to emotion than to reason—but that offer critical readers important evidence of the bias of the text.

Authors draw on a broad arsenal of devices to make their portrayals convincing. In most cases, the motives and techniques are forthright and honorable: the product is of value and the claims are legitimate. Sometimes, however, things are not as they are made to seem.

LABELING

We respond to things in accordance with the labels that we attach to them. Label a plant that occurs naturally a weed, and people will mow it down. Call the same plant a regional flower, and people will cultivate it. The difference between an antique and a piece of garbage is, all too often, in the eye of the labeler. The same oil spill can be a "marginal release of material" or "an environmentally catastrophic outpouring of pollutants." In the letter of the Birmingham clergy protesting the Reverend Martin Luther King, Jr.'s nonviolent protests [Texts for Analysis 6], the clergy distinguish between "outsiders" and the "responsible citizens" of Birmingham, thereby shaping the reader's perception of the participants. In like manner, the letter distinguishes between the "extreme measures" of King and the "calm manner" and "restraint" of the local community.

In any text, terms are chosen according to the image the writer wishes to convey. Through this process of **labeling**, writers seek to shape the reader's perceptions. At the point at which such terms also affect the reader's acceptance of ideas, they incorporate aspects of **persuasion**.

For years dentists received a newsletter from Princeton Dental Resource Center—a prominent sounding organization seemingly associated with the prestigious Princeton University. Not until the newsletter suggested that "your favorite chocolate bar . . . can be good-tasting and might even inhibit cavities" did dentists realize that the group was financed by M&M/Mars, makers of M&M's, Mars, Snickers, and Milky Way chocolate bars.

• Barry Meier, "DUBIOUS THEORY: CHOCOLATE A CAVITY FIGHTER"[2] •

Euphemisms: A Form of Labeling

Euphemisms are inoffensive expressions substituted for those with disagreeable connotations. As such, they represent a form of labeling. For example, "passing away" (dying), and "Montezuma's revenge" (diarrhea) are euphemisms. As a means of enabling polite conversation on topics such as death, sex, and toilet training, euphemisms play an important role in human communication. "Etiquette cannot do without euphemisms," the columnist Miss Manners observed. "Actually, one of etiquette's major missions is to disguise what people actually mean."[3] Once euphemisms entice acceptance of otherwise unacceptable ideas, they become an aspect of persuasion.

Some Limitations of Labeling

Labeling is subject to a number of problems. First of all, labeling seemingly can bring something into existence simply by talking about it. The "peace dividend" following the end of the Cold War in the early 1990s is a case in point. As the United States moved to scale down military spending, many people assumed that these cuts would make additional funds available for domestic problems. But just as talking about unicorns does not make them exist, debating how to spend a peace dividend did not make one appear. The expense of destroying old weapons, new military priorities, and the growing budget deficit quickly absorbed any newly available funds. Drawing on the same principles, a British judge in 1993 rejected a claim of computer-related repetitive strain injury (RSI) based on his acceptance of a hand surgeon's claim that "R.S.I. is not a disease or diagnosis, but a label."[4]

Labeling problems can also arise in the selection of concepts in a description or analysis. For example, any discussion of a society in terms of lower, middle and upper classes assumes that the society is actually structured that way or is, at least, best understood that way. Labeling groups this way, or any another way, does not necessarily make it so.

Calling the homeless "the underhoused" doesn't give them a place to live; calling the poor "the economically marginalized" doesn't help them pay the bills. Rather, by playing down their plight, such language might even make it easier to shrug off the seriousness of their situation.

Instead of allowing free discussion and debate to occur, many gung-ho advocates of politically correct language seem to think that simple suppression of a word or concept will magically make the problem disappear.

• Michiko Kakutani, "THE WORDS POLICE ARE LISTENING FOR
'INCORRECT' LANGUAGE"[5] •

Euphemisms present another problem. Although euphemisms are often picturesque and harmless, they can also be deceptive and outright dishonest. When, for example, a large corporation speaks of "downsizing" or "streamlining," it obscures the harsh reality of many people facing sudden unemployment and a potentially bleak economic future. Not only are the emotional overtones removed by the choice of terms, but the true implications as well. When, as in this example, important social issues are reduced to bureaucratic considerations, euphemisms can function as a subtle form of thought control.

Yet another problem is that, when we label something, we focus on only one of a variety of possible characteristics. This, psychologist Gordon Allport points out, results in an inherent prejudice: "that every label applied to a given person refers properly only to one aspect of his nature."[6] Highlighting one aspect, we ignore other perspectives. To refer to the Nobel Prize–winning writer Toni Morrison as a "black novelist," for example, suggests that her writing is somehow limited in scope or appeal. On the other hand, the classification, when understood to refer to her subject matter, not her race, does distinguish her subject matter from that of other novelists.

Readers must distinguish when a label is useful for descriptive purposes and when it serves more to pigeonhole individuals, groups, or ideas, thereby reducing the level of discussion. In either case, labels can signal the values advanced in the text. Critical readers will be alert to the presence of euphemisms and other forms of labeling, and to the role such labeling plays in shaping the discussion.

•••••••••••••••••••• LABELING ••••••••••••••••••••

Which of the following labels are accurate in their description and which suggest qualities that do not exist?

1. progressive education
2. the free world
3. an unbreakable record
4. lite popcorn
5. user-friendly software
6. all-purpose tires

•••

Bestowing Authority by Labeling

Authors persuade by endowing assertions with acceptable or unacceptable qualities. To convince readers, texts confer on their conclusions the authority associated with well-reasoned arguments. Evidence in favor of an argument is labeled *scientific, logical, factual,* or *informed opinion;* opposing evidence is attributed to *unscientific* or *emotional* considerations. Information to be accepted is portrayed as *reliable, consistent, well researched, authoritative;* evidence to be rejected is portrayed as *unsubstantial* or *reflecting bias* or *opinion.* Favorable evidence is said to *conclude* or

There is an old story about three baseball umpires. One said, "I call 'em like they are." This view may be described philosophically as naive realism. The next said, "I call 'em like I see 'em." He may be described as a relativist, aware of the subjective element in any judgment. The third said, "They ain't nothing until I calls 'em." He is no grammarian, but he can be said to be a semanticist, deeply aware of the way in which the reality we live in is largely created by the language with which we describe it.

> • S. I. Hayakawa, THROUGH THE COMMUNICATION BARRIER: ON SPEAKING, LISTENING AND UNDERSTANDING[7] •

prove; unfavorable evidence is said to *allege* or *claim*. There is, of course, a very real distinction between a report that is well researched and a report that is thrown together. Yet, in all-too-many instances, these terms are only subjective labels rather than accurate descriptions. In such cases, things are not as they are said to be. As readers, we may or may not be aware of such distortion. Either way, the first step is to recognize exactly how things are portrayed within the text.

EXAMPLE: "Facts, Not Species, Are Periled"

In 1993, defenders of the Rio Accord, an international agreement to protect the environment reached at a global conference in Rio de Janeiro, Argentina, argued that plant and animal species were disappearing at what was, for them, alarming rates. The following is the opening of a guest editorial in *The New York Times*:

Facts, Not Species, Are Periled

If President Clinton signs the Rio accord to protect rare and endangered species, he will place scientific truth in greater danger than endangered species.

A fair reading of the available data suggests a rate of extinction not even one-thousandth as great as doomsayers claim. If the rate were any lower, evolution itself would need to be questioned.

The World Wildlife Fund, the main promulgator of alarm about biodiversity and the extinction of species, frames the issue in the starkest terms: "Without firing a shot, we may kill one-fifth of all species of life on this planet in the next 10 years." This assertion is utterly without scientific underpinning and runs counter to all the existing evidence.

Such apocalyptic claims are used to bludgeon the Federal Government for money and action. A long-running fund-raising pitch from World Wildlife Fund's president, Russell E. Train, describes how the organization rallied support for reauthorization of the Endangered Species Act by telling Congress that "some scientists believe that up to one million species of life will become extinct by the end of this century" unless governments "do something."[8]

Sounds serious—and convincing! But consider more closely what is going on:

Facts, Not Species, Are Periled

If President Clinton signs the Rio accord to protect rare and endangered species, he will place scientific truth in greater danger than endangered species. [**catchy opening—sets out a position against the Rio Accord by suggesting that "scientific truth" would be in "greater danger" than endangered species—for the moment, an unsubstantiated claim that appeals to the the belief in "scientific truth"**]

A fair reading of the available data [**implies contrary opinions are not accurate**] suggests a rate of extinction not even one-thousandth [**belittles the extent of the opposing prediction with the phrase "not even"**] as great as doomsayers claim. [**labels opponents as "doomsayers," implying their predictions are hysterically pessimistic**] If the rate were any lower, evolution itself would need to be questioned. [*reductio ad absurdum*—**an unsubstantiated claim suggesting the logical implications of an argument are absurd—again, a device to belittle the claim**]

The World Wildlife Fund, the main promulgator of alarm [**further belittles the notion of danger by implying alarm is irresponsible**] about biodiversity and the extinction of species, frames the issue in the starkest terms: "Without firing a shot, we may kill one-fifth of all species of life on this planet in the next 10 years." [**lends authority to the refutation by challenging a major spokesperson of the other side**] This assertion is utterly without scientific underpinning and runs counter to all the existing evidence. [**double labeling of the opposition's claims as inaccurate without evaluating the claim or offering counterevidence**]

Such apocalyptic [**term suggesting excessive pessimism again**] claims are used to bludgeon [**term suggesting the use of force rather than reason**] the Federal Government for money and action. [**explains opposition's claims by attributing ulterior motives to them**] A long-running fund-raising pitch [**adverse labeling to suggest a false claim**] from World Wildlife Fund's president, Russell E. Train, describes how the organization rallied support for reauthorization of the Endangered Species Act [**subtle implication that such a stand is inappropriate**] by telling Congress [**again, suggesting a falsehood**] that "some scientists believe that up to one million species of life will become extinct by the end of this century" unless governments "do something." [**the quotation lends authority to the text**]

To the uncritical reader, the text may seem an authoritative argument against the Rio Accord. The success of the text can be traced to its discrediting of the hysterical, unscientific claims of environmentalists. To the critical reader, the text clearly opposes the Rio Accord—but any sense of authority is a result of how positions are labeled. The text relies on persuasive devices that, while appealing, do not in themselves prove anything—but certainly make the argument clear. To determine the truth of the situation, readers must go beyond the present text.

The use of persuasive devices is as much a part of language as any other aspect. "Language manipulation is a natural, neutral human activity," one critic notes, "I expect *everyone* to intensify, to downplay, to manipulate language for their own benefit and advantage. This is what human beings do. This is what they've always done, always will do."[9] Most importantly for the critical reader, these devices provide concrete evidence of the bias of the text, and thus clues for interpretation.

• MISUSE OF LABELING •

In 1991, Rep. Newt Gingrich (R-Ga.) headed a group that published a booklet entitled "Language: A Key Mechanism of Control," a work that advised Republican officeholders to use "optimistic, positive governing words" like "environment, peace, freedom, fair, flag, family and humane" to describe their own party, and to define opponents with words such as "betray, sick, pathetic, lie, liberal, hypocrisy, permissive, attitude, self-serving."[10]

The problem here is that the advice assumes words can be employed simply for their emotional effect without concern for the truthfulness of the assertion, for their connotations rather than their content, for the purpose of manipulation rather than enlightenment. The greater problem for the reader is that labeling often reflects this very abuse—and that it works!

Analyzing Labeling

An analysis of labeling involves three steps: (1) identifying the terms in question, (2) identifying their implications, and (3) indicating how such terms contribute to the overall meaning.

Suppose a text refers to an opposing argument as "lame" and "infirm." The first step is to notice the use of such terms; the next step is to recognize the nature of those terms. Here we might observe that the opposing arguments are labeled in unflattering terms of physical weakness and disability.

The final step is to suggest how the use of such terms is consistent with our overall interpretation of the text. Here, we might conclude the labeling portrays the opposition arguments as lacking power and believability.

Students often express such observations in terms of the author or the author's intentions. An author is said to label opposing arguments in unflattering terms of physical weakness and disability for the purpose of portraying them as lacking power and believability. As noted earlier, thinking in terms of an author can help one recognize what is going on, but the discussion should be stated in terms of the text because it is evidence within the text that ultimately supports the inference.

Labeling often provides the additional evidence necessary to assure a proper classification of patterns of content. Readers unsure whether the earlier quotation by the president of the World Wildlife Fund is evidence of sanity or irresponsible pessimism can find evidence in the labeling of the environmentalists as irresponsible doomsayers, since the text portrays the president of the World Wildlife Fund as a spokesperson for that group.

•••••••••••• **IDENTIFICATION OR PORTRAYAL?** ••••••••••••

Does the following excerpt from the article "New Military Way of Life and Strife" actually identify liberals? Explain.

> Liberals—those broad-minded people who define a bigot as anyone who disagrees with them—have decided that homosexuals are to be officially defined as a victimized group.[11]

•••

APPEALS TO THE INTELLECT VERSUS INTELLECTUAL INTIMIDATION

Claims of Rationality

A claim of rationality can be made in ways other than labeling the discussion as reasonable and objective. To suggest a reader accept information or conclusions, a text can:

- Appeal to known authority (by title, position, background, and so on)
- Assert the presence of evidence
- Indicate no evidence to the contrary
- Claim consistency with accepted values
- Indicate consistency of argument
- Claim extensive supporting research
- Claim broad acceptance

To suggest a reader reject information or conclusions, a text can:

- Indicate lack of reputable spokespeople
- Attribute remarks to discredited sources, fanatics, or superstition
- Deny the existence of supporting evidence
- Indicate evidence to the contrary
- Claim inconsistency with common values
- Assert inconsistency of argument

- Suggest a lack of supporting research
- Claim a lack of public acceptance

By so doing, texts endow some assertions with the authority of logic and denigrate others as subjective and inconsistent.

EXAMPLE: **The Brady Bill**

The following excerpt from an article in *American Rifleman* magazine illustrates how claims of rationality can lend credence—whether warranted or not—to an argument.

> "Too Many Kids Are Getting a Real Bang Out of Life," announces a full-page ad in *The New York Times*—"Help Save the Next Generation."
>
> The ad, purchased by Handgun Control, Inc., reflects the theme of the organization's latest push for the Brady bill [requiring a waiting period for handgun purchases]. In a February press conference, Sarah Brady, Handgun Control's chairwoman [and wife of James Brady, President Reagan's press secretary who was seriously wounded in an assassination attempt on the president], noted that nearly 4,000 Americans under the age of 20 had been murdered in 1991. . . . Brady did not suggest how many lives the Brady bill might save. Nor did she cite studies showing how similar laws, enacted by more than 20 states, have reduced crime. That's because there are no such studies. All the scholarly research has found that laws like the Brady bill have no statistically significant impact on crime.[12]

Has all truly scholarly research in fact found that laws like the Brady bill have no statistically significant impact on crime? From the text alone, we have no way of knowing. But notice the following about the excerpt:

- It does not claim that the Brady bill would not save lives, only that Mrs. Brady did not say how many.
- It does not claim that similar laws in twenty states have not reduced crime, only that there are no such studies—which, if true, explains why Mrs. Brady did not quote any.
- It restricts its claim to "scholarly" research, thereby allowing it to select which studies to accept and which to reject.

The excerpt is, nevertheless, consistent in its attack on the claims of Handgun Control, Inc. and Mrs. Brady as unsubstantiated and unscholarly, and hence as irresponsible.

Readers who check the endnote for the source of this article will, it seems, find evidence to substantiate the analysis. Care must be taken, however; we cannot simply assume that the ideas associated with a publication or the political agenda of an author are necessarily present in a text. While such knowledge can be a catalyst for analysis, or, as here, evidence seemingly in support of an interpretation, evidence for the interpretation must come from the text itself.

Other Forms of Appeal

Techniques of persuasion do not concentrate solely on the negative. While half the job is making what one wants the reader to reject look bad, the other half is to make arguments one wants readers to accept look good. Texts project a variety of positive qualities besides rationality or objectivity to persuade readers to accept their conclusions. Examples include patience, perseverance, resourcefulness, respectfulness, and humility.

In the Petition of the Inmates of the 9th Floor, Tombs City Prison [Texts for Analysis 7], as with any petition, the inmates must show that they are familiar with the law, have tried less confrontational means, and are not making unreasonable requests. To the ingredients of any petition (a request from someone to someone for something that they have the power to grant), we can add additional ingredients necessary for a *successful* petition (such as humility and respect). Here again, there is a fine line between something being so and simply making it appear so. While we can recognize the petition's claim that prisoner's basic needs have not been met, we cannot tell, from the petition alone, whether those needs have in fact gone unmet.

Where the text's claims are true, well and good. However, readers often have no way of distinguishing reason from nonsense, or accurate data from unsubstantiated claims. When readers cannot verify the claims, suggestions of reason and objectivity function as a form of intellectual intimidation. This is not to say they are inaccurate or distorted, but merely that the appeal becomes more emotional than intellectual as the reader is badgered into acceptance. While this may be a problem as far as taking sides is concerned, it need not hinder the interpretation of texts. Whether the claims are legitimate or not, critical readers recognize such claims as indicating how a text portrays the situation, as devices that highlight the text's values.

•••••••••••••• ASSERTION AND PERSUASION ••••••••••••••

Do the statements below make the same assertion? Do they have the same persuasive qualities? In what ways do they differ?

1. The commission's so-called study claimed to reach the appalling conclusion that the defendant was in some way innocent.
2. I believe the commission erred in finding the accused to be free of guilt.
3. The commission erred when it found the accused innocent.

QUOTATIONS: EVIDENCE OR INTIMIDATION?

Quotations as a Device for Persuasion

Quotations contribute to a text in various ways. They can add important evidence or suggest avenues for further examination of an issue. They can enable authors to acknowledge the contributions of others, to repeat particularly striking comments without fear of plagiarism, or to consider biased viewpoints without being accused of bias themselves. Indeed, a commonly held belief is that quotations, by their very nature, lend support to an argument. If someone else can be found to make an observation, the observation somehow gains validity. This technique is particularly common in televised news broadcasts. It is not enough for an anchorperson to assert something; an eyewitness must be produced to verify the assertion. Rightly or wrongly, outside verification lends credence to ideas.

Quotations become a powerful persuasive device when the person quoted is not just anyone, but an **authority**. The power of a quotation lies in the authority of the speaker being transferred to the assertions within the quotation. On the issue of world hunger, for example, we might prefer to trust statements advanced by an official of the United Nations over those attributed to the uncle of a local grain merchant. Yet, as we have seen, the apparent authority of a source is often merely a matter of labeling. Indeed, one person's expert is often another person's fool.

Certainly, some people may have more experience in a field, may have done more reading, or may have talked with more people about a topic. We should recognize and respect such background. But that does not necessarily endow those people with complete knowledge. It need not even give them special insight. Ideally, an idea held by only the author, Thoreau's "majority of one," should be deserving of as much attention and respect as one held by many.

Quotations as a Tool for Interpretation

Much of what a text argues is apparent in the selection and presentation of quotations. In many cases, the underlying perspective is actually clearer from the way the quotation is presented (an aspect of the use of language) than from the quotation itself (an aspect of choice of content).

When a text accepts the views expressed in a quotation, it obviously has an interest in portraying that source as authoritative. When a text rejects the views expressed in a quotation, it still has a stake in establishing that the views are authoritative as far as the other side is concerned. The notion of "authority," then, does not necessarily mean someone who is correct in his or her views. Rather, it refers to someone of prestige and respect in the eyes of those accepting that particular viewpoint.

Texts reflecting the view of a political party will belittle the opinions of opposition spokespeople and applaud the views of their own members. When a text quotes a spokesperson from the United Nations or any other source, our real concern is how the text portrays that source: whether as "that respected world body, the United Nations" or as "the world's busybody debating society, the United Nations." In the latter case, the text is obviously denying the vaidity of the testimony, and hence using the quotation as a claim to be denied. If an essay portrays a remark from the Sierra Club as biased and another from an industrialist as objective, odds are the text is not taking a strong environmental position.

Arguing for a bill to limit the number of years politicians could serve in a specific office, for example, the columnist George Will took *The New York Times* to task for what he saw as obvious slanting in its labeling of incumbents as "seasoned professionals" and newcomers as "inexperienced 'citizen politicians'" and "casual amateurs." But when it came to identifying the newspaper *Roll Call*, which agreed with his position, he referred to it as "the splendid newspaper that covers Congress."[13]

In the case of the Rio Accord excerpt, the source is endowed with authority in two ways:

> A long-running fund-raising pitch from World Wildlife Fund's president, Russell E. Train, [**head of an international environmental organization**] describes how the organization rallied support for reauthorization of the Endangered Species Act [**with "long-running fund-raising pitch," reinforces the fact that the position has been held for a long period of time**] by telling Congress that "some scientists believe that up to one million species of life will become extinct by the end of this century" unless governments "do something."

Here, of course, the source serves as a negative example rather than a positive one. It is refuted, not supported.

Let's look at one more example, from the Brady Bill passage:

> In a February press conference, Sarah Brady, Handgun Control's chairwoman, noted that nearly 4,000 Americans under the age of 20 had been murdered in 1991.

• REAL VERSUS INVENTED QUOTATIONS •

In a court case to determine whether a journalist could invent quotations reflecting someone else's thoughts, Federal Appeals Judge Alex Kozinski sided with the journalist, arguing that "an article devoid of [quotes], one that consists entirely of the author's own observations and conclusions, will generally leave readers dissatisfied and unpersuaded, as well as bored." Unfortunately for the journalist—and happily for readers—this was a minority decision![14]

The notion of authority is achieved here by quoting someone obviously close to the bill in question (named for her husband) and by portraying her as holding high office (chairwoman) in the group making the claims. Once again, however, the quotation is offered up as an example to be refuted.

Finally, notice that texts using quotations for evidence often fall victim to the *ad hominem* fallacy of attacking (or praising) the speaker rather than the idea.

Interpreting the Use of Quotations

To use quotations as an interpretive tool, readers must recognize:

- The nature of the remarks in the quotation
- The source of the quotation and the degree of authority inherent in, or attributed to, that source
- The impact of using such a quote from such a source within the discussion

From a recognition of how a certain quotation is used, readers infer additional meaning about the text as a whole:

> The World Wildlife Fund, the main promulgator of alarm about biodiversity and the extinction of species, frames the issue in the starkest terms: "**Without firing a shot, we may kill one-fifth of all species of life on this planet in the next 10 years.**" This assertion is utterly without scientific underpinning and runs counter to all the existing evidence.

Here, a quotation suggesting extremely dire consequences (the nature of the remark) from an environmental group that is portrayed as a leading spokesperson for the cause (the source and authority of the quotation) is used to suggest the degree of irrationality of the environmentalists' arguments (the impact within the discussion).

Statistics

Statistics function within texts with much the same authority as quotations. People tend to accept statistical information as truth. Numbers, they say, don't lie.

Statistics refers to the collection and analysis of numerical information. The field of statistics is concerned with how we obtain and explain measurements or other numerical data. As a scientific tool, statistics can be a powerful aid in investigating complicated phenomenon. Statistics are, however, subject to a wide variety of abuses and misunderstandings. Statistical evidence alone does not necessarily provide additional insight. While numbers can provide objective information, measurements can be deceptive. At its worst, statistics are "used when other methods are of no avail . . . [as] a last resort and a forlorn hope . . . [as] a delicate dissection of uncertainties, a surgery of suppositions."[15] Nonetheless, statistics remain an extremely seductive persuasive device. For a more complete discussion of the issues in the uses and abuses of statistics, see Appendix F, "Logic and Statistics."

LOGICAL FALLACIES

Logical fallacies are instances in which, for one reason or another, reasoning is corrupted. It is worth noting that instances of poor logic are sufficiently common, and alluring, that they have been given names and become required study for generations of students. While deficient in logic, these emotional appeals often make effective persuasive devices. A sample of these fallacies follows:*

arguments from unknown facts: an argument based on information that is not presently known (such as predictions) or even information that is unknowable:

If the ban on homosexuals is lifted, the number will increase tenfold. Every time a homosexual soldier receives even a slightly negative report he will be able to claim sexual preference discrimination.

ad hominem **argument**: an attack on the speaker rather than the substance of his or her argument, such as labeling someone subversive, ill-informed, or perverted to refute them:

I believe the military is supposed to represent the finest ideals of American society not the opinions of a deviant minority.

ad populum **argument**: an argument based on snob appeal or people's desire to follow the crowd or accepted beliefs:

If you do not believe me, believe [Chairman of the Joint Chiefs of Staff] General [Colin] Powell, this is not a good idea.

hasty generalization: similar to reasoning by anecdote, a generalization based only on exceptional cases or on a limited or unrepresentative sample of the available evidence:

Heterosexual male soldiers will not follow homosexual leaders. I base this claim, not just on hypothesis but examples in units in which I have served. . . . Comrades of mine in the Navy are particularly worried about their rights as heterosexuals, when they are forced to share crowded ship-board quarters with known homosexuals.

My wife served for four years in the Marines and was approached by lesbians several times. . . . How much more common will this scene become when homosexuality is condoned?

---

*The examples are from Texts for Analysis 3A, Letter to Senator John McCain (R-Ariz.).

faulty analogy: a conclusion drawn from an analogy, especially one that has not been established:

The military discriminates against the handicapped, drug users, and criminals, with good reason. Imagine the consequences of nearsighted pilots, chemically dependent tank drivers or soldiers who are forced to depend on the actions of a known criminal. They do not belong in the military and neither do homosexuals.

the "red herring": a diversionary tactic of changing the subject:

If the military is not allowed to discriminate against "sexual preference," will homosexuality be the limit or will the other sexual preferences like bestiality and pedophilia be accepted as well?

To these might be added *reductio ad absurdum*, noted in our interpretation of the Rio Accord passage, and several others:

false cause: the assumption that one event is the cause of another simply because it came before the latter, without establishing a causal connection

argument from ignorance: an argument based on the absence of evidence against an idea, while failing to show evidence for it

As with other persuasive devices, fallacies offer the critical reader additional insight into the underlying values and perspective of an argument. They are, in effect, examples of the writer as charlatan showing his or her hand. (For a more complete discussion of logical fallacies, consult any of the texts recommended at the conclusion of Appendix F.)

EXAMPLE: **There He Goes Again—Ronald Reagan's Reign of Error**

In a classic exercise in preventive critical listening prior to a press conference by President Reagan, two writers offered examples of persuasive devices from his earlier speeches:

1. **Exaggeration.** Mr. Reagan is a master of what Huck Finn called "stretchers." Yes, taxes (measured as a percentage of gross national product) rose from 1960–1981, but they did not double, as he claimed. (In fact, they rose from 10.4 percent to 12 percent.) As in many of his statements, there was a kernel of truth in his comments, but not much more.

2. **Omission.** Mr. Reagan brings to mind Franz Kafka's remark about the theologian Martin Buber: "No matter what he says, something is missing." In 1982, he said that the poor wouldn't suffer from budget cuts because the Federal budget was increasing by $32 billion. He neglected to point out that all of the increase was for military spending.

3. **Anecdotage**. Mr. Reagan is apparently unfamiliar with the Talmudic observation that "for example is not evidence." Thus, he would have us believe that one bizarre example of a "welfare queen" using aliases to collect multiple benefits is typical of all welfare recipients. Is this a telling story, or is he telling stories?

4. **Repeat offenders**. "As I have said before . . ." is a Reagan perennial. Most of the time, he really has said it before, though it's no more true the 20th time than the first. Other times, he has never said it before.

5. **Voodoo statistics**. Remember when he said that it costs the Department of Health and Human Services $3 to deliver $1 of services, when in fact it costs 12 cents?

6. **Historical clincher**. His invocation of past events is often historical revisionism. History does not show, for instance, that Vietnam was two countries for centuries.

7. **Stonewalling**. When you hear him say, "Well, that's just not true," in a tone of pained innocence, the odds are good that in fact it is true. For example, he denied that his civil rights program hurts blacks and that his tax program favors the rich.

8. **Rhetorical question**. Often used as a substitute for genuine evidence, his questions frequently contain unproved assumptions and illogical leaps. Trying to defend our Marines' presence—and Marine casualties—in Lebanon, he said, "Didn't we assume a moral obligation to the continued existence of Israel as a nation back in 1948?" (In fact, propping up the fragile government of [Lebanese] President Amin Gemayel has very little to do with the existence of Israel, which has withdrawn its troops from Beirut.)[16]

Recognizing both the persuasive power and logical limitations of such tactics, the authors noted the comment by Reagan's press secretary, Larry Speakes, who observed after admitting that the president had used a misleading anecdote: "But it made the point, didn't it?" They concluded the article by recalling Abraham Lincoln's remark about an opponent, "that he had such a high regard for the truth that he used it sparingly."

• DOUBLESPEAK •

In 1971, the National Council of Teachers of English founded a Committee on Public Doublespeak concerned with the use of language as "an instrument of social control."[17] With primary targets of advertisers and politicians, they initiated annual awards in 1974 to increase awareness of the use of language designed to confuse rather than enlighten. The 1991 award went to the U.S. Department of Defense for its "armed situation" (war) in the Persian Gulf, a war in which bombs did not kill, but rather "degraded, neutralized, attrited, suppressed, impacted, decapitated or took out" their targets.[18]

IMPLICATIONS

Language is a tool of communication. Admittedly, however, language is often used to mislead, deceive, distort, or otherwise portray things as they are not to justify certain actions or beliefs.

Overall, the devices texts use to persuade are often the same as those used in casual conversation. In texts, as in all human communication, reason is a tool all too often absent or abused. Critical reading calls for the same common sense and skepticism normally employed with speech.

• **TRUTH IN ADVERTISING** •

An interesting Catch-22 arises with the case of advertising **puffery**—extravagant statements that are nonetheless seductive, such as the claim that a product is "the best that money can buy!" When such statements are obviously false, they are not deceptive—and, hence, are legal. But when obviously false, no one believes them, and they are not effective. They only contribute to mistrust of advertising claims. If such statements are phrased in a way that they might be believed, they become deceptive—and, hence, illegal.

EXERCISES/DISCUSSION

A. Quotations

Indicate how the quotation in each of the following excerpts contributes to an overall meaning. (*Note:* You may have to read the original texts to understand the references.)

> Malcolm X had always been an extravagant talker, a demagogue who titillated slum Negroes and frightened whites with his blazing racist attacks on the "white devils" and his calls for an armed American Mau Mau. [Texts for Analysis 2B]

> Some Senators of that [1948] era feared that allowing negroes and whites to serve together would have grave public health consequences. "The mandatory intermingling of the races," one said, would be "sure to increase the number of men who will be disabled through communicable diseases." [Texts for Analysis 3C]

> The circuitous logic evinced in this case history, which cites as proof of success the fact that the patient ultimately came to share the psychiatrists' views, must be rejected. Nor does the self-righteous assertion that the psychiatrists' motivation is benevolent mitigate the invidiousness of involuntary treatment. As Thomas Szasz has pointed out in *Law, Liberty and Psychiatry:* "Treating patients against

their wishes, even though the treatment may be medically correct, should be considered an offense punishable by law . . ." [Texts for Analysis 4D]

It is the order of the day for the assigned legal aid, on first meeting his client, to open the conversation by saying "I suggest that you take a guilty plea" or "I can speak to the District Attorney and get you (this or that) plea." [Texts for Analysis 7]

The mindset of some officials was illustrated by Gen. Merrill A. McPeak, the Air Force chief of staff, who testified that he would choose.a male pilot vying for a combat position over a woman even if she were a person of superior intelligence and in every way more qualified. He admitted his remark "doesn't make much sense," but said "that's the way I feel." [Texts for Analysis 15]

B. Good Reasoning versus Logical Fallacies

The following arguments were presented in a debate in the New York State Legislature on a bill to overturn a law prohibiting abortion.

Evaluate the legitimacy of each of the arguments. The question is not whether you agree with the view expressed, but whether the argument is relevant and rational. Where possible, indicate the nature of the appeal.

1. The present abortion law encourages butchery. We torture the fetus and we allow them to be born in stunted and twisted form. This law presses down unmercifully on the poor. Is this equality under God?

2. Today, gentlemen, we measure our own morals and only God knows if what I do today in voting for this bill is the right thing because I really don't know. But the arguments of the poor and disadvantaged are so compelling and you see standing here a son whose father is dead set against abortion, but I must vote yes.

3. If this bill passes, our society will be filled with childless families and society as we know it will perish and succumb. I wonder, if we could let God in here today whose side he would be on? Would he be on the side of the affluent pseudoin-tellectual who says "abortion on demand"?

4. I have noticed something about the debate here today. From those of us oppos-ing this bill I hear a buoyancy and a luminous debate. But from those on the other side I hear plaintiveness and anguish. And it must be this way for we are for life and they are against it.

5. From any viewpoint it's a good thing to relax the law and that's that. It's a good thing because the law is discriminatory against women. And I can see no way in which repeal of a law barring abortion could destroy the family or morality or religion. I see no harm at all, and I just do not agree that abortion means murder.

6. It seems to me to be the right of any rational women to make the decision to terminate pregnancy so long as it can be done within medically sanctioned cir-cumstances.

7. The social effects of legalizing abortion will be judged to be good or bad largely in terms of the way one judges social development in a framework of one's moral

values. In the framework of my own values, the legalizing of abortion is another indication of a loss of sensitivity around the basic issue of human life about which I cannot be optimistic.

C. Euphemisms

The following euphemisms were cited by the Committee on Public Doublespeak of the National Council of Teachers of English in the press release announcing their 1992 Doublespeak Awards. See if you can indicate the actual reference. (Answers are provided in endnote 19.)

1. "spatial anchoring" of people
2. when college students "expedite their progress toward alternative life pursuits"
3. "weeding books"
4. "unique retail biosphere"
5. "synthetic glass"
6. "high-velocity, multi-purpose air circulator"
7. "immediate permanent incapacitation"

D. Texts for Analysis: Techniques of Persuasion

Indicate techniques of persuasion employed in the following articles:

1. An Open Letter to the Press About a Real Threat to Medical Progress [Texts for Analysis 8]
2. Letter to Senator John McCain (R-Ariz.) [Texts for Analysis 3A]
3. Petition of the Inmates of the 9th Floor, Tombs City Prison [Texts for Analysis 7]
4. "Let Women Fly in Combat" [Texts for Analysis 15]

Critical Thinking— Going Beyond an Interpretation

If a democratic society is to remain free, citizens should not be encouraged to be docile, trusting and naive. If any statement can be a lie, any behavior deceptive, and all lies and deceptions defended for their good intentions, we're not likely to find simple solutions. Our best defense may be in our ability to analyze language, to make critical judgments, to transform vague trust or distrust into specific acceptance or rejection.

• Hugh Rank
THE PEP TALK: HOW TO ANALYZE
POLITICAL LANGUAGE[1] •

Critical reading, alone, is not enough. In choosing what to believe and what to reject, readers must engage in various aspects of critical thinking as well.

CRITICAL READING AND CRITICAL THINKING

This book has been concerned with critical reading—with achieving the fullest possible understanding of a text. Yet critical reading is not an end in itself. We read not simply for the sake of reading, but to learn about the world, to discover information and ideas for future actions and decisions. In the process, texts can reinforce or challenge our prior understanding. Ultimately, we must either accept or reject their portrayals and conclusions. To do that, we must think critically about the information and ideas before us. Interpreting a text is, then, only the first step in a larger process of evaluation and decision making. Having read and interpreted a text, we must decide what to believe.

Testing That a Text Makes Sense

To accept the ideas of a text, we must first make sense of that text. The text must "add up." We must be able to find consistency in the presentation. Examples must be consistent with generalizations, and choice of language consistent with the ideas conveyed. We must find rational argument underlying devices of emotional persuasion.

All of these concerns are part of an analysis and interpretation. Here, however, we go one step further to *evaluate* the text—to judge whether to accept the assertions. Should a text appear inconsistent in its arguments, we would, presumably, be disinclined to trust its conclusions.

Testing That a Text Is Believable

Consistency and rationality are requirements of good thinking, but they are not, by themselves, enough. As noted previously, false evidence can lead to well-argued but nevertheless false conclusions. The selection of evidence and illustrations shapes the conclusion. A presentation that is consistent and well reasoned may still ignore relevant evidence or fail to consider all possible explanations consistent with that evidence.

To protect themselves from being led down a path of outlandish claims to seemingly reasonable conclusions, readers evaluate the assertions on the basis of their prior knowledge and experience—what they have come to believe to be true. The role of prior knowledge in reading is thus double-barreled. As we saw in Chapter 2, readers draw on prior knowledge to interpret sentences according to what they imagine might make sense. On an unconscious level, prior knowledge influences—one might even say shapes—our understanding. On a more conscious level, readers employ prior knowledge to weigh that understanding against what they know of the world. In practice, of course, the processes overlap and reinforce each other.

Some of the questions considered in testing the believability of a text might include:

- Has information we have come to accept been ignored?
- Is evidence relevant (the right kind), sufficient (the necessary amount), and reliable (itself unquestionable)?
- Are the causes suggested capable of producing the effects described?
- Do the people held responsible for events actually have the power to determine the outcome they are charged with?
- Have alternative causes or explanations been considered?
- Do the author's background, motives, prior works, or experience suggest actual knowledge of, and authority in, the matter?

Obviously, the more knowledge we bring to bear, the better we can evaluate claims in our reading.

• Recognizing Qualifications •

The deeper one thinks about issues, the less one thinks in terms of black and white. The more thoughtful the writing, the more it draws subtle distinctions and limits its remarks. Assertions are qualified by time, condition, extent, reason, cause, situation, and purpose; the text discriminates between all, many, some, and a few. One need not, for instance, be either for or against a particular policy. A wealth of conditions or qualifications can be argued, resulting in a broad spectrum of opinion.

Example: The Rio Accord

Consider once more the excerpt in the previous chapter on the Rio Accord. If we have come to trust the enviromental analyses of the World Wildlife Fund, we would tend to accept their argument in the text. Our acceptance might be further buttressed by the recognition of the degree to which the refutation relies on intimidation rather than evidence. If, however, our experience tells us that environmentalists tend to overstate the dangers, our reactions might differ. We might wish to go along with the article's claims but, as critical readers, still feel an obligation to explain the article's apparent reliance on intellectual intimidation. The more we know (or think we know), the better we can evaluate new claims.

• THE TWO ROLES OF PRIOR KNOWLEDGE •

A simple example can demonstrate the two modes of thinking involving the use of prior knowledge.

> Since the sun appears every morning in the east and sets in the west, the sun must revolve around the earth.

On an unconscious level, we draw on our prior knowledge of the words and grammar, and on our ability to imagine heavenly bodies moving around one another, to make sense of the sentence. The grammar is fine; the reasoning seems to follow. On a more conscious level, we evaluate the statement based on our prior knowledge of astronomy and recall that the same effect results from the earth revolving on its axis.

Reading with Emotion as Well as Reason

The discussion so far presents an ideal case. In practice, acceptance or rejection of a text is not based solely on matters of intellect. Readers are human, and hence subject to various prejudices—to say nothing of gullibility, ignorance, and emotionalism. Readers tend to see things the same way they always have unless confronted with contradictions. They agree with presentations that share their prior values and perspectives. Their judgments are shaped by personal biases, whether political beliefs or simply faith in certain authors.

Belief goes hand in hand with motive. All other things being equal, we believe what we perceive to be to our advantage, whether that be in terms of mental laziness or economic gain. We are motivated by distinct needs, desires, motives, and goals. We each have our own agenda for society, our own vision of the role of government, and our own standards of public and private behavior. New ideas are a nuisance to be avoided, an inconvenience to be rationalized away. Readers seek justification for prior beliefs and filter out information or ideas that might challenge their initial understanding. While such tendencies are hardly laudable, they do serve as a warning against our more emotional and irrational side.

Considering All Possibilities

Properly done, critical reading involves inventiveness and imagination. We must see alternative possibilities—much as when someone once observed that the wonder is not that people who are hungry steal, but that those who are hungry don't! We must question whether models accurately portray the topic as we know it. (Is America a class society? Is drug addiction properly a question of cultural behavior, physical addiction, or illegal actions?) We must question assumptions, whether they be of fact, interpretation, or the labeling inherent in the choice of terms. (Can the issue of gays in the military be fairly discussed as analogous to blacks in the military? Did Columbus really "discover" America? Are women a "minority"? What is the dividing line between "artistic vision" and "mental illness"?)

• GUILTY OR INNOCENT •

If people are presumed innocent until proven guilty, why is there a system of bail to allow people out of jail while awaiting trial?

THINKING CRITICALLY

Broadly speaking, critical thinking is concerned with reason, intellectual honesty, and open-mindedness, as opposed to emotionalism, intellectual laziness, and closed-mindedness. Thus, critical thinking involves:

- Following evidence where it leads
- Considering all possibilities
- Relying on reason rather than emotion
- Being precise
- Considering a variety of possible viewpoints and explanations
- Weighing the effects of motives and biases
- Being concerned more with finding the truth than with being right
- Not rejecting unpopular views out of hand
- Being aware of one's own prejudices and biases, and not allowing them to sway one's judgment

While we may have no prior knowledge of the specific issues of the Rio Accord, we are not without any ability to evaluate the remarks. All readers should recognize that authorities might differ in how they count species, which species they consider endangered, and how they evaluate whether certain events affect others. All readers should realize that people associated with wildlife organizations tend to want to maintain biological species, while people primarily associated with business might be more inclined to sacrifice animals for jobs. And just as we try to figure out the sentence structure, so we should also seek to recognize personal or professional interests that might be involved in an issue such as this.*

EXAMPLE: **Public Statement by Eight**
Alabama Clergymen

The following example suggests some of the additional factors considered in evaluating a text.

April 2nd, 1963, Dr. Martin Luther King, Jr., began nonviolent demonstrations in Birmingham, Alabama. On April 12, the city of Birmingham took legal steps to enjoin Dr. King and roughly 150 supporters from participating in those demonstrations. That same day, eight prominent white clergymen issued a public statement calling for an end to the demonstrations. [Texts for Analysis 6]. The headlines in the *Birmingham News* read, "City seeks to hold mixers in contempt" and "White clergymen urge local Negroes to withdraw from demonstrations." Four days later, while in jail, Dr. King, wrote his famous *Letter from the Birmingham Jail* as a reply to what he perceived as "criticism of [his] work and ideas" in the clergymen's statement.

Over the years, Dr. King's *Letter* has won universal acclaim as a statement of the goals and tactics of the nonviolent, direct-action civil rights movement. The public statement of the clergymen, on the other hand, has acquired a reputation as a misguided challenge not only to the strategy of desegregation but to the civil rights movement itself. And yet, Rabbi Milton Grafman, an original signer, noted many years later, "I'm sure that everyone who signed that request agreed with the 'Letter from Birmingham Jail,' even though they questioned his tactics."[2]

Have the eight clergymen gotten a bad rap? An answer depends on questions of critical reading of a number of documents. Insofar as the clergymen offer their earlier response to Alabama Governor George Wallace's "Segregation now, segregation forever!" inaugural speech as evidence of their conviction, we can examine that text as well for evidence of their stand against segregation. By examining King's *Letter*, we can determine whether he misunderstood their concerns, failed to recognize them, or misstated them for his own advantage.

We must be careful, however, to recognize what we can and cannot prove. We cannot determine the clergy's thoughts or goals from the documents alone, but we can determine what we take those documents to mean. We cannot say what might have happened had King not intervened, but we can discuss what the different participants predicted and how that affected their action. Finally, the clergymen's statements and Dr. King's response must ultimately be read within the

---

*For the record, the authors of the Rio Accord passage, Julian Simon and Aaron Wildavsky are, respectively, professor of business at the University of Maryland and professor of political science at the University of California.

> The art of reading is in great part that of acquiring a better understanding of life from one's encounter with it in a book.
>
> • André Maurois[3] •

context of the civil rights movement of the 1960s; we must be careful not to read in information or insight that was not available at the time.

Aspects of an Evaluation

Responsible evaluation involves more than merely complaining or praising, condemning or applauding, the remarks in a text. Properly viewed, evaluation involves more than agreement or disagreement. Criticizing a text involves not only making clear what you like or dislike about it, what you agree with or disagree with, but supporting these comments with an analysis that both explains the text and makes clear the basis of your judgments. Just as we stress the value of interpreting the underlying assumptions and perspectives of a text, so we should be sensitive to assumptions and values underlying our own understanding. Our reader must be able to distinguish our analysis of a text from our assertion of our own belief. We must clearly articulate both the evidence for our judgments and our standards of judgment so that our reader can challenge our final evaluations.

SOME FINAL THOUGHTS ON FREEDOM AND RESPONSIBILITY

Authors write, presumably, because they believe they have something to say that others should recognize and accept. Consciously or unconsciously, we have argued, they attempt to shape the reader's consciousness. Just as citizens are responsible for the morality of their actions, so readers are responsible for the degree to which they allow others to shape their understanding, and, with that, their very identity.

At its worst, writing takes the form of propaganda. Propaganda is concerned more with manipulation than enlightenment. It attempts to override or short-circuit reflection and thought, playing instead on fears or desires. It is simplistic in its arguments. It demands acceptance, not evaluation.

Political advertising often exhibits a number of the characteristics of propaganda: a lack of reason, a tendency toward stereotyping, a reluctance to draw distinctions, a tendency to generalize. Advertising, however, lacks the political implications. Saying "Crest is best!" is not the same as saying "Caucasian is best." The former has the minor consequence of a choice of toothpastes; the other leads to denials of legal rights.

In many ways, critical reading is not so much a matter of learning a new and more sophisticated way of reading as it is one of regaining a freedom and responsibility that is often sacrificed in early reading and writing instruction. As suggested in the previous chapter, critical reading often involves little more than bringing to *all* written texts the same skeptical questioning and analysis, the same sensitivity to nuance, that we commonly employ with speech.

In critical reading, we recognize each text as the creation of an individual author and thus a presentation of a particular view of reality. We weigh and evaluate each text not only so that we might recognize charlatans and purveyors of intellectual snake oil, but also so that we might assess a wide array of outlooks on a particular topic, the better to challenge and revise our own understanding of the world.

TACTICS AND TECHNIQUES— PUTTING IT ALL TOGETHER

[D. E.] Rumelhart contends that the question to be asked of readers is not "Did you understand?" but "What did you understand?" To this could be added, "What are the grounds for your understanding?"

• Janice Lewis
"REDEFINING CRITICAL READING FOR COLLEGE
CRITICAL THINKING COURSES"[1] •

Restatement, Description, and Interpretation— A Review

A review of techniques of analysis at the three levels of discussion.

This chapter reviews the techniques of analysis discussed in the preceding chapters. An excerpt from a newspaper article is examined at the three levels of discussion: restatement, description, and interpretation. Sample interpretations of other texts are offered in Chapter 13.

Throughout the following discussion, focus your attention on the *process* of investigation rather than the results. And keep in mind that the specific remarks merely represent the way one particular reader might respond. Other readers might see the text quite differently.

Moscow Subway Defies the Odds

Every Moscow subway station has a digital clock that if it were mounted in a New York subway station would be a source of endless public razzing. The clocks time the intervals between trains. Each has only three digits: two that count seconds and one for minutes. The message is that trains are never more than 10 minutes apart, a boast the New York subway system does not dare to make.

The Moscow subway system—carrying eight million riders a day, more than any other subway in the world—works, and works well. In a city where very little does function well, the subways are almost a haven from gray winter days, rundown buildings and rutted, slushy streets. The social forces that made New York subways a world marvel in the early 20th century still appear to be powerfully at work in Moscow.

Rapid escalators bring people deep underground to arching granite and marble stations, elegantly lighted, with statues, murals and mosaics set in the walls. Graffiti are unknown, fatal accidents are rare and crime is just beginning to be a problem. However disorderly people might be in the streets, a code of behavior, a respect, keeps them subdued in the subways—except during rush hours, when trains are as jammed as in New York and people elbow their way aboard.[2]

THE INITIAL READING

An initial reading requires you to ask several key questions:

- Can you make sense of what you are reading?
- What kind of text do you have before you?
- What are your goals, and how will you satisfy them?

The answers reflect a number of discoveries and decisions.

Can You Make Any Sense of What You Are Reading?

This question is not as silly as it might seem. If you do not understand the words or the references, further analysis is pointless. Additional preparation is needed to unlock the meaning of unfamiliar words, references, and associations. If the text in question is part of a larger work, reread any earlier material that might prepare you for an understanding. If the text still makes no sense, consult another text for background information or ask someone about the topic.

What Kind of Text Do You Have Before You?

To answer this question, you need to describe both the content and the structure of the text. This process involves answering another series of questions.

- **What is the text about?** This question is simply asking what the overall topic is.

  The text discusses the Moscow subway system, comparing some aspects to those of the New York City system.

- **What kind of discussion does the text offer?** This question asks for an initial description of what the text "does."

  The discussion is a description with comparisons that suggest an evaluation.

- **What might be involved with a discussion of the particular topic?** The question requires you to identify the "ingredients" suggested by the format and/or topic—to pinpoint what issues or ideas might be relevant.

  Any evaluation of a subway system might look at such issues as efficiency, facilities, speed, comfort, size, and expense. Discussions of American subway systems often include concern about noise, dirt, crime, and a general lack of courtesy.

- **Is the text purely informational, or does it express opinions and defend ideas?** The question here is whether the issues are such that reasonable people might differ in their presentation. These questions address the type of response that might be appropriate. The more subjective the discussion, the more interpretation may be called for.

  The article appears to present facts, but the choice of facts may result in praise or condemnation.

- **What is taken as given? What is to be explained or resolved?** This question asks for further analysis of the content and further description of the direction of the discussion.

  The article assumes common dissatisfaction with the New York subway system.

All of these questions are concerned with "the lay of the land," a description of the overall content and structure of the discussion. They ask the reader to speculate on issues and concerns inherent in the topic. Notice that there is no attempt at this point to suggest an overall meaning. That task requires a more in-depth analysis.

What Are Your Goals, and How Will You Satisfy Them?

Readers read for different purposes. How they read is influenced by the available time, by the type of text, and by what they hope to—or are expected to—get from their reading. We can read to discover what a text says, does, and/or means—one by one or all three at once. Each reading produces its own form of understanding corresponding to the highest level of reading attempted: restatement, description, and interpretation.

During an initial reading, you must decide on a desired level of understanding. Is your goal to be able to repeat the remarks or to discover an underlying perspective? Are you to read for understanding, enjoyment, accountability—or all of the above?

WHAT A TEXT SAYS: PRESENTING A RESTATEMENT

A restatement merely summarizes the main idea of the text—as you no doubt know by now. This usually means repeating the conclusion without the reasons, or the final thought without the supporting evidence. While many texts will have a single sentence that sums up the main idea, many more won't—or different readers might take different sentences as the main idea.

Finding the Main Idea

If no statement seems to sum up the overall idea or to serve as a conclusion toward which the rest of the text is directed, the following technique is often helpful. Select from each paragraph the sentence that best summarizes the thought of that paragraph. These sentences can be pieced together to form a new paragraph, and that paragraph, in turn, can be reduced to a single sentence.

While you cannot expect to find a main idea or topic sentence in each and every paragraph, you can usually find something close enough for the process to work. With magazine articles or other texts with very short paragraphs, it may be necessary to group a few paragraphs into one for the sake of the analysis. Newspaper articles tend to indicate the main idea in the first sentence and continue with progressively less important information to allow the article to be cut to fit the available space. Paragraphs that are clearly digressions need not be included in the search for the main idea.

In reviewing the sample text, paragraph by paragraph, we can identify several main ideas (indicated here by boldface):

Every Moscow subway station has a digital clock that if it were mounted in a New York subway station would be a source of endless public razzing. The clocks time the intervals between trains. Each has only three digits: two that count seconds and one for minutes. **The message is that trains are never more than 10 minutes apart, a boast the New York subway system does not dare to make.**

The Moscow subway system—carrying eight million riders a day, more than any other subway in the world—**works, and works well.** In a city where very little does function well, the subways are almost a haven from gray winter days, rundown buildings and rutted, slushy streets. The social forces that made New York subways a world marvel in the early 20th century still appear to be powerfully at work in Moscow.

Rapid escalators bring people deep underground to arching granite and marble stations, elegantly lighted, with statues, murals and mosaics set in the walls. Graffiti are unknown, fatal accidents are rare and crime is just beginning to be a problem. **However disorderly people might be in the streets, a code of behavior, a respect, keeps them subdued in the subways**—except during rush hours, when trains are as jammed as in New York and people elbow their way aboard.

Gathered together, our highlighted sentences produce the following:

The message is that trains are never more than 10 minutes apart, a boast the New York subway system does not dare to make. The Moscow subway system works, and works well. However disorderly people might be in the streets, a code of behavior, a respect, keeps them subdued in the subways.

These statements might then be distilled still further:

The Moscow subway system works well, better than New York's subway system.

Once a main idea has been isolated, you should restate it in your own words to assure an understanding:

The Moscow subway provides good, clean, efficient service to its riders.

Common Problems in Restatement

The process of isolating topic sentences is actually fairly sophisticated. Readers must distinguish between general and specific remarks. They must distinguish between evidence and conclusions. They must decide on the relative importance of assertions. Successful restatement relies on some of the skills involved in describing a text: recognizing the roles individual sentences play and discovering the overall structure.

Restatements commonly "go off track" in a number of ways. The statement of the main idea may encompass only a portion of the discussion, be inconsistent with some remarks in the text, or reflect the reader's final thoughts on the topic, not the text's. One cannot claim, for instance, that the sample text says that one should visit Moscow just to see the subways, much as a reader may come away with that feeling. (One might argue this as an interpretation, but it would be a stretch!)

Students often highlight topic sentences with a marker as they read. Highlighting is useful not because it directs attention for subsequent review, but because it forces the reader to analyze structure. Separating the main idea from the supporting evidence is a learning/decision-making process. Reading someone else's markings does not achieve the same purpose. Similarly, highlighting broad portions of a text serves little purpose since active selection is no longer involved.

WHAT A TEXT DOES: PRESENTING A DESCRIPTION

To tell the difference between a summary and a description, you have only to examine the topic of your remarks. A summary is about the same topic as the text; a description is about the text itself.

Summary: **The Moscow subway system** runs well.

Description: **The article** describes the Moscow subway system as running well.

Describing the Text

A description indicates both the topic of the text and the way that topic is presented. The following elements are included:

- How the topic is broken up for discussion (how the text is structured)
- What is asserted about that topic, and how evidence and claims are presented

The models and terminologies for paragraph analysis examined in Chapter 1 and the Appendices can be applied here.

The opening remarks of a description should focus on the major divisions of the text. For the most part, the description will follow the sequential development of the text:

The news article discusses the Moscow subway system, comparing it to the New York subway on such concerns as the punctuality of trains, the aesthetics of the train stations, and the behavior of the riders. The Moscow system is said to be on time far more often and devoid of the graffiti and crime associated with the New York system. At times this contrast relies on the reader's knowledge of other subway systems.

For long or complicated texts, additional analysis at lower levels will be appropriate. The initial divisions offer you a table of contents, as it were, for further commentary. Once completed, a description will usually both restate and describe. It will indicate what the text says as well as how it goes about saying it:

> The news article discusses the Moscow subway system [**topic of discussion**], comparing it to the New York subway on such concerns as the punctuality of trains, the aesthetics of the train stations, and the behavior of the riders [**description**]. The Moscow system is said to be on time far more often and to have less graffiti and crime than the New York system [**restatement**]. The presence of a digital clock to verify train schedules is cited as evidence of this punctuality [**description**]. The text talks about those aspects people commonly dislike [**description**] and suggests that the Moscow subway does not have the problems associated with the New York subway system [**restatement**]. The Moscow system is described as having well-lit stations and no graffiti [**restatement**]. The system is efficient and courteous [**restatement**]. People are portrayed as civil to each other [**description**]. The article concludes that, especially in comparison to other systems, the Moscow subway system works and works well [**restatement of main idea**].

Again, notice that this discussion is not about the Moscow subway; it is about the article discussing the Moscow subway.

Common Problems in Description

The most common problem with a description of a text is the tendency to lapse into restatement:

> (1) The news article discusses the Moscow subway system, comparing it to the New York subway on such concerns as the punctuality of trains, the aesthetics of the train stations, and the behavior of the riders. (2) The system is efficient and courteous. (3) Trains run on time; people are civil to each other.

Sentence 1 is about the text, but sentences 2 and 3 are about the subway system. Restatement is fine as long as it is clear to your reader that you are presenting the ideas of the text, not making claims about the topic yourself. You can direct your comments to the text with only a slight change:

Restatement: The system is efficient and courteous.

Description: The system is described as efficient and courteous.

Once framed as a description, this latter statement can lead to an examination of how that description is achieved.

Descriptions can go awry in other ways. As with restatement, they may err by dealing with only a portion of the text. Or they may rely entirely on terms, such as *says, states,* or *talks about,* that do not really describe what is going on—terms that are useful for offering supporting evidence but vague as overall descriptive terms.

Ideally, comments should draw on all three of the models (and their terminology) discussed in Chapter 1—the role, descriptive, and relationship models. And the descriptive categories should describe "what is going on," not how a reader might react. A description may assert that a text pleads for sympathy, but it cannot claim that a text makes the reader sorry for someone. Finally, a longer description may fail to identify major areas within the text that can serve to outline both the text and the description itself.

WHAT A TEXT MEANS: PRESENTING AN INTERPRETATION

The goal of an interpretation is an assertion of overall meaning, supported and justified by a description of the text. Interpretation is distinguished from restatement and description in several ways:

- Concentration on patterns throughout the text, rather than on the sequential development of the discussion
- An awareness of language and persuasive devices
- The inference of an overall meaning

The overall strategy of interpretation reflects the ingredients necessary for inference equations:

- Classifying patterns of content and language usage
- Identifying relationships between those patterns
- Drawing inferences from the above relationships

As a check on your interpretation, verify that persuasive devices are consistent with the preceding analysis

Characterizing Patterns of Content

We have established that our sample passage contrasts the Moscow and New York subway systems. How, then, is each portrayed? (Information on the Moscow subway is in boldface.)

Every Moscow subway station has a digital clock that if it were mounted in a New York subway station would be a source of endless public razzing. **The clocks time the intervals between trains. Each has only three digits: two that count seconds and one for minutes. The message is that trains are never more than 10 minutes apart,** a boast the New York subway system does not dare to make.

The Moscow subway system—carrying eight million riders a day, more than any other subway in the world—works, and works well. In a city where very little does function well, **the subways are almost a haven** from gray winter days, rundown buildings and rutted, slushy streets. The social forces that made New York subways a world marvel in the early 20th century still appear to be powerfully at work in Moscow.

Rapid escalators bring people deep underground to arching granite and marble stations, elegantly lighted, with statues, murals and mosaics set in the walls. Graffiti are unknown, fatal accidents are rare and crime is just beginning to be a problem. However disorderly people might be in the streets, **a code of behavior, a respect, keeps them subdued in the subways—except during rush hours, when trains are as jammed as in New York and people elbow their way aboard.**

The Moscow subway system is depicted as efficient, clean and generally pleasant. It is said to possess good qualities and to lack certain bad ones. This depiction is emphasized by comparison to aspects of the New York subway system

Do these comments cover all of the content? Not quite. The city of Moscow is also described: as having "gray winter days, rundown buildings and rutted, slushy streets," with the people acting "disorderly in the streets." The third element of content, then, is the description of the city of Moscow itself, a portrayal depicting a somewhat depressing and disorderly environment.

Each of these three parts can now be examined more closely. Further evidence for each pattern can be sought in the language usage and persuasive devices.

Characterizing Patterns of Language

The choice of words in the Moscow text supports the preceding analysis. The Moscow system is said to be able to "boast" about achievements the New York subway system cannot "dare" to make—language of a decisive victory by one competitor over another. The lack of punctuality of the New York subways is described as "a source of endless public razzing," a phrase suggesting both unanimous and constant ridicule. The phrase "works, and works well" emphasizes its point through repetition. And the positive qualities of the Moscow subway are further highlighted by a series of adjectives and adverbs: "*rapid* escalators . . . *arching* granite and marble stations, *elegantly lighted*."

Identifying Relationships and Drawing Inferences

As noted previously, the discussion is based on comparison:

positive portrayal of Moscow subways	contrasted with	downplaying of New York subways

On a lower level, the text presents another contrast:

positive portrayal of Moscow subway	contrasted with	negative image of Moscow city

Utilizing the notion of inference equations, we can infer meaning from these relationships. From the first, we infer the superiority of the Moscow subway system:

positive portrayal of Moscow subways	contrasted with	downplaying of New York subways ⟶	superiority of the Moscow subway system

From the second relationship, we infer the uniqueness of those virtues in an otherwise drab city:

positive portrayal of Moscow subway	contrasted with	negative image of Moscow city ⟶	uniqueness of the subway system's virtues

This latter inference is supported by the use of the term *haven*—"the subways are almost a haven from gray winter days"—a term suggesting escape from adversity.

Verifying the Consistency of Rhetorical Devices

The primary persuasive device employed in the sample text is the evidence itself. There are neither obvious appeals to the reader's common sense nor logical fallacies appealing to the emotions. The basic appeal is simply to qualities that are commonly accepted as good: punctuality, neat appearance, civility.

Completing An Analysis and Interpretation

One additional element of the text has yet to be confronted. We must come to terms with the title: "Moscow Subway Defies the Odds." What "odds" are being defied? How can a subway defy odds? If "odds" is taken to indicate the likelihood of success, the title reinforces the notion that the Moscow subway breaks from the mold of the city at large.

Our final analysis might read as follows:

The text argues the virtues of the Moscow subway system. Overall, the text describes the Moscow system as more efficient and user friendly than the New York system. The superiority of the Moscow system is highlighted by dramatizing the differences in the punctuality of trains. The Moscow system is said to be able to "boast" about achievements the New York system cannot "dare" to make—language of a decisive victory by one competitor over another. The scope of this victory is emphasized with the claim that the Moscow system is the biggest in the world, a claim that suggests an even tougher burden on the system. While New York is credited with achievements in the past, Moscow is portrayed as continuing similar achievement in the present, further stressing Moscow's present superiority. This superiority is limited, however, to the subway system.

Whatever the interpretation, it will be defended by the evidence cited in the description.

Extending the Main Idea

Readers wishing to extend the meaning of the text might suggest additional interpretations:

- That being able to provide an efficient system of public transportation is an example of the superiority of the Russian economic system
- That the emphasis on the Moscow subway system as its greatest achievement implies that the rest of the Russian system is wanting

Any evaluation of such interpretations would depend on a closer examination of the text. Evidence for and against such interpretations would have to be carefully weighed.

Ensuring Completeness and Consistency

Serious problems result from analyzing only a portion of a text. Thus, when you confront any written material, be sure to identify patterns of content and language *throughout* the text. Circle, underline, or highlight what you find. (When reading sections or chapters in a library book, make a photocopy of the text to mark up.) By the time you are done, most of the text should be covered with markings. While you want to be very selective in highlighting passages as main ideas for a restatement, you must account for every bit of content in an interpretation.

An interpretation can range from a single sentence to several pages. Ultimately, however, there is no such thing as a truly complete analysis of a text. Even if the analysis extends well beyond the length of the original text, it cannot encompass all possible observations at all levels—unless you have a very short text! On the other hand, an analysis should be complete insofar as it makes sense of all that you have observed.

Once you have considered the complete text, your task is to ensure that the pieces fit together in a coherent way. Here again, an underlying assumption is that the text has done a good job. If you can show that the text makes a consistent presentation, that everything within the text serves a common purpose, then an interpretation becomes possible.

In the case of our sample text, we must be able to account for the inclusion of the observations that at rush hour the people of New York and Moscow both push onto the trains, and that the subway system is uncommonly efficient in Moscow. These items would seem to preclude the notion that the article makes a broad statement of the superiority of communism over capitalism. Rather, the issue is specifically the subway systems, not political or economic systems, and not human behavior.

• FOCUSING ON THE TEXT •

Confronted with examples, phrases, or other elements of the text, readers ask: Why might the author have included this, or why did the author phrase it this way? Such questions are not really addressed to the motive or intent of the author; they are simply a means of questioning the effectiveness of that element within the text: What is the nature of this statement, and what is achieved by making it? What does it signify or imply? Speculation on why an author "said it that way" should be in terms of the nature and effect of the wording, not in terms of the author's possible motives or intentions.

Common Problems in Interpretation

As with description, the most common problem in interpretation is not carrying out the task at hand. Thus, you need to verify that you have presented an interpretation. This interpretation must go beyond restatement and description to infer meaning based on the relationships of evidence within the text.

It is not enough, however, simply to indicate patterns of content and language; the whole idea is to classify their nature and to draw inferences from their presence.

Incorrect: The Moscow system is said to be able to "boast" about achievements the New York system cannot "dare" to make.

Correct: The Moscow system is said to be able to "boast" about achievements the New York system cannot "dare" to make—language of a decisive victory by one competitor over another that emphasizes the superiority of the Moscow system.

Common problems of interpretation thus include the following:

- The use of overly vague or inaccurate language to classify patterns of content or language.
- Discussion of one's feelings rather than the ways elements of the text invoke those feelings.
- A failure to indicate how persuasive devices slant the discussion.
- Claiming the validity of an interpretation without supplying evidence or explaining how that interpretation is consistent with seemingly discordant elements. Finally, as with the other forms of discussion, an interpretation must cover all of the text, not selected portions.

• DEMONSTRATING CONFIDENCE IN YOUR INTERPRETATIONS •

Students commonly introduce their remarks with "I think" or "It seems to me," thereby emphasizing that what follows is merely an opinion. But what else could it be? In the end, such phrases reflect insecurity or indecision. Rather than resort to such vague phraseology, cite the specific evidence from which the impression rises. Similarly, phrases like "I get the feeling that" tend to reflect a focus on your emotional responses. Instead, isolate the language that evokes your reactions and indicate how you might account for such terms in the overall interpretation of the text. Reserve "I think" and "it seems to me" as devices to signal indecision, when appropriate.

Sample Analyses

All reading is an act of inquiry, and all analysis an exercise in problem solving. The interpretations that follow should be read more for the spirit of the investigation than for the end result. They do not claim to offer an authoritative or final meaning of the texts. They do, however, serve as examples of the approach and thinking involved in critical reading.

The first three examples offer analyses of a complete text and two excerpts. The fourth example looks at a special concern of critical analysis.

TIME *MAGAZINE: "A GRADUATION GIFT FROM UNCLE SAM"*

This might be a good point to return to the article on armed-forces recruiting in Chapter 1.

A Graduation Gift from Uncle Sam

(1) Armed-forces recruiters are catching flak for paying schools to get scouting information about students. (2) The city of Los Angeles board of education passed a measure last week that stops the district from selling the names and addresses of high school students to military recruiters. (3) The board was responding to complaints from parents, who consider the practice an invasion of student privacy. (4) Since 1971 the district has been selling the names of juniors and seniors for 3¢ apiece. (5) Last year it made $8,081 from the list, which school officials say was used to cover clerical costs. (6) The Pentagon acknowledges that buying lists from high schools is a common way for the military to target potential recruits.

Let us make a fresh examination of the text based on the strategies introduced in previous chapters.

Content

The article is about three groups of people: the school administration, army recruiters, and parents. (The students seem to be pawns in both the real-life event and the presentation in the text. In any event, their interests are supposedly voiced by the parents.)

How are the groups portrayed? The school board and the armed-forces recruiters are shown to have a mutually beneficial relationship (sentences 4–6). The parents are portrayed as challenging that relationship (sentence 3).

Sentences 1 and 2 offer evidence of a controversy. Sentence 3 indicates who initiated the latest move. Sentences 4–6 give evidence of how long the practice has been going on and its scope.

Language

Discussing the possible violation of rights, the text states that the parents "consider" the policy an infringement of student privacy, not that they have "proven" it or "shown" it. The term could suggest that the assertion is a personal interpretation, and hence questionable.

The text could have referred to the need to "identify" students instead of to "target" them. It could have referred to the armed-forces recruiters being "criticized" or "condemned" instead of "catching flak." Thus, a pattern of overdramatized language is revealed.

Structure

The text contrasts the interests of the recruiters and school board with those of the parents, a format that suggests an unresolved dilemma.

Inference Equations

In terms of inference equations, we have the following:

| showing gain by one group | coinciding with | showing gain by another group | $\longrightarrow$ | mutual benefit |
| showing gain by some groups | contrasted with | the denial of rights of another group | $\longrightarrow$ | a dilemma |

Evidence that a questionable policy has been in effect for a long time (twenty years; sentence 4) may suggest that it was kept secret, that it simply was never questioned, or that it is perfectly legitimate. Once that evidence is coupled with evidence that the policy is standard practice elsewhere (sentence 6), the pattern suggests that the policy is legitimate:

| acceptance for years | together with | acceptance elsewhere | $\longrightarrow$ | legitimacy |

Indeed, the text does not provide evidence that the policy *does* infringe on students' right to privacy, only that some have questioned it (sentence 3).

Miscellaneous Observations on Content and Language

What does the reference in the title to a "gift" mean? Three possibilities present themselves. The gift could be (1) the donation of one's name to the recruiters, (2) an approach by the Army, or (3) the money given the schools.

A "graduation gift" generally refers to a gift received by a student at the completion of a period of schooling. But in case 1, the student receives nothing. Were that the intended meaning, the usage would be a bit ironic. In case 2, the student receives something, but hardly a "gift." Again there would be irony in the usage. The phrase could refer to a gift to a school (case 3), but that might make more sense if the gift were from a graduating student and the school were not a public high school. In that case, "gift" would, at best, be a euphemism for "payoff" or "fee." Is the term used more as a metaphor than for its literal meaning? Possibly the choice of the term "gift" is more careless than subtle. At best the choice seems somewhat ironic. One way or another, it does not refer to a normal gift to a student or the usual way in which schools receive money.

Content Again

There is one other element of content to look at: the numbers. The text indicates that the recruiters paid 3 cents per student name (sentence 4) and that the school board made $8,081 last year (sentence 5). What are these numbers examples of? The text indicates the significance of the latter number. It was less than or equal to the amount of their clerical costs (sentence 5). Which is to say, it is an example of not enough money for a profit. And 3 cents is just one penny more than 2 cents, traditionally an insignificant amount. The numbers are examples of an insignificant amount of money being exchanged.

Nature of the Text

Since the article does not state agreement with one side or the other in the dispute, it would seem to be presenting an unresolved dispute and leaving it to the reader to make a judgment. On closer examination, the text seems to treat the controversy, and the school board's actions, in an ironic fashion, as sort of a tempest in a teapot. The picturesque language and the title lend support to this interpretation.

Putting all of these observations and inferences together, we might offer an interpretation such as the following:

Interpretation

The article "A Graduation Gift from Uncle Sam" suggests a recent confrontation between the Los Angeles school board and parents over the selling of student names to armed-forces recruiters is a tempest in a teapot in which the school board has bowed unnecessarily to parent pressure.

The article contrasts an assertion by parents that a real issue of student privacy is at stake with evidence of the length of time the policy has been in place and the existence of similar policies elsewhere. In this way the text suggests that no real denial of rights exists.

The controversy is satirized through overstatement. Recruiters are said to be "catching flak" while students are said to be "targeted" by the recruiters. The ultimate irony is the suggestion in the title that by giving their names to the recruiters the government is giving the students a graduation present.

Further evidence of the lack of substance of the parents' complaint is supplied by the mathematics of the arrangement. Citing a fee of 3 cents per name suggests that no real money is involved. This is further supported by the assertion that the income only covers the school board's clerical costs. In other words, the school board does not really gain anything, so nothing is wrong in what they are doing.

Much of this sample interpretation is description supporting the inferred meaning.

Finally, notice that the interpretation does not deny the reader the option of being outraged that the sale of names went on. The interpretation only says that the text excuses it, not that everyone else should.

PAUL SAMUELSON: EXCERPT FROM ECONOMICS

Strikes and Collective Bargaining   Both sides realize that failure to reach agreement will mean a costly strike. It may sometimes happen that management refuses to go above $9.50 an hour while labor refuses to take less than $9.60. A "work stoppage" will result.

Should we call this an "employees' strike" or an "employer's lockout"? Popularly, it will be referred to as a strike. But since each side knows it can end the work stoppage by agreeing to the other party's terms, we could call it either.

Journalists ask why workers go out on strike just because of a 10-cent disagreement. They point out that it might take two or three years for the workers to recover—at 10 cents an hour—their loss of earning during the strike. But workers look at it differently. To them the employer caused the strike by stubbornness. They point out that the amount the employer will also lose by the strike is greater than what would be saved by refusing to pay the extra 10 cents.

Actually, a strike is *not* over just the last 10 cents of wage disagreement! The workers believe that the employer would not have been forced from $9 up even to $9.50 except for the threat of a strike, which hangs over the negotiations like a time bomb. To keep the bomb from going off, both sides must agree.

Threats become hollow unless occasionally carried out. Both parties must show that they are truly prepared to incur at some point the costs of a strike. Thus, suppose the employer was deprived, voluntarily or by law, of the right to refuse any wage demand if it would bring on a strike. Would this cost the employer only 10 cents an hour? Obviously not. There would then be no reason why the union might not hold out for a 90- rather than a 55-cent wage increase. Similarly, if the union could never exercise the right to strike, why should not the employer offer $7 rather than $9?[1]

What is this text about? What is at issue here? Is this text to be taken as purely informational, or is it deserving of critical analysis and interpretation?

If an informational reading is sufficient, the focus is on restating the meaning and, possibly, briefly describing the passage. If an interpretation is desired, further analysis of how aspects of the text are portrayed is called for. Once again, the observations that follow might have been made in some other order, and other readers might have other observations.

Topic

What do we have here? A discussion of strikes.

Nature of the Text

How does the text progress? It discusses what each side can win or lose and why workers might still want strikes. It offers description and narrative, with no obvious argument of a position. It is seemingly objective.

Patterns of Content

The next step might be to look more closely at the content. Into what parts can the content be divided? How are strikes portrayed? How are the actions of each side portrayed?

Note the pattern of claims (content):

- An initial example of 10-cent difference is given as sufficient grounds for a strike.
- Both sides are said to be hurt by a strike.
- Strikes are not labeled as an action of one side or the other.
- It is implied that journalists are unable to figure out why workers would strike over 10 cents when they lose so much by striking.
- Workers are said to justify striking as a response to employer stubbornness.
- Both sides, it is claimed, must show they will undergo the costs of a strike.

And finally, the text suggests that were it not for strikes, both sides would be totally unreasonable in their demands on the other.

As in earlier cases, numbers matter. It pays to do the calculations. The specific difference cited, 10 cents, is an example of an almost petty difference. It is as though the money doesn't really matter. After all, the text seems to suggest, what's 10 cents an hour anyway?

What are the examples examples of? Strikes are initially presented as fights over wages, and then as part of a psychological process of proving one will fulfill a threat. The two sides' demands are considered equal—equally justified or equally ridiculous. The encounter is portrayed as a game of "chicken" necessary to keep one's bargaining power.

Ingredients Inherent in the Topic

Prior knowledge of strikes might suggest other characteristics of strikes that are not included in this discussion. There is no suggestion that a situation might exist in which workers deserved more and the employer refused, or the workers were overpaid and their demands simply unjustified. There is no discussion of the workers striking for any reason other than increased wages—such as work conditions, seniority rights, benefits, protection from layoffs, or any other labor/management issues. Strikes are presented as essentially economic battles. Are worker wage demands to be viewed the same when the company is losing money as when it is making enormous profits? There is no room here for a "justified" strike—by either side.

Patterns of Language

The earlier classification of the content can be checked by looking more closely at the language used to describe strikes and strike actions.

The text plays up the human drama of negotiation with terms like "time bomb" and references to "hollow" threats and "stubbornness." The text plays with a proper name for a strike ("employees' strike" or "employer's lockout"), refusing to even say who starts one.

Structure

In terms of major portions, the discussion focuses on the actions and concerns of the workers and the employer. The two are contrasted in their demands but shown to behave similarly.

Interpretation

Strikes are portrayed as a game of psychological warfare between parties with equally valid demands attempting to prevent the other side from thinking it can achieve what are considered unreasonable demands. The text finds strikes a necessary but ridiculous part of the bargaining process of workers and management in a world in which each would make unreasonable demands were it not for the other's power.

Pointing out that either side can start a strike and either side can end it suggests almost a macho game. When this is presented as a situation in which both parties ultimately lose, the game is presented as almost silly.

The human drama of negotiation is played up, but with no mention of the human situation of the working conditions and wages as issues. The text neglects any discussion of possible justice in the demands and ignores issues of economic or physical well-being that might be involved in the dispute. The only motivation suggested for either side is greed or the opportunity to make the other side suffer economically. The notion that strikes do not make sense is emphasized by the phrase "journalists ask" when talking about workers going on strike, since journalists are supposedly intelligent people. In this way, the text suggests that it does not make sense for workers to go out on strike in the short run. Such a portrayal paints a strike as an often irrational psychological power game for purely economic advantage. On the other hand, the text finds strikes a necessary evil to prevent the other side from being able to enforce unreasonable demands.

Admittedly, the recognition of what is missing requires prior knowledge. But this is, after all, only one reader's interpretation. Finally, while the author might have striven for objectivity in portraying the world, a careful reader will recognize that just as strikes can be viewed quite differently by workers and owner, so they can be presented in different ways by different academic texts.

VINE DELORIA: EXCERPT FROM CUSTER DIED FOR YOUR SINS

After Lyndon B. Johnson had been elected he came before the American people with his message on Vietnam. The import of the message was that America had to keep her commitments in southeast Asia or the world would lose faith in the promises of our country.

Some years back Richard Nixon warned the American people that Russia was bad because she had not kept any treaty or agreement signed with her. You can trust the Communists, the saying went, to be Communists.

Indian people laugh themselves sick when they hear these statements. America has yet to keep one Indian treaty or agreement despite the fact that the United States government signed over four hundred such treaties and agreements with Indian tribes. It would take Russia another century to make and break as many treaties as the United States has already violated.

Since it is doubtful that any nation will ever exceed the record of the United States for perfidy, it is significant that statesmen such as Johnson and Nixon, both professional politicians and opportunists of the first magnitude, have made such a fuss about the necessity of keeping one's commitments. History may well record that while the United States was squandering some one hundred billion dollars in Vietnam while justifying this bloody orgy as commitment, it was also busy breaking the oldest Indian treaty, that between the United States and the Seneca tribe of the Iroquois Nation, the Pickering Treaty of 1794.[2]

Nature of the Discussion

The text compares America's respect for Indian treaties with its actions in Southeast Asia and the record of Russia. A distinct interpretive element is present: In addition to information, the text offers conclusions and judgments. Evaluation is included as part of the overall presentation.

Patterns of Content

The basic pattern of content is a contrast between current American justification of the need to adhere to treaties and past history. The first part of the contrast occurs in the opening paragraphs, in terms of both America's commitments and Russia's lack of commitment to treaties:

> After Lyndon B. Johnson had been elected he came before the American people with his message on **Vietnam**. The import of the message was that **America had to keep her commitments in southeast Asia or the world would lose faith in the promises of our country**.
>
> Some years back Richard Nixon warned the American people that **Russia was bad because she had not kept any treaty or agreement signed with her**. You can trust the Communists, the saying went, to be Communists.

The second part of the contrast appears in the next paragraph:

> Indian people laugh themselves sick when they hear these statements. **America has yet to keep one Indian treaty or agreement despite the fact that the United States government signed over four hundred such treaties and agreements with Indian tribes.** It would take Russia another century to make and break as many treaties as the United States has already violated.

This contrast is played up in the subsequent paragraph:

> Since it is doubtful that any nation will ever exceed the record of the United States for perfidy, it is significant that statesmen such as Johnson and Nixon, both professional politicians and opportunists of the first magnitude, have made such a fuss about the necessity of keeping one's commitments. **History may well record that while the United States was squandering some one hundred billion dollars in Vietnam while justifying this bloody orgy as commitment, it was also busy breaking the oldest Indian treaty, that between the United States and the Seneca tribe of the Iroquois Nation, the Pickering Treaty of 1794.**

The passage also contrasts what America said (indicated by italics) and what it did (indicated by boldface):

> After Lyndon B. Johnson had been elected he came before the American people with his message on Vietnam. The import of *the message was that America had to keep her commitments in Southeast Asia or the world would lose faith in the promises of our country.*
>
> Some years back *Richard Nixon warned the American people that Russia was bad because she had not kept any treaty or agreement signed with her.* You can trust the Communists, the saying went, to be Communists.
>
> Indian people laugh themselves sick when they hear these statements. **America has yet to keep one Indian treaty or agreement despite the fact that the United**

States government signed over four hundred such treaties and agreements with Indian tribes. It would take Russia another century to make and break as many treaties as the United States has already violated.

Since it is doubtful that any nation will ever exceed the record of the United States for perfidy, it is significant that statesmen such as *Johnson and Nixon,* both professional politicians and opportunists of the first magnitude, *have made such a fuss about the necessity of keeping one's commitments*. History may well record that while the United States was squandering some one hundred billion dollars in Vietnam while justifying this bloody orgy as commitment, **it was also busy breaking the oldest Indian treaty, that between the United States and the Seneca tribe of the Iroquois Nation, the Pickering Treaty of 1794.**

Patterns of Language

Several out-of-the-ordinary language choices emphasize the text's message or contribute to its persuasive effect.

> After Lyndon B. Johnson had been elected he **came before** the American people with his message on Vietnam.

"Came before" conveys a sense of pontification or self-righteousness.

> Indian people **laugh themselves sick** when they hear these statements.

"Laugh themselves sick" is an idiom suggesting the utter ridiculousness of the situation. This notion is reemphasized with the phrase "have made such a fuss about the necessity of keeping one's commitments," which suggests the ludicrousness of American claims. And the labeling of American actions as "perfidy" and of two presidents as "professional politicians and opportunists of the first magnitude" completes the pattern.

Persuasive Devices

Overstatement and exaggeration are both used to strengthen the persuasive appeal:

> . . . **Indian people laugh themselves sick** when they hear these statements. America has **yet to keep one** Indian treaty or agreement despite the fact that the United States government signed **over four hundred** such treaties and agreements with Indian tribes. **It would take Russia another century** to make and break as many treaties as the United States has already violated.
>
> Since it is **doubtful that any nation will ever exceed the record of the United States for perfidy**, it is significant that statesmen such as Johnson and Nixon, both professional politicians and opportunists of the first magnitude, have made **such a fuss** about the necessity of keeping one's commitments. History may **well record** . . .

Inference Equations

In terms of inference formulas, we have the following:

examples of claimed behavior	contrasted with	examples of actual behavior	→	hypocrisy
examples of behavior	similar to	behavior of those condemned	→	condemnation

Interpretation

The essay condemns the United States for hypocrisy by contrasting her respect for treaties with foreign countries with her actions toward Native Americans. The depth of this hypocrisy is emphasized by a comparison of the actions of two presidents with those of Russia, references to vast numbers of unkept treaties, and phrases that exaggerate the depth of America's violation of Indian treaties, as well as by phrases emphasizing the irony of America's duplicity.

"I'M 38, AND RUNNING OUT OF TIME"

Different readers, we have argued, may respond differently to a text. The commentaries [Texts for Analysis 4B–4D] that accompany Texts for Analysis 4A are included to suggest how readers can examine the same text from a variety of viewpoints. "I'm 38, and Running Out of Time" [Texts for Analysis 12], as the following discussion suggests, is also open to different interpretations. The "final" interpretation, in this case, is still left to the reader—and again, the discussion is offered more as an example of the spirit and method of investigation than as an authoritative reading.

Background

In the 1992 presidential campaign, Republican Vice President Dan Quayle ran with President George Bush for reelection. In a campaign speech espousing traditional family values, Quayle cited the television character Murphy Brown's having a baby out of wedlock as an negative example of family values. The essay "I'm 38, and Running Out of Time" responds to that allegation.

A Variety of Viewpoints

What are we to make of this essay? Does it express an overall point of view? Readers are often better off asking, "What is going on here?" rather than "What does it say?" The first question leads to a broader recognition of recurring features.

The essay can be analyzed from various perspectives. At various times, it seems to be a narrative of past actions, an analysis of a personal problem, a description of a societal problem, and a discussion of family values. What is it really talking about, and what is it saying about that topic? Is the text an attack on Dan Quayle's ignorance or insensitivity? Is it a lament on the lack of social supports? Or is it simply the lament of a crybaby who has gotten in over her head?

Option 1: An essay of personal trials

Through a narrative of her experiences, a woman describes her problem. As an essay of a personal trial, the text offers evidence of responsibility (attempts to prevent pregnancy), resourcefulness (efforts to locate solutions), a desire for acceptance (pleas not to be thought ill of), innocence (ignorance of her pregnancy), unpreparedness (the lack of sex education), and humanity (the need for love, the desire to raise a child, and the agony involved in making a tough decision). Together, this evidence argues that the problems cannot be excused by blaming them on the individual:

| individual with problems | and | individual is good | ⟶ | problems arise from other source |

Option 2: An essay of social problems

As a description of a societal problem, the essay stresses the need for a speedy solution while portraying the inadequacy of social agencies (the medical insurance system, the public health care system, the welfare system, the courts, and the Catholic Church) in responding to a real person's very real needs:

| examples of need | paired with | examples of failure to meet need | ⟶ | inadequancy of solutions |

Option 3: A discussion of family values

Structurally, the text contrasts three views of family values. One view, espoused by Vice President Quayle using the example of Murphy Brown, claims that single-parent families reflect a lack of family values. Another view, represented by the father of the child, is the pragmatic or realistic one that family values depend on one's ability to "support and nurture" a child, irrespective of whether one is married (reflected in the nature of the father's concerns).

Throughout, however, the text seems to plead for a third view: that an unwed mother of good character but lacking resources should be able to find help to enable her to raise a child. Throughout, the text seeks to resolve this issue of the appropriate view of family values:

| unacceptable view 1 | contrasted with | unacceptable view 2 | ⟶ | dilemma |

Option 4: A condemnation of the absent father

The text presents the case of an unwed woman confronting pregnancy alone and recounts her trials and tribulations in attempting to find aid from social or governmental services. The text presents the woman as accepting the father's desire not to be involved in or responsible for her choices about her pregnancy. By documenting the woman's problems of going it alone, however, the text vehemently condemns the father's uncaring behavior. While it shows the woman turning to the community for help, it neither excuses her predicament nor shows *why* the community should solve her problems for her. It thus focuses on individual, not social, responsibility, with the father condemned for his lack of accountability.

Inferring an Overall Meaning

Some readers might feel that the text is a fabricated story, that the abundance of details indicates a collection of case histories. For the purposes of analysis, however, we must take the examples as offered, as the personal experience of a single individual.

Which of the earlier interpretations is "correct"? None of them—and all of them. Ultimately, the test of any interpretation is that it is consistent and complete—that it can account for all aspects of the text in a consistent manner.

Since the text has presented the issues with depth and breadth, a reader might be reluctant to conclude that it simply raises questions. Surely the way in which the text discusses the situation offers clues to an underlying perspective.

The preceding analyses cover patterns running through paragraphs 1–10. Paragraphs 11–13 add a new form of content: the description of the alternative to having the baby: an abortion. A key test of any of the previous interpretations is the ability to explain this last section.

With regard to language, the closing paragraphs are laced with terms of questioning and lack of resolution:

> . . . Do you think you can take good care of a child? That's really the question . . . agonizing me. . . . I think about . . . and about . . . and about. . . . When I think about . . . wondering . . . and if . . . And I think, What would Dan Quayle want me to do?

Insofar as an abortion is presented as an uncomfortable and traumatic event with no redeeming outcome, the text argues against terminating out-of-wedlock pregnancies. And insofar as the text presents the woman as credible, determined, and undeserving of rebuke, the text argues that she should be able to successfully bear and raise a child. It is the contrast between the portrayal of the woman and a seemingly uncaring society, including the vice president, that shapes the overall point: society forces unwed mothers into untenable choices.

The text does not resolve the individual woman's final choice because, one can argue, that is not really the issue. The issue, as far as the text is concerned, is the existence of the larger problem. Throughout, the text has implied that the solution to the problems of poor, unwed, pregnant women lies in adequate support from social welfare agencies.

With this interpretation, a reader can now go back and see if all of the evidence is consistent with such an analysis. The use of Quayle's statement takes on increased meaning since, as vice president, he represents governmental authority.

Some readers might not see the essay as extending its argument so far, but rather regard it simply as a reply to and condemnation of one person's remarks. Others might take it as an attack on the capitalist system as a whole, although evidence for extending the meaning this far seems scarce.

For different readers, the essay can legitimately mean different things. How each reader responds personally will depend on the degree to which their understanding of the text meshes with their own values.

TEXT FOR ANALYSIS

I. Contrasts

II. Petitions, Arguments, and Pleas

III. Contemporary Issues

Contrasts

1. *The Ku Klux Klan*

1A
from *The Simms History of South Carolina*

• Mary C. Simms Oliphant •

TO KEEP THE THIEVING RADICALS or Republicans in power in South Carolina, the Republican leaders in Congress had more and more United States troops sent to the State to overawe and threaten its citizens. From the start, the rascally Republicans realized that they would be driven out by the people of the State unless they had United States troops at their backs. The Republicans organized and armed companies of negro soldiers in the State militia, but refused to allow militia companies to be formed by white men. With the arming of the negroes, crime increased greatly. Houses were burned in the night. White women were often insulted if they appeared alone on the streets.

As the year 1870 drew to a close, conditions in South Carolina became more and more terrible. Crimes among the negroes—murder, burglary, and house burning— were frequent. The negro militia grew more insolent each day, encouraged as they were by the "Carpet Bag" government with United States troops at its back.

This dreadful condition of affairs forced the white people of the State to organize secretly for their own protection. They formed small bands called Ku-Klux Klans whose purpose was to frighten the negroes from their evil doing. The Ku-Klux met only at night. They dressed in long white robes and caps. They were always mounted, and the very sight of these ghostly riders galloping by in the night was usually enough to terrify the superstitious negroes. Many of the best men in South Carolina belonged to the Ku-Klux Klan.

The negroes in the town of Union were the first to suffer punishment at the hands of the Klan. In January, 1871, a one-armed Confederate soldier was cruelly beaten and then murdered by a company of 40 negro militiamen. The Klan forced the militia to disarm and put in jail thirteen of the negroes believed to have taken part in the murder. The negroes in Union became so threatening that the Klan visited the jail and shot the murderers, except three who escaped.

Wherever the negro militiamen became intolerable, the Klan set itself to work to frighten or punish them. Seeing the determination of the white people to take justice into their own hands, Governor Scott finally disbanded the negro militia in the counties where they were giving the most trouble. The Ku-Klux Klan then stopped its work.

When everything was quiet again, Congress started an investigation of the Ku-Klux. General Grant, who had succeeded Andrew Johnson as president, declared Spartanburg, Union, York, Laurens, Chester, Newberry, Fairfield, Lancaster, and Chesterfield counties in a state of rebellion and put them under military government. Troops were sent into these counties and hundreds of citizens accused of belonging to the Ku-Klux were thrown into jail. Here they stayed for weeks, sometimes months. Some were never brought to trial. A few were finally found guilty, but even with the courts in the hands of the Radicals so little evidence could be found against the Ku-Klux that the greater number of them were freed.

In 1872, Franklin J. Moses, Jr., a "Scalawag" from Sumter, succeeded Scott as the second Radical governor of South Carolina. During his administration, the State sank to its lowest depths of misery. President Grant openly sympathized with the government in the hands of the negroes, "Scalawags," and "Carpet Baggers." He furnished all the soldiers needed to keep them in power. Legislature, governor, courts, and juries were equally corrupt. Seats in Congress were openly bought. Moses was known as the "Robber Governor" because of his open stealing of the State's money. No white man felt that his life or property were safe any longer.[1]

1B

from *Report of the National Advisory Commission on Civil Disorders*

On July 27, 1967, President Lyndon B. Johnson appointed a National Advisory Commission on Civil Disorders, chaired by Governor Otto Kerner of Illinois, to report on the racial disturbances of the summer of 1967 that were punctuated by extensive rioting in Newark and Detroit.

RECONSTRUCTION WAS A TIME OF HOPE, the period when the 13th, 14th, and 15th Amendments were adopted, giving Negroes the vote and the promise of equality.

But campaigns of violence and intimidation accompanied these optimistic expressions of a new age, as the Ku Klux Klan and other secret organizations sought to suppress the emergence into society of the new Negro citizens. Major riots occurred in Memphis, Tennessee, where 46 Negroes were reported killed and 75 wounded, and in the Louisiana centers of Colfax and Coushatta, where more than 100 Negro and white Republicans were massacred.

Nevertheless, reconstruction reached a legislative climax in 1875 with passage of the first Civil Rights law. Negroes now had the right to equal accommodations, facilities, and advantages of public transportation, inns, theaters, and places of public amusement, but the law had no effective enforcement provisions and was, in fact, poorly enforced. Although bills to provide federal aid to education for Negroes were prepared, none passed, and educational opportunities remained meager.

But Negroes were elected to every Southern legislature, 20 served in the U.S. House of Representatives, two represented Mississippi in the U.S. Senate, and a prominent Negro politician was Governor of Louisiana for 40 days.

Opposition to Negroes in state and local government was always open and bitter. In the press and on the platform they were described as ignorant and depraved. Critics made no distinction between Negroes who had graduated from Dartmouth and those who had graduated from the cotton fields. Every available means was employed to drive Negroes from public life. Negroes who voted or held office were refused jobs or punished by the Ku Klux Klan. One group in Mississippi boasted of having killed 116 Negroes and of having thrown their bodies into the Tallahatchie River. In a single South Carolina county, six men were murdered and more than 300 whipped during the first six months of 1870.

The federal government seemed helpless. Having withdrawn the occupation troops as soon as the Southern states organized governments, the President was reluctant to send them back. In 1870 and 1871, after the 15th Amendment was ratified, Congress enacted several laws to protect the right of citizens to vote. They were seldom enforced, and the Supreme Court struck down most of the important provisions in 1875 and 1876.[2]

1C

from *The Pursuit of Liberty: A History of the American People*

• R. Jackson Wilson et al. •

THE "NEGRO RULE" OF RADICAL RECONSTRUCTION was a myth. In no state did blacks dominate or control the government. There was not a single elected black governor, and only in South Carolina was there ever a black legislative majority. Moreover, the range of ability, education and competence among black officeholders was not wildly different from the range among most white officeholders in the North or South. The Reconstruction governments certainly contained corruption, but they were no more corrupt than their "lily-white" counterparts before or after the war. Although black suffrage was essential for keeping these regimes in power, their electoral base, especially in the beginning, extended beyond the ex-slaves. Many former Whigs, Southern Union men, and antisecessionists initially allied themselves with the new Republican governments. Many whites in nonslaveholding regions who had always resented the rule of the planter elite voted for and participated in the Reconstruction governments. These governments were in many ways reform governments. But they spent comparatively little time trying to achieve social equality between whites and blacks. Instead, they concentrated on such things as public education and eliminating the undemocratic features of the antebellum political system, by which the planter elite had maintained its dominion—things that benefitted poor whites as well as the freedmen.

But this is not how the former slaveholders and old planter elite saw radical Reconstruction. Illiterate black field hands who could vote while former planters could not, blacks who held office, "uppity" ex-slaves who mocked their former masters, black soldiers who now patrolled whites—all these things in the eyes of the former slaveholders turned radical Reconstruction into "Black Reconstruction." "Negro rule" became the galling symbol of all the horrors of radical Reconstruction, of all they had lost, of the defeat they had suffered and the degradation they now felt. They struck back against the Reconstruction governments with all the means at their disposal. They appealed to white supremacy to draw support of the poorer whites away from the Republicans, casting themselves as saviors who would "redeem" the South from the twin specter of black rule and Yankee domination. In states like Tennessee, Virginia, and North Carolina, where white voters held a clear majority, the "redeemers" gained control in 1871. For the most part they relied on the ballot box for victory, but in some areas they used intimidation and violence against blacks and their allies.

Where the racial balance was even or blacks held a majority, the battle for control was often violent. Carpetbaggers (whites from the North) and scalawags (white Southerners who collaborated with the Yankees) were ostracized and boycotted. Blacks were threatened with loss of jobs, credit, and access to lands for sharecropping. Secret organizations like the Ku Klux Klan were set up. Striking at night, dressed in robes and hoods, they beat, mutilated, and often murdered their victims. Directing their attacks mostly against scalawags and black leaders, they tried to terrorize blacks into withdrawing from political activity. The campaign of terror shocked Northerners and a number of Southerners. Two "force bills" and a Ku Klux Klan Act were passed by Congress, and in 1871 President Ulysses S. Grant initiated federal prosecutions in Mississippi. In South Carolina, Grant placed a few counties under martial law. But the laws were unevenly enforced and violence continued. "White legions," semimilitary organizations that intimidated whites into voting Democratic and forcibly kept blacks from voting, helped redeem Texas, Arkansas, and Alabama. As the 1875 Mississippi election approached, whites were determined to keep blacks and Republicans away from the polls, and the governor feared a bloodbath if he used black militia to oversee the elections. When he asked for federal help, the Grant administration refused, declaring that "the whole public are tired of these annual autumnal outbreaks in the South." The Democrats swept to power, aided by the white legions, and Mississippi too joined the ranks of the redeemed.[3]

1D
Letter to the Editor, *American Heritage*

• C. P. Hall II •

Note: Material from the original letter that was dropped for publication is indicated in italics.

I READ WITH INTEREST Bernard A. Weisberger's article ["When White Hoods Were in Flower"] about the Ku Klux Klan in the April issue ("In The News"). I generally agree with everything he says after the first two paragraphs but *while I do not wish to debate* I would offer the following additional information about one brief period of time. This information is admittedly third hand, gathered by my mother from, and about, her grandfather and passed on to me. An allowance must be made for distortion under these circumstances, a point offered in the spirit of full disclosure.

My great-grandfather was a citizen of Tennessee from the Nashville area, a soldier in the Confederate Army, and, immediately following the Civil War, a member of the Ku Klux Klan. According to him the Klan was a reaction to efforts to exploit postwar regional economic collapse by manipulating the unelected local government to confiscate the farms of land-poor Confederate veterans for failure to pay taxes. The Klan, in the Nashville area, did more mass parading in broad daylight than night riding, but both occurred. Although hoods were worn, membership was hardly a secret, since the members rode their own horses, as easily identifiable to the locals then as sports cars with vanity plates would be today. Within two years the crisis was over and the Klan formally disbanded; members burned their regalia and swore an oath that the Klan was ended, never to return.

When approached by those who claimed to be "resurrecting" the Klan in the 1880's, my great-grandfather declined to join, based on his oath. Although exceptions to this generalization can presumably be cited, members of the original Klan were conspicuous by their absence from the later bastard klan organizations *founded in the 1880's which still exist today.*

It may be possible to construct a continuum of illegal organizations, perhaps with Robin Hood's band at one end and anarchist types at the other. On such a continuum I would like to think that history might judge the Klan **of the 1860s** to be an organization undeniably outside the law but organized to combat a specific injustice, restrained in its lawless activities by men neither enamored of lawlessness nor coming to enjoy such behavior, who, when the injustice ended, shut down their organizations rather than search out excuses to justify continued lawless ways. *Such a group belongs above the mean of that continuum, as faint as that praise may be.*

This was the Klan grotesquely romanticized by D. W. Griffith in *Birth of a Nation*, not the rascals who sold memberships to rednecks and nincompoops for twenty dollars each, beginning in the 1880s. The point to all of this is that if my friends and I bought pointed hats and declared ourselves to be the Immortals of Darius the Great, it would not make it so. The reputation of the armed forces of the ancient Persian Empire should not be burdened by our follies, and competent historians would not speak of the two groups in the same breath, even if we charged twenty dollars a pop for our silly hats.[4]

2. The Assassination of Malcolm X

On February 22, 1965, the black leader Malcolm X was assassinated as he started to address a rally in New York City. Malcolm X, whose life has recently been portrayed in a movie by Spike Lee, was a controversial figure. He had spent time in jail as a street criminal. As spokesman for Elijah Muhammad's Nation of Islam, he articulated a virulently antiwhite program of black self-help. After a trip to Mecca, he broke with Elijah Muhammad and his antiwhite policies to form an independent political group addressing both national and international concerns.

2A

from *The New York Times*

MALCOLM X, THE 39-YEAR-OLD LEADER of a militant black nationalist movement, was shot to death yesterday afternoon at a rally of his followers in a ballroom in Washington Heights.

Shortly before midnight, a 22-year-old Negro, Thomas Hagan, was charged with the killing. The police rescued him from the ballroom crowd after he had been shot and beaten.

Malcolm, a bearded extremist, had said only a few words of greeting when a fusillade rang out. The bullets knocked him over backward.

Pandemonium broke out among the 400 Negroes in the Audubon Ballroom at 166th Street and Broadway. As men, women and children ducked under tables and flattened themselves on the floor, more shots were fired. Some witnesses said 30 shots had been fired.

The police said seven bullets had struck Malcolm. Three other Negroes were shot.

About two hours later the police said the shooting had apparently been a result of a feud between followers of Malcolm and members of the extremist group he broke with last year, the Black Muslims. However, the police declined to say whether Hagan is a Muslim.

The Medical Examiner's office said early this morning that a preliminary autopsy showed Malcolm had died of "multiple gunshot wounds." The office said that bullets of two different calibers as well as shotgun pellets had been removed from his body.

One police theory was that as many as five conspirators might have been involved, two creating a diversionary disturbance.

Hagan was shot in the left thigh and his left leg was broken, apparently by kicks. He was under treatment in the Bellevue Hospital prison ward last night; perhaps a dozen policemen were guarding him, according to the hospital's night superintendent. The police said they had found a cartridge case with four unused .45-caliber shells in his pocket.

Two other Negroes, described as "apparent spectators" by Assistant Chief Inspector Harry Taylor, in command of Manhattan North uniformed police, also were shot. They were identified as William Harris, wounded seriously in the abdomen, and William Parker, shot in a foot. Both were taken to Columbia Presbyterian Medical Center, which is close to the ballroom.

Capt. Paul Glaser of the Police Department's Community Relations Bureau said early today that Hagan, using a double-barrelled shotgun with shortened barrels and stock, had killed Malcolm X.

Malcolm, a slim, reddish-haired six-footer with a gift for bitter eloquence against what he considered white exploitation of Negroes, broke in March, 1964, with the Black Muslim movement called the Nation of Islam, headed by Elijah Muhammad . . . .[5]

2B
from *Newsweek*

HE WAS BORN MALCOLM LITTLE, an Omaha Negro preacher's son. Before he was out of his teens, he was Big Red, a Harlem hipster trafficking in numbers, narcotics, sex, and petty crime. He was buried as Al Hajj Malik Shabazz, a spiritual desperado lost between the peace of Islam and the pain of blackness. His whole life was a series of provisional identities, and he was still looking for the last when, as Malcolm X, 39, apostate Black Muslim and mercurial black nationalist, he was gunned to death by black men last week in a dingy uptown New York ballroom.

He had seen the end coming—predicted it, in fact, so long and so loudly that people had stopped listening. Malcolm X had always been an extravagant talker, a demagogue who titillated slum Negroes and frightened whites with his blazing racist attacks on the "white devils" and his calls for an armed American Mau Mau. His own flamboyant past made it easy to disregard his dire warnings that he had been marked for murder by the Muslims, the anti-white, anti-integrationist Negro sect he had served so devoutly for a dozen years and fought so bitterly since his defection a year ago.

His assassination turned out to be one of his few entirely accurate prophecies. Its fulfillment triggered an ominous vendetta between the Malcolmites and the Muslims—ominous in its intensity even though it was isolated on the outermost extremist fringe of American Negro life.

Death came moments after Malcolm stepped up to a flimsy plywood lectern in Manhattan's Audubon Ballroom, just north of Harlem, to address 400 of the faithful and the curious at a Sunday afternoon rally of his fledgling Organization of Afro-American Unity. The extermination plot was clever in conception, swift and smooth in execution. Two men popped to their feet in the front rows of wooden folding chairs, one yelling at the other: "Get your hands off my pockets, don't be messing with my pockets." Four of Malcolm's six bodyguards moved toward the pair; Malcolm himself chided, "Let's cool it."

Volley: Then came a second diversion: a man's sock, soaked in lighter fluid and set ablaze, flared in the rear. Heads swiveled, and, as they did, a dark, muscular man moved toward the lectern in a crouch, a sawed-off shotgun wrapped in his coat. *Blam-blam!* A double-barreled charge ripped up through the lectern and into Malcolm's chest. From the left, near the spot where the two men had been squabbling, came a back-up volley of pistol fire.

Malcolm tumbled backward, his lean body rent by a dozen wounds, his heels hooked over a fallen chair. The hall was bedlam. Malcolm's pregnant wife, Betty, rushed on stage screaming, "They're killing my husband!" His retainers fired wildly through the crowd at the fleeing killers. Four assailants made it to side doors and disappeared.

The man with the shotgun, identified by police as 22-year-old Talmadge Hayer of Paterson, N.J., dashed down a side aisle to the stairway exit from the second-floor ballroom. From the landing, one of Malcolm's bodyguards winged him in the thigh with a .45-caliber slug. Howling in pursuit ("Kill the bastard!"), the ballroom crowd caught Hayer on the sidewalk, mauled him, and broke his ankle before police rescued him.

Hayer was charged with homicide. Five days later, police picked up a karate-trained Muslim "enforcer," Norman 3X Butler, 26, as suspect No. 2.

The arrest of a Muslim surprised almost no one. For all his many enemies, Malcolm himself had insisted to the end that it was the Muslims who wanted him dead. They seemed to dog him everywhere he went; a bare week before his death, he was firebombed out of his Queens home, the ownership of which he had been disputing with the Muslims. Increasingly edgy, he moved with his wife and four children first to Harlem's Hotel Theresa, finally—the night before his death—to the New York Hilton in the alien world downtown. When he died, Manhattan police assumed that Muslims were involved. . . .[6]

2C
"I Saw Malcolm Die"

• Thomas Skinner, from *The New York Post* •

THEY CAME EARLY TO THE Audubon Ballroom, perhaps drawn by the expectation that Malcolm X would name the men who firebombed his home last Sunday, streaming from the bright afternoon sunlight into the darkness of the hall.

The crowd was larger than usual for Malcolm's recent meetings, the 400 filling three-quarters of the wooden folding seats, feet scuffling the worn floor as they waited impatiently, docilely obeying the orders of Malcolm's guards as they were directed to their seats.

I sat at the left in the 12th row and, as we waited, the man next to me spoke of Malcolm and his followers:

"Malcolm is our only hope," he said. "You can depend on him to tell it like it is and to give Whitey hell."

Then a man was on the stage, saying:

". . . I now give you Brother Malcolm. I hope you will listen, hear, and understand."

There was a prolonged ovation as Malcolm walked to the rostrum past a piano and a set of drums waiting for an evening dance and stood in front of a mural of a landscape as dingy as the rest of the ballroom.

When, after more than a minute the crowd quieted, Malcolm looked up and said, "A salaam aleikum (Peace be unto you)" and the audience replied "Wa aleikum salaam (And unto you, peace)."

Bespectacled and dapper in a dark suit, his sandy hair glinting in the light, Malcolm said: "Brothers and sisters . . ." He was interrupted by two men in the center of the ballroom, about four rows in front and to the right of me, who rose and, arguing with each other, moved forward. Then there was a scuffle in the back of the room and, as I turned my head to see what was happening, I heard Malcolm X say his last words: "Now, now brothers, break it up," he said softly. "Be cool, be calm."

Then all hell broke loose. There was a muffled sound of shots and Malcolm, blood on his face and chest, fell limply back over the chairs behind him. The two men who had approached him ran to the exit on my side of the room shooting wildly behind them as they ran.

I fell to the floor, got up, tried to find a way out of the bedlam.

Malcolm's wife, Betty, was near the stage, screaming in a frenzy. "They're killing my husband," she cried. "They're killing my husband."

Groping my way through the first frightened, then enraged crowd, I heard people screaming, "Don't let them kill him." "Kill those bastards." "Don't let him get away." "Get him."

At an exit I saw some of Malcolm's men beating with all their strength on two men. Police were trying to fight their way toward the two. The press of the crowd forced me back inside.

I saw a half-dozen of Malcolm's followers bending over his inert body on the stage, their clothes stained with their leader's blood. Then they put him on a litter while guards kept everyone off the platform. A woman bending over him said: "He's still alive. His heart's beating."

Four policemen took the stretcher and carried Malcolm through the crowd and some of the women came out of their shock long enough to moan and one said: "I don't think he's going to make it. I hope he doesn't die, but I don't think he's going to make it."

I spotted a phone booth in the rear of the hall, fumbled for a dime, and called a photographer. Then I sat there, the surprise wearing off a bit, and tried desperately to remember what had happened. One of my first thoughts was that this was the first day of National Brotherhood Week.[7]

3. Gays and the Military

3A
Letter to Senator John McCain

In February 1993, the U.S. Senate debated newly elected President Clinton's proposal to allow homosexuals to serve openly in the armed forces. In the debate, Senator John McCain (R., Ariz.) placed the following letter into the record.

HON. JOHN McCAIN,   JANUARY 12, 1993
WASHINGTON, D.C.

Dear Senator McCain:

I am an Army Captain, and I want to encourage you to do everything possible to stop President-Elect Clinton's proposal to lift the ban on homosexuals in the military. I believe this action would have a dramatically negative effect on military morale, discipline and readiness as well as undermining public confidence in our armed forces.

Everyone has rights, but not everyone has the right to serve in the military. The military discriminates against the handicapped, drug users, and criminals, with good reason. Imagine the consequences of nearsighted pilots, chemically dependent tank drivers or soldiers who are forced to depend on the actions of a known criminal. They do not belong in the military and neither do homosexuals.

In ten years I have seen hundreds of training hours lost to sexual discrimination cases. If the ban on homosexuals is lifted the number will increase ten fold. Every time a homosexual soldier receives even a slightly negative report he will be able to claim sexual preference discrimination. This will only further detract from training and add to an already burdensome amount of paperwork.

Heterosexual male soldiers will not follow homosexual leaders. I base this claim, not just on hypothesis but examples in units in which I have served. Soldiers, especially those in combat arms, will not tolerate known homosexuals in their unit. It is detrimental to morale and order to have soldiers worry about their bunkmates' sexual preferences. The result of such situations is usually violence. Comrades of mine in the Navy are particularly worried about their rights as heterosexuals, when they are forced to share crowded ship-board quarters with known homosexuals.

The military is aware that there are homosexuals presently serving and this has already created unit disruptions. My wife served for four years in the Marines and was approached by lesbians several times. One even threatened to kill herself if my wife did not give in to her advances. That did not improve the morale of her unit. The trust that creates cohesion and fighting spirit is lost. How much more common will this scene become when homosexuality is condoned?

I believe the military is supposed to represent the finest ideals of American society not the opinions of a deviant minority. Basic biology demonstrates that homosexuality is unnatural. If the military is not allowed to discriminate against "sexual preference," will homosexuality be the limit or will the other sexual preferences like bestiality and pedophilia be accepted as well? Will they soon be considered normal behavior too? Will the military soon be unable to discriminate against anyone? Like dozens of other officers I have spoken with, I will seriously consider resigning if this new measure is put into effect.

I adamantly urge you to do everything you can to stop this proposed measure. If you do not believe me, believe [Chairman of the Joint Chiefs of Staff] General [Colin] Powell, this is not a good idea,

Sincerely,

———

Captain, U.S. Army[8]

3B
"Between Fear and Fantasy"

• Ken Corbett •

MILITARY OFFICIALS AND CONGRESSIONAL LEADERS cite the possible threat of violence to homosexuals as a reason to continue discriminating against gays in the military. This raises the obvious question of whether we should be governed by threat. But we also are left to ask what fuels such aggression.

Throughout the debate, straight military men keep voicing concern that they will not be able to control their aggression against gay men. Gay soldiers and sailors are threatened with the prospect of being beaten, even murdered. As if to prove the point, three marines beat a homosexual man outside a gay bar in Wilmington, N.C., Saturday morning while shouting, "Clinton must pay!"

Why is this aggression almost exclusively focused on gay men? Newspaper articles are full of the anger and concerns of male soldiers. Talk shows feature verbal slugfests between gay and straight military men. Women are almost never mentioned. This no doubt reflects military demographics, but it also reflects the manner in which the hatred of male homosexuality is founded on fears of femininity. The equation is simple: male homosexuality equals femininity, which produces fear, which produces aggression.

More specifically, hatred of gay men is based on fear of the self, not of an alien other. This was expressed by Martin Jones, a 22-year-old airman quoted in this paper as saying he wouldn't be able to sleep at night if the ban were lifted because he would be "worried that some homosexual is going to sneak over and make a pass."

Seemingly unaware of the slippery slope between fear and fantasy, he conveyed a suspicion that gay men will not be able to control their sexual appetite, and rape will ensue. Leaving aside the fact that rape is largely a heterosexual phenomenon (and a prevalent heterosexual male fantasy), Airman Jones's concern smacks of the pernicious misconception that gay men and women have a devouring sexual appetite—that they are hungry sirens eager to bite.

More to the point, Mr. Jones imagines himself the object of a man's desire. He anxiously pictures himself wanted in a way that most men feel only a woman should be wanted. In so fantasizing, he must, if ever so briefly, put himself in the place of a man who desires another man.

But Mr. Jones quickly sheds this threatened desire: He and his like-minded colleagues turn the object of desire into a hated, threatening object. Mr. Jones creates a distinct border between "them" and "us." He is not one of them, he hates them.

Hatred thrives on rigid order. Armed with hatred and protected by institutional values, Mr. Jones doesn't have to take responsibility for his aggressive impulses. Mr. Jones, his commanders and many in Congress would have us believe this kind of phobic behavior should guide military policy. But what kind of policy is built on a phobic solution? What kind of law is built on hatred?

Apparently these are not questions that Mr. Jones is asking himself when he can't fall asleep. He thinks sneaky homosexuals cause his insomnia. But it is really his own fears and fantasies that keep him awake.[9]

3C
from Address to the Senate

• Sen. Carol Moseley-Braun (D-Ill.) •

MR. PRESIDENT, FEW MATTERS ARE more vital to America's security than the readiness of the military forces who defend the values which we all cherish.

One of those values, Mr. President, is the protection of individual rights.

Yet even as our new President and Commander in Chief seeks to advance those rights by removing the unfair and outdated ban on gays and lesbians in the military, we hear disturbing voices across the land.

As we listen to those who tell us that gays and lesbians will destroy the military, the simple truth is that this debate is not about military capability at all. It is about irrational fears and prejudices. It is about civil rights and leadership in a democratic society.

The issue today, Mr. President, is simple: Do we move forward as a society, recognizing the talents and dignity of all of our citizens? Or do we allow our differences to pit one American against the other and take this country down a painful road we have traveled before?

The Pentagon tells us flatly that homosexuality is incompatible with military service. As a military leader, the Commandant of the Marine Corps, asked in defending the ban presently: "How would you react if your son called and informed you that his roommates for the next 2 years were two homosexuals ***?"

This is not the first time the military has had such concerns. I want to quote a 1942 Navy memorandum.

"Men on board ship live in particularly close association," warned a 1942 Navy memorandum. "In their messes one man sits beside another; their hammocks or bunks are close together; in their common tasks they work side by side. ***"

"How many white men would choose, of their own accord, that their close associates in sleeping quarters, at mess and in a gun's crew should be of another race?" the Navy's top admirals asked.

In 1948, speaking in favor of a measure to guarantee to any American the right to serve in a military unit comprised exclusively of members of his own race, one Member of this body said: "I know that perspectives are often blurred by the desire to capture the votes of a highly organized and vocal minority."

Some Senators of that era feared that allowing negroes and whites to serve together would have grave public health consequences. "The mandatory intermingling of the races," one said, would be "sure to increase the number of men who will be disabled through communicable diseases."

And Senators in opposition to President Truman's directive insisted that they were in no way opposed to basic civil rights for all. They simply felt duty-bound, Mr. President, to defer to the Pentagon's expert judgment on the issue.

How many of those very same arguments have we heard repeated this year with regard to President Clinton's proposed directive to integrate gays and lesbians in the military?

While the discrimination faced by African-Americans often takes different form from that faced by gay and lesbian Americans, this much we can say with absolute certainty: The military has no more of a rational basis for banning gays and lesbians in 1993 than it did for segregating African-Americans in 1943.

Old beliefs die hard, Mr. President. But when they stand in the way of equal opportunity for any American, die they must. . . .

In 1948, the military leadership felt that black and white could not and would [not] serve together. We now know, Mr. President, that since 1948 millions of white Americans have made such a choice. They have fought, eaten, and slept side by side with African-Americans with no impairment of military readiness whatsoever.

And from those experiences, Mr. President, they have forged an America that is stronger now than at any time in its history. Stronger now because its people are more unified and more respectful of their glorious diversity than ever before.

Despite my disagreement with the Joint Chiefs of Staff on this issue, I have confidence in our military leadership's ability to carry out the orders of their Commander in Chief.

I can even appreciate General Powell's dilemma when he said: "I've got to consider what you say to a youngster who might come and say, 'General, in the most private of my accommodations, I prefer to have heterosexuals around me than homosexuals.'"

This is what you say to that youngster, General Powell. Tell him that he's in our Armed Forces now. Tell him that he's a proud member of the greatest fighting forces in the world.

Remind him that his homosexual platoonmates have also volunteered to give their lives for their country and the values we all hold dear. Remind him that they, like all members of our military, will be held to the strictest codes of conduct and behavior.

But most importantly, General Powell, tell him that the greatest danger he faces is not in his private accommodations. It is from the forces of hate and fear in this country that 40 years ago would have denied to you the opportunity to lead.

Tell him that if he can defeat the enemy within himself he will be ready to confront any enemy abroad. Wish him a long and distinguished career in the service, and tell him that by the end of his 40 years in uniform you hope he will have seen as many changes for the better in our military and the imperfect society it defends as you have in yours.[10]

3D
"Issue of Gays Really Needs Deep Thought"

• Samuel Francis •

FOR TWO HOURS IN LATE JANUARY, the brass hats of the Pentagon cloistered themselves with President Clinton to try to explain to him why lifting the ban on alternative lifestyles in the military is not a terribly swift idea. Since the closest Clinton has even come to people in uniform is quipping with the burger jockeys at McDonald's, the brass took on no enviable mission.

Nevertheless, with help from Sen. Sam Nunn of Georgia, the chairman of the Senate Armed Services Committee, the Joint Chiefs seem to have penetrated the bunker of presidential consciousness. Now there has been a "compromise," but no outright reversal of the ban—at least not for a while.

Yet most of the arguments the generals offered boil down to pragmatic and administrative reasons. The *New York Times* reports that Joint Chiefs Chairman Colin Powell brought up several: Accepting homosexuals in the military would create problems for "morale and discipline, recruiting, cohesiveness among combat troops, personal privacy and even the spread of AIDS."

These are good reasons, but none touches the heart of the issue, which is whether the social normalization of homosexuality is a good idea. Unless that issue is resolved in the negative, unless Americans and their leaders decide it's not a good idea, most of the reasons Powell mentioned become irrelevant.

If homosexuality is "normal," if it is no different from heterosexuality, then problems of morale and discipline, recruiting and cohesiveness wither away as the stereotypes of homosexuals as "abnormal" become outdated. The spread of AIDS would be no more serious than that of other venereal diseases, and personal privacy has never been much of a consideration in an Army that doesn't even have toilet stalls. Powell and his colleagues in khaki did their best, but by all accounts they missed the bull's-eye.

Nor are many of the reasons that the religious right offers much more compelling. It's true the Bible condemns sodomy; the Old Testament inflicts the death penalty for it. And other church and rabbinical traditions condemn it as well. But America no longer even pretends to be a Christian society, and unless we make that pretense, there's no reason to write Jewish or Christian Scriptures into our secular law.

Moreover, God may not like sodomy, but reportedly he also doesn't much care for lying, gluttony or any of a wide range of vices that abuse the flesh he created. As abhorrent as such sins are in the eyes of the Almighty, it doesn't follow that our public laws should punish them. To reach that position, you have to engage on other ground.

The main argument homosexuals use to justify repealing laws against sodomy among consenting adults and voiding the ban in the military is that homosexuality does no harm. They claim (I'm not convinced they're right) that homosexuals are no more inclined to commit sex crimes than heterosexuals and that the homosexual act itself hurts no one. Hence, under a commonly accepted standard, the state has no business using legal force to prevent or punish such acts. It is on the validity of that argument that the case for normalizing homosexuality must stand or fall.

It is not a valid argument. One of its flaws is its very narrow conception of what constitutes "harm." The lesson of 4,000 years of social history is that sexual behavior, consensual or not, has consequences for others, that it often affects (and hurts) others in ways society needs to control, and that unregulated sex renders social bonds, especially in the family but also beyond it, impossible. We can regulate it through law or through socially enforced moral custom or both, but we have to do it somehow.

History knows of no society that has not regulated sexual behavior and forbidden some kinds of it, nor is there any reason known to social science to suppose that a society that fails to do so is possible. A "society" that makes no distinction between sex within marriage and sex outside it, that does not distinguish between continence and debauchery, normality and perversion, love and lust, is not really a society but merely the chaos of a perpetual orgy.

It is to just such an orgy that the proponents of normalized and unrestricted homosexuality invite America. Maybe most Americans have reached the point at which they are ready to immerse themselves in the illusion that a perpetual orgy pretending to be a society really doesn't hurt anybody.

Or maybe most Americans haven't thought it through. It's clear that their leaders haven't and don't know how to make the case against normalization. That's one more reason why Clinton ought to hold off on his executive order until Americans and their leaders have a chance to think about it some more.[11]

4. A Question of Ethics
Cases in Bioethics from The Hastings Center Report

The Hastings Center in Hastings-on-Hudson, New York, is an institute specializ-ing in bioethics, the study of ethical issues related to the practice of medicine. Its month-ly magazine, The Hastings Center Report, *frequently includes case studies with commentaries. The following appeared in the February 1976 issue.*[12]

4A
Fear of Flying: The Psychiatrist's Role in War

THE FOLLOWING REPORT IS REPRINTED *from the Air Force's PACAF Surgeon's Newsletter, December 1966, p. 5.*

Fear of Flying: A twenty-six-year-old staff sergeant AC-47 gunner with seven months' active duty in Vietnam, presented with frank admission of fear of flying. He had flown over one hundred missions, and loss of several crews who were well known to the patient, precipitated his visit. He stated he would give up flight pay, promotion, medals, etc., just to stop flying. Psychiatric consultation to USAF Hospital, Cam Ranh Bay, resulted in thirty-six days' hospitalization with use of psychotherapy and tranquilizers. Diagnosis was Gross Stress Reaction, manifested by anxiety, tenseness, a fear of death expressed in the form of rationalizations, and inability to function. His problem was "worked through" and insight to his problem was gained to the extent that he was returned to full flying duty in less than six weeks. This is a fine tribute to the psychiatrists at Cam Ranh Bay. (633 Combat Spt Gp Dispensary, Pleiku AB.)

4B
from *Commentary*

• Perry London •

AS THE NEWSLETTER SAYS, success in returning the gunner back to duty is a fine trib-ute, indeed, to psychiatrists' efficiency as technicians. The question is: does it also tes-tify to their deficiency as moralists? Proper morality, in some views, would have made them work against the official position of the government and the military in the Vietnam War; and holders of such views are outraged that physicians would sell their services in such an unjust cause. . . .

Yet most of humankind, most of the time, are too busy trying to manage the routines of daily living to spend much energy on moral calculations. Most morals get borrowed from the neighbors, the organization, or the big shots of our other-directed society. Just as politics is the exercise of leadership, and most of us are rather passive followers, morality is the exercise of normative behavior, and most of us are rather passive actors in the creation of our norms. The Children of Israel liked Egypt and did not mind slavery in principle; it was the beatings, the strawless bricks, and the baby snatchers that did them in. So it is with most of us, most of the time.

I do not mean to argue that people should never be held individually accountable for their acts, or that the Vietnam war was a just one. I do not mean to say that a decent society makes the individual the last arbiter of morality, not the first one. In 1966 (when the *Newsletter* was published), I thought, like many others, that we were on the right side of the Vietnam war. By 1969, like many others, I had changed my mind. In 1975 [when this commentary was written], it is unseemly, if not immoral, to retrospectively condemn the doctors of last decade's war for doing what then looked like their duty in a cause which they probably supported. Physicians are no more ignorant, or ill-intentioned, or immoral, than the rest of us. The case is a study in tragedy, not morality.

4C
from *Commentary*

• H. Tristram Engelhardt, Jr. •

IN READING THIS CASE, one might be tempted to consider it simply an example of the misuse of medicine in the service of a political goal. That would be an oversimplification because the individuals concerned, the psychiatrist, the persons who asked for their consultation, and in the end perhaps the patient, probably saw themselves as acting in accord with reality. The case illustrates the role that value judgments play in the concept of disease. The judgment that someone has a disease presupposes, among other things, (1) that the person afflicted is the subject of phenomena that are abnormal and (2) that those phenomena are explainable in terms of the laws of pathophysiology and psychology. That is, the statement that some condition is a pathological state presupposes more than a mere description. The condition must be held in some sense to be a state of suffering and to be abnormal, where "abnormal" means other than "unusual." . . .

In "Fear of Flying" the flier was appreciated as being ill in that he was in distress (that is, suffering—afraid that he would be shot down in combat) and was unable to function normally. Normal function was here defined as the ability to engage in combat. Moreover, the failure to function was held to be caused rather than to be a chosen pattern of conduct. To consider a state of affairs a disease is to hold that it is caused by pathological processes, not freely willed action. Diagnosing the flier as ill with "Gross Stress Reaction" thus (1) authorized the use of medicine to restore health and the ability to function normally, and (2) excused the individual from responsibility for not having functioned. . . .

One should recognize this case as a flamboyant example of the generally value-laden character of talk about disease and health. It is not as if one could simply isolate those diseases which are objectively disease categories and those that are not. Rather, some disease concepts fail (and should fail) because they conflict with general human values.

4D
from *Commentary*

• Robert Newman •

THIS CASE ILLUSTRATES THE INHERENT DANGERS of psychiatrists' equating deviance with psychopathology and proceeding unquestionably from the premise that "curing" such deviance is a universally valid goal. . . .

When the patient does not have the unequivocal option to refuse treatment, one must proceed from the assumption that voluntarism is lacking. Under these circumstances the concept of success and failure loses all meaning. Whether the "problem" is fear of flying, drug abuse, homosexuality, masturbation, or any other behavior, it must be left to the individual to decide if it is acceptable or not, and whether change is a desired goal. The attitudes of the psychiatrist regarding the behavior, and the value which the psychiatrist may personally place on modifying that behavior, are irrelevant. The circuitous logic evinced in this case history, which cites as proof of success the fact that the patient ultimately came to share the psychiatrists' views, must be rejected. Nor does the self-righteous assertion that the psychiatrists' motivation is benevolent mitigate the invidiousness of involuntary treatment. As Thomas Szasz has pointed out in *Law, Liberty and Psychiatry:* "Treating patients against their wishes, even though the treatment may be medically correct, should be considered an offense punishable by law. . . . Let us not forget that every form of social oppression has, at some time during its history, been justified on the ground of helpfulness toward the oppressed."

Petitions, Arguments, and Pleas

5

Gettysburg Address

• Abraham Lincoln •

FOURSCORE AND SEVEN YEARS AGO our fathers brought forth on this continent a new nation, conceived in liberty, and dedicated to the proposition that all men are created equal. Now we are engaged in a great civil war, testing whether that nation, or any nation so conceived and so dedicated, can long endure. We are met on a great battlefield of that war. We have come to dedicate a portion of that field, as a final resting place for those who here gave their lives that that nation might live. It is altogether fitting and proper that we should do this. But, in a larger sense, we cannot dedicate—we cannot consecrate—we cannot hallow—this ground. The brave men, living and dead, who struggled here, have consecrated it, far above our poor power to add or detract. The world will little note, nor long remember, what we say here, but it can never forget what they did here. It is for us, the living, rather, to be dedicated here to the unfinished work which they who fought here have thus far so nobly advanced. It is rather for us to be here dedicated to the great task remaining before us,—that from these honored dead we take increased devotion to that cause for which they gave the last full measure of devotion—that we here highly resolve that these dead shall not have died in vain—that this nation, under God, shall have a new birth of freedom—and that government of the people, by the people, for the people, shall not perish from the earth.

6

Public Statement by Eight Alabama Clergymen, April 12, 1963

In 1963, the Reverend Martin Luther King, Jr., went to Birmingham, Alabama, to lead nonviolent demonstrations in support of the local effort to desegregate stores and restaurants. He was arrested for trespass, and, while in jail, wrote his famous defense of the tactic of nonviolent direct action, Letter from the Birmingham Jail. *That letter was in response to the following statement by leaders of the Birmingham clergy.*

WE THE UNDERSIGNED CLERGYMEN are among those who, in January, issued "An Appeal for Law and Order and Common Sense," in dealing with racial problems in Alabama. We expressed understanding that honest convictions in racial matters could properly be pursued in the courts, but urged that decisions of those courts should in the meantime be peacefully obeyed.

Since that time there has been some evidence of increased forebearance and a willingness to face facts. Responsible citizens have undertaken to work on various problems which cause racial friction and unrest. In Birmingham, recent public events have given indication that we all have opportunity for a new constructive and realistic approach to racial problems. [A new mayor, Albert Boutwell, was to be sworn in on April 15.]

However, we are now confronted by a series of demonstrations by some of our Negro citizens, directed and led in part by outsiders. We recognize the natural impatience of people who feel that their hopes are slow in being realized. But we are convinced that these demonstrations are unwise and untimely.

We agree rather with certain local Negro leadership which has called for honest and open negotiation of racial issues in our area. And we believe this kind of facing of issues can best be accomplished by citizens of our own metropolitan area, white and Negro, meeting with their knowledge and experience of the local situation. All of us need to face that responsibility and find proper channels for its accomplishment.

Just as we formerly pointed out that "hatred and violence have no sanction in our religious and political traditions," we also point out that such actions as incite to hatred and violence, however technically peaceful those actions may be, have not contributed to the resolution of our local problems. We do not believe that these days of new hope are days when extreme measures are justified in Birmingham.

We commend the community as a whole, and the local news media and law enforcement officials in particular, on the calm manner in which these demonstrations have been handled. We urge the public to continue to show restraint should the demonstrations continue, and the law enforcement officials to remain calm and continue to protect our city from violence.

We further strongly urge our own Negro community to withdraw support from these demonstrations, and to unite locally in working peacefully for a better Birmingham. When rights are consistently denied, a cause should be pressed in the courts and in negotiations among local leaders, and not in the streets. We appeal to both our white and Negro citizenry to observe the principles of law and order and common sense.

Signed by:

C. C. J. Carpenter, D.D., LL.D., Bishop of Alabama
Joseph A. Durick, D.D., Auxiliary Bishop, Diocese of Mobile-Birmingham
Rabbi Milton L. Grafman, Temple Emanu-El, Birmingham, Alabama

Bishop Paul Hardin, Bishop of the Alabama–West Florida Conference of the Methodist Church

Bishop Nolan B. Harmon, Bishop of the North Alabama Conference of the Methodist Church

George M. Murray, D.D., LL.D., Bishop Coadjutor, Episcopal Diocese of Alabama

Edward V. Ramage, Moderator, Synod of the Alabama Presbyterian Church in the United States

Earl Stallings, Pastor, First Baptist Church, Birmingham, Alabama[13]

7

Petition of the Inmates of the 9th Floor of Tombs City Prison

In August 1970, prisoners in the Manhattan House of Detention for Men, commonly called "The Tombs," took several guards hostage and demanded to see the mayor and the press. At a meeting with the correction commissioner, the inmates, all of whom were awaiting trial, issued the following hand-lettered petition.

WE, THE INMATES OF THE 9TH FLOOR of Tombs City Prison, Manhattan, N.Y., submit this petition of grievances and we solicit your attention in this matter.

Grievances

1. We address ourselves to what we feel to be the injustices we suffer in the courtrooms of the Criminal Court and the Supreme Court of Manhattan County;

   (a) Many of us have been denied preliminary hearings in Criminal Court;

   (b) Those of us who do receive hearings are usually given sham hearings that border on a system of Kangaroo Courts in which we are not given a chance to take the stand in our own behalf, nor are we ever advised of our rights by the judges at these so-called hearings;

   (c) Many of us find ourselves the victims of excessive bails;

   (d) Many of us are brought to court and wind up sitting in the detention cells all day and never get to enter the courtroom (This is generally regarded as a move by the people's representative, the district attorney, to wear the man down so that he will be willing to plead guilty);

   (e) Many of us have submitted writs and petitions to the court asking that the court rectify some error in procedure. We are denied hearings on our writs even though constitutional questions are involved, or, as is usually the case, the writs go unanswered;

   (f) Many of us have been waiting for trial dates for an average of eight months to a year or more and our motions for speedy trials are ignored by the courts.

In conclusion of grievance No. 1, it appears that each and every one of us has been denied some basic constitutional right and we stand before the public at large guilty until we prove ourselves innocent.

2. In relation to grievance No. 1, in most instances we find that the Legal Aid Society aids and abets the incursions and abuses of our rights in the courtrooms. It is the order of the day for the assigned legal aid, on first meeting his client to open the conversation by saying "I suggest that you take a guilty plea," or "I can speak to the District Attorney and get you (this or that) plea."

All this without even asking the client in confidence whether he is in fact guilty of the charge. Those of us who have to rely on the Legal Aid Society to represent us find that though they are paid by the state they will not thoroughly investigate the case or subpoena witnesses in our behalf.

In conclusion of grievance No. 2, we feel that under the present system of the courts that we cannot receive any justice and can only suffer threat, coercion and intimidation disguised as law and justice.

3. We now address ourselves to the physical brutality perpetrated by the officials of Tombs Prison against the inmates thereof. This unnecessary brutality has been largely directed against the black and Puerto Rican inmate population. We vehemently denounce this policy of inhumane treatment.

It is common practice for an inmate to be singled out by some Correction Department employee because he did not hear the officer call his name or because the officer did not like the way this or that inmate looked or because of the manner in which the inmate walked or because the officer brings the turmoil of his own personal problems to work with him, and together with other officers, beat the defenseless inmate into unconsciousness, often injuring him for life physically and mentally or both.

The attacks on the inmates are made by the officers wielding blackjack, night sticks, fists and feet. After such attacks it is the policy of the officials in collusion with any one of the institution doctors to fix up fake accident reports to cover up the mayhem that has been committed against the person of the inmate.

We reject all official denials that such things do not happen here as there are those of us who have experienced these sadistic attacks and there are witnesses to verify the fact. It is common knowledge by thoughtful men that "Not one leaf of a tree could turn yellow without the silent knowledge and consent of the tree itself."

That is in relation to the officers who daily brutalize and maim us. These acts would not and could not happen without the knowledge and consent of the Commissioner of Correction, the Assistant Commissioner of Correction, the Warden of Tombs Prison, the Deputy Wardens of Tombs Prison, and the Captains of Tombs Prison.

In conclusion of grievance No.3, we DEMAND that this policy of physical brutality cease immediately.

4. In relation to grievance No. 3, it has come to our attention that our wives, sisters and mothers have been variously insulted and indecently proposed to by the officers of Tombs Prison when they come to visit us. We DEMAND that this abuse to our women be discontinued.

5. We now address ourselves to the food which we are fed. Molded bread; only enough jelly to put on one slice of bread; rotten potatoes, always half-cooked; powdered eggs with the consistency of overcooked tapioca; not enough desserts; THE FOOD IS GENERALLY UNPALATABLE WITHOUT SEASONING AND NOT FIT FOR HUMAN CONSUMPTION. In conclusion to this grievance we DEMAND BETTER PREPARED FOOD.

6. Because many of us feel that we cannot get a fair shake between the Legal Aid Society and the courts, we find that we must prepare our own briefs and motions. This institution has law books in its library, but the institution does not allow the inmates to use the law books for reference data. In conclusion of grievance No. 6 we DEMAND USE OF THE LAW BOOKS IN THE LIBRARY.

7. This entire institution is ridden with body lice, roaches, rats and mice and we DEMAND THAT ADEQUATE MEASURES BE TAKEN TO ALLEVIATE THIS CONDITION.

8. As has been stated, a great majority of the men here spend about an average of eight months to a year here with their cases and a good portion of them, due to circumstances, have no other clothes to wear save those which they had when they entered the institution. We feel that the institution should supply each inmate with adequate clothing and facilities to maintain the upkeep of their civilian attire.

9. We ask that there be an improvement in the medical staff here at the institution. As the matter now stands, the doctors prescribe an assortment of pills for every individual ailment without adequate diagnosis of the patients' complaint. The doctors even relegate responsibility by having an institution nurse listen to prisoners complaint of ailment and prescribe pills for that ailment contrary to standard medical practice and the law in that regard.

10. We ask that there be no repercussions against any of the inmates involved in this protest, and that each and every point in the above list of grievances be given your personal attention. We also ask that this entire petition, without deletion, be made public by giving access to it to the press.

In Conclusion

We are firm in our resolve and we demand as human beings the dignity and justice that is due to us by right of our birth. We do not know how the present system of brutality and dehumanization and injustice has been allowed to be perpetuated in this day of enlightenment, but we are the living proof of its existence and we cannot allow it to continue.

The manner in which we chose to express our grievances is admittedly dramatic, but it is not as dramatic and shocking as the conditions under which society has forced us to live. We are indignant and so, too, should the people of society be indignant.

The taxpayer, who just happens to be our mothers, fathers, sisters, brothers, sons and daughters should be made aware of how their tax dollars are being spent to deny their sons, brothers, fathers, and uncles justice, equality and dignity.

Respectfully submitted
WE ARE ONE PEOPLE
THE INMATES OF THE 9TH FLOOR TOMBS PRISON[14]

8

An Open Letter to the Press About a Real Threat to Medical Progress

• Susan E. Paris, President, Americans for Medical Progress •

MANY OF YOU SAW *60 MINUTES'* first-rate report on the ordeal of Dr. Michael Carey, a neurosurgeon whose important brain-injury research was derailed by so-called animal rights activists (January 24th). The story was nothing short of a media breakthrough.

Millions of Americans were exposed to the true agenda and cult-like ideology of extremists who oppose all use of laboratory animals in medical research. In the eyes of these "animal zealots," to borrow a term used on the program, the life of a laboratory rat, or cat, or pig, or dog, is equal to the life of a child.

Ironically, as *60 Minutes'* viewers learned, the same movement that claims compassion for all living creatures is totally lacking in compassion for human beings. Animal rights activists threaten, harass, and malign scientists who are dedicated to saving human life and easing human suffering. Dr. Carey's work, for example, was aimed at saving combat soldiers' lives.

The time has come to relentlessly report the animal rights movement's threat to medical progress. The time has come to pull back the mask of moderation behind which the movement has long hidden its fanatical face. The time has come to tell the public that animal *rights* has nothing to do with animal *welfare* . . . and everything to do with a set of dangerously bizarre beliefs.

A single network television exposé, even one viewed by a huge national audience, should mark the beginning, not the end, of the truth-telling. I urge you to follow the example set by *60 Minutes*. Nothing less than the future of medical research—and medical progress—could be at stake.

Yours truly,
Susan E. Paris
President, Americans for Medical Progress[15]

9

Address to the Senate on the National Endowment for the Arts

• Senator John Danforth •

The National Endowment for the Arts (NEA), a government agency, awards funds to artists to support their development. In 1989, following claims that a number of NEA-sponsored artists (including photographer Robert Mapplethorpe and sculptor Andres Serrano) were exhibiting obscene works, hearings were held on a bill to reauthorize funding for the NEA. Jesse Helms (R-N.C.) offered an amendment to "prohibit the use of appropriated funds for the dissemination or production of obscene or indecent materials or materials denigrating a particular religion."

The following speech was given on the floor of the Senate by Sen. John Danforth (R-Mo.) on September 29, 1989.

MR. PRESIDENT, I HAVE UNFORTUNATELY HAD the opportunity to look very briefly at the exhibits that the Senator from North Carolina has brought to the floor and everything that has been said about them is true. These are gross. These are terrible. These are totally indefensible. I do not think they are art.

Mr. President, however I do not believe that the issue before us tonight is whether we like or do not like these pictures. I do not like them and my guess is that not a single resident of my State would like them. They would not like the idea of the Government paying for them. I am sorry Government did pay for them.

That is not the issue before us. The issue is very simple: The Senator from Texas used the expression, and I think it was very well chosen, the question is: What is suitable art? And the issue before the Senate is very simple, and it is whether we in the U.S. Senate should attempt to make definitions of what we consider to be suitable art.

Maybe there should not be any National Endowment for the Arts. Maybe the Government should never be in the business of making judgments of taste, because that is what the NEA does. I think that is an arguable position. But the question is not whether the NEA should do it or not do it. We have already decided that the NEA is in that business.

The question is whether we in the Congress of the United States should try to establish some criteria by which we define what is or is not suitable art. That is what the Senator from North Carolina does by this amendment. His amendment does not say that the Mapplethorpe exhibition is pornography and it should not be funded. He does not say that. He goes much more broadly than that. He does not say that Mr. Serrano should or should not be funded by the NEA.

He goes much more broadly than that in the terms of his amendment, and I want to read a couple of paragraphs because we have been focusing on obscenity and I think everybody knows that obscenity has been a problem for the Supreme Court of the United States. But he also says in paragraph 2 that the amendment covers material which denigrates the objects or beliefs of the adherents of a particular religion or nonreligion.

Mr. President, consider what that means: material which denigrates the object or beliefs of the adherents of a particular religion or nonreligion.

Does it denigrate the object of a religion to portray Christ as a clown? Well, the musical *Godspell* did just that. It portrayed Christ as a clown. Could it be found by some administrator that the portrayal of Christ as a clown denigrates the object of somebody's religion? Of course it could.

Godspell probably would be covered by the breadth of this amendment.

How about a portrayal of Christ as a wild animal? Would that portrayal denigrate a person's religion? Well, C. S. Lewis did that in *The Lion, the Witch and the Wardrobe*. It was a book about Christianity and the Christ figure was a lion and some administrator, some bureaucrat could have said that denigrates a person's religion. C. S. Lewis spent his academic and literary life describing his religious beliefs, which were very, very profound beliefs.

How about in the world of music? Could it be said that the beliefs of the Quaker faith [who are against all war] are denigrated by "Onward Christian Soldiers Marching As to War" [a traditional Christian hymn]?

And then how about the question of race. I remember from my own part of the country, *Tom Sawyer* and *Huckleberry Finn*. There have been those throughout the last number of decades who have tried for one reason or another to get *Tom Sawyer* and *Huckleberry Finn* off of the shelves of our schools.

This amendment would say that *Tom Sawyer* would not have qualified for a NEA grant and *Huckleberry Finn* because it could be argued that they denigrated an individual, namely Nigger Jim, as he was called according to his race.

Or how about creed? Can we think of anything in the annals of literature that denigrates an individual because of his religion? How about the *Merchant of Venice*? How about William Shakespeare himself? Would that be covered by this amendment? I think it would be. This amendment is not just about Mapplethorpe. It is also about Shakespeare.

And in our own time in American literature Alice Walker's great little book, *The Color Purple*, made into a movie, clearly denigrates men.

And this amendment says that material that denigrates or reviles a person on the basis of sex falls within the parameters. I take it that *The Color Purple* would not have qualified for an NEA grant.

How about age? I do not remember the name of the book, but I do remember that Bill Cosby, the famous comedian, wrote a book about kids. It is a spoof of children, and his television programs are always doing that. And I take it that those programs and the book denigrate people on the basis of age.

Then there is national origin which is also covered material that denigrates or reviles on the basis of national origin. Perhaps *The Godfather*. The head of Paramount Theaters was visiting me recently. I said, "What is the greatest movie you ever made?" He said, "The two Godfather movies taken together, absolutely the essence of American art" and it would be covered by this amendment.

I am not for Mapplethorpe. I am sick that a dollar of taxpayer money went to pay for this kind of junk. I am sick about it. I could just see the faces of the people of Sedalia, or Cabool, or Mountain Grove, MO, if they were told that they had to pay for this. It truly is outlandish. That is not the issue.

The issue is: How good are we at defining whether something is suitable art or not-suitable art and how do we draw those definitions? And should we really write definitions on the floor of the Senate which cover *Godspell*, and *Tom Sawyer*, and the *Merchant of Venice*, and *The Color Purple*, and *The Godfather?* Mr. President, I think the answer is no.[16]

10
"Latino, Sí. Hispanic, No."

• Earl Shorris •

WHEN THE KING OF SPAIN was asked last year what name he used for those people in the U.S. who were related to him by language, he is reported to have said, with regal certainty, "Hispanic."

Ricardo Gutiérrez, a salesman from the east side of Los Angeles, faced with the same question, answered with equal certainty, "Latino."

Although Mr. Gutiérrez would seem to have superior knowledge of cultural issues in the U.S., many people and institutions, including the Census Bureau, side with the King. I am not one of them.

Of course, there are those who think that the King and the salesman are wrong. They oppose the use of any single word to describe all of the King's linguistic relatives—a lawyer whose family came from Puerto Rico, a waiter who emigrated from Spain, a Quiché Indian farmworker from Guatemala, a poet from the Dominican Republic and a taxi driver from Colombia.

They raise a serious issue. The use of a single word to name a group including people as disparate as Mexicans and Cubans conflates the cultures. And whatever conflates cultures destroys them. Nevertheless, there will have to be a name, for political power in a democratic society requires numbers, and only by agglomeration does the group become large enough to have an important voice in national politics. Agreement on one encompassing name is therefore vital. And possible, for any set that can be defined can be named. Which brings up another problem.

The group cannot be defined racially, because it includes people whose ancestors came from Asia to settle in the Western Hemisphere thousands of years ago, as well as people from Europe, the Iberian Peninsula and Africa. Religion won't do either. The group comprises Roman Catholics, many Protestant denominations, Jews and people who still have deep connections to Mixtec, Nahua and other native American religious rites and beliefs.

Economically, the group ranges from the chairman of the Coca-Cola Company to undocumented farmworkers who sleep in burrows dug into the ground in the hills east of Oceanside, Calif.

Nothing is left to define the linguistic relatives of the King but the language itself. There must be some connection to the Spanish language, if not in use, then in memory. If the language was not acquired from Roman soldiers who landed in Spain 2,000 years ago, then it was acquired from Spanish soldiers who landed in the Western hemisphere 500 years ago.

During preparations for the 1980 U.S. Census, several names for the group were discussed. Latino won out, according to people who took part in the discussions, but at the last minute someone said it was too close to Ladino, an ancient language of Spain, now spoken by only a few Spanish Jews. Hispanic was chosen instead.

Since then, Hispanic and Latino have taken on political, social and even geographical meaning. Latino is used in California. In Florida, Hispanic is preferred by Cubans no matter what political, social or educational views they hold. Hispanic is used more often than Latino in Texas but neither word is used much; Mexican, Mexican-American and Chicano dominate there. Chicago, which has a mixture of people from the Caribbean and the mainland, has adopted Latino. In New York City, both names are used, depending largely on one's politics.

Hispanic belongs to those in power; it is the choice of establishments, exiles, social climbers and kings. Latino has been adopted by almost everyone else. Latino and Hispanic are the left and right, commoner and king of names. Democrats are generally Latinos, Republicans are Hispanics. Many Anglos, people who oppose bilingual education and those who support English-only laws prefer Hispanic, which is an English word meaning, "pertaining to ancient Spain."

But neither politics nor economics should determine the choice of a name. Language defines the group, provides it with history and home; language should also determine its name—Latino. The vowels of Latino are a serenade, Hispanic ends like broken glass. Latino/Latina has gender, which is Spanish, as against Hispanic, which follows English rules. Perhaps the course of democracy and assimilation dictates that someday this linguistic connection to culture must die, but there is no hurry; we need not be assassins now.[17]

11

On Abortion

• William F. Buckley Jr. •

In June 1992, the U.S. Supreme Court upheld a provision of the Pennsylvania Abortion Control Act that required women seeking an abortion to listen to a doctor's speech about the operation twenty-four hours before it could take place. In November of that year, the editors of Harper's Magazine *asked a number of writers for the words they would speak in such a situation. The following was one of the submissions.*

WHAT YOU ARE DOING IN OPTING for an abortion has been legal since 1973. Before that it was illegal. You are entitled to wonder why it was illegal. Well, the consensus was that the mistake made by a woman who conceives without intending to do so shouldn't be rectified by snuffing out the life that was created, which is what you now have undertaken to do. The process is exactly that: to kill the fetus and arrange for it to be extruded from your womb. If it were left alone, in due course it would be a baby; eighteen years from now, it could become a young woman. It wouldn't be a great surprise if she looked very much like her mother.

Babies are most awfully inconvenient, taking up time and money, and during the period of pregnancy they are often the cause of morning sickness and always the cause of a distortion, however temporary, of your weight and your girth. It is a genuine pity that babies weren't made to just materialize when they are, say, two years old. But since the medical profession can't contrive this, our choices are limited. We deliver the baby whole and alive in nine months, or we deliver it today embryonically and oblige our primary client, which is you. The other potential client has no voice in our deliberations, and that is all to the good, as we can imagine what he/she would be saying, assuming "it" had a day in court. . . . So shall we get on with it?[18]

Contemporary Issues

12
"I'm 38, and Running Out of Time"

• Paulette Mason (pseudonym) •

I NEED SOME ADVICE. I'm pregnant—15 weeks pregnant. And I'm not married. Please don't think I don't believe in family values. I do. I'm not promiscuous; it's just that I was lonely and I liked this man a lot. We used birth control but it failed. I didn't know I was pregnant because I didn't have the usual symptoms. Everything that a woman expects to have happen on a monthly basis continued to happen. I never learned that this was possible in high school hygiene; we didn't have sex education, just the seven food groups.

The man I got pregnant by doesn't want to have anything to do with me or the child. I want to have the baby; I'm 38 and I'm running out of time. I've been thinking about how and when and whether I could have a child for a couple of years now. I agree with [the vice president's wife] Marilyn Quayle; for a woman like me, it's an essential part of my nature to make a home with a man and raise a child.

The father of my baby also believes in family values. That's why he wants me to get an abortion. He feels children should be raised in a two-parent home, and since he has no intention of being that other parent, it would be unfair to the child to raise it alone. He's an active Democrat, but he doesn't think Murphy Brown is a good role model.

"You're not Murphy Brown," he said to me. "You're not a rich independent yuppie who can afford to scoff at convention and go it alone. You've been reading too many women's magazines loaded with feminist junk. You barely make a living. How can you support and nurture a child? You don't even have a steady job." (I work freelance.) "I bet you don't even have health insurance," he said. As a matter of fact, I don't have health insurance.

After I got off the phone, I looked into getting insurance. It turned out that no one would insure me; my pregnancy was considered a previous condition. Then I looked into Medicaid and city health clinics. The social worker I talked to said I made too much money to qualify. I called a hospital and found out that if I required a C-section it would cost about $12,000. I didn't have that much in the bank. If the baby were born prematurely, it would cost about $1,000 a day to keep her alive in the hospital nursery. If something was wrong with the baby, I'd be in debt to the hospital for the rest of my life. But I didn't want to let money be the critical factor in this decision.

Finally, I was able to find one insurance company that was willing to insure me and the baby for possible complications. "Boy am I glad I found you guys," I told the insurance agent. He agreed I was lucky; his company was the only one he knew of that would insure pregnant women.

I thought maybe I could go on welfare so that I could stay at home during those all-important first two years. But when I looked into welfare, it turned out that even with food stamps I wouldn't be able to live on it. The social worker I spoke to said that most women on welfare have some income off the books and live with family members. My parents live on Social Security and small pensions. My brother is unemployed. He says that since the recession, it's been hard to find work.

I made up a budget. After I factored in health insurance for me and the baby ($4,000) and child care help ($300 a week for full-time baby-sitting), I was many thousands of dollars short.

I looked into child support. The man I got pregnant by lives out of state. The lawyers and court officials I spoke to said that it could easily take two years for me to get a court order. I was at wit's end. Then I got a brainstorm. I called the Catholic church. I figured it was against abortions and so was I. I asked the woman who answered the phone, Can you help me keep my baby? She told me that her agency primarily helped girls from the South Bronx and what they offered them was infant foster care. That was the very day the newspapers in New York were filled with stories about a foster family that had starved a child to death. I mentioned this to the social worker. She said: "We're very careful. All our families are fingerprinted and their records checked."

Things seemed so hopeless by then. I went to a doctor who did second-trimester abortions, which are a good deal more complicated than first-trimester abortions. In the second trimester, the fetus is sufficiently large so that it has to be dismembered to be removed. When I heard the doctor use the word dismember, I started to cry—for myself and my baby and what might have been my future.

If a surgeon isn't skilled, the uterus can be perforated, leading to infection, sterility, even hysterectomy. The procedure takes two days. On that first day, the woman's cervix is dilated. I asked the doctor, "Will it hurt?" The doctor said that sometimes it doesn't hurt but other times it hurts a lot, and women leave sobbing and doubled over in pain. "It's very traumatic to many women," he said, "because they know that they've started a process that will end in termination and there's nothing that can be done to stop it once it starts."

On the second day, the actual procedure is carried out. The woman undresses, puts on a paper gown, is wheeled into an operating room, her legs are put into stirrups and an anesthesiologist puts her under. When she wakes up in the recovery room, the baby is gone. When the doctor explained all this to me, I started to cry again. "I don't know what to do," I told the doctor. The doctor said it was my choice. He said: "Nobody likes to get an abortion, especially a late abortion. I've performed thousands of operations and I've never met a woman who was happy about it. Do you think you can take good care of a child? That's really the question."

This has been agonizing for me. I think about the way I want to have a baby, and about paying someone to act like a mother to my child, and about what I'll say when my child asks why her father didn't want her, and about what I'll feel like during the 24 hours my cervix is dilating and I'm waiting for the end. When I think about adoption, I think about spending the rest of my life wondering where my baby, the baby I wanted, is, and if she's happy and how she turned out. And I think, What would Dan Quayle want me to do?[19]

13
"One Size Fits All the Way to Middle Age"

• Stephanie Strom •

DROP THE PERSONAL TRAINER. Lose the rice cakes. No amount of pain is going to maintain that perfect size 8 figure the way a clothing maker can just by fiddling with labels.

As the sylphs of the 60's have aged, clothing sizes have slyly filled out, too. A baby boomer with three kids can safely brag that she still wears the same size she did in college. But if she tried to slip into a 20-year-old dress, chances are she couldn't get it over her hips.

"I hate to say it, but it's a con job on women," said Bruno Ferri, president of the Wolf Form Company, which has been making dress forms since 1931.

Sixty years ago, he said, a size 10 dress form had a 34.5 inch bust, a 24.5 inch waist and a 34.5 inch hipline. Today, there is no standard size 10, and the smallest size 10 form Wolf makes has a 35.5 inch bust, a 26 inch waist and a 37 inch hipline. "And in many cases, it's almost an inch larger than that," Mr. Ferri said.

Manufacturers say they aren't pulling one over on women, but adjusting to the market's reality, which is that, as the population has aged over the last decade, the average woman—like the average man—has more, on average, to love.

"Older women are bigger and fatter, but they still want to be a size 4 or 6 even though they're really an 8 or 10," said Bud Konheim, president of Nicole Miller Ltd. "We will cut a big size for the older women and call it a 4 or a 6 and everyone will be happy."

That's good business. Older women have more money, and retailers say they punish manufacturers who make them feel fat.

A few years ago, said Richard Conrad, president of Castleberry Knits, which sells dresses for older women, market research on a major competitor showed that its most loyal customers quit buying when they grew into larger sizes. "We all took new measurements and adjusted sizing to a woman who now had a backside and some hips and came up with a fuller 8," he said. "*We* weren't going to be the ones to tell her she really was a 10."

(The theory, incidentally, works in reverse when bras are the garment in question. A woman who has usually worn a 34B may be amused to find herself suddenly filling out one marked 36C.)

There was a time when there were legal limits to this. Sort of. The National Bureau of Standards developed sizing standards for clothing in the early 1940's. They were voluntary, but virtually all manufacturers hewed to them.

But by the 1970's manufacturers began to cheat as the pre–World War II statistics stopped reflecting real American bodies. Then in the early 1980's, the Reagan Administration decided deregulation would save money. Federal measuring stopped.

Now there seems to be some movement, if not to reregulate, then to re-establish standards.

The American Society for Testing and Materials, a nonprofit group of scientists and statisticians, is measuring women of the 1990's to establish new norms. One of its studies, on about 7,000 women over 54 years old, is challenging old assumptions.

It found that even women who gain no weight may change shape dramatically from shifts in bone structure and from the relentless tug of gravity. Their shoulders, for example, rotate forward, so blouses stretch across the shoulder blades and are loose in the chest.

"Women are embarrassed by their body changes because they blame themselves," said Ellen Goldsberry, the University of Arizona professor running the study. "Our data show that body changes are a function of aging, not diet and exercise. It's as normal as a young girl graduating to junior sizes."

Sirvart Mellian, who heads the society's study, would like to see labels give bust, waist and hip sizes. Some European countries require it.

Makers of men's clothing usually can't play the sizing game, since men buy pants by waist size and shirts by neck and arm sizes.

But Mr. Konheim's company, Nicole Miller Ltd., doesn't discriminate against male vanity. Its silk boxer shorts are cut extra generously because Mr. Konheim prefers feeling like his old Medium self to admitting his de facto Large self.

"I have that psychological thing in my head that I just can't possibly be a Large," he said. "If I feel that way, I figure the best thing to do is size the damn things up so that every large guy can put on a Medium and feel great that he's still as fit as he was when he played lacrosse at Yale."[20]

14

"Alarm Clocks Can Kill You. Have a Smoke."

• Elizabeth M. Whelan •

BELIEVING WHAT YOU READ about preventive medicine in popular women's magazines can be hazardous to your health. A review of the July, August and September issues of 10 such publications reveals not only that the health "advice" is a distortion of scientific reality, but that the disinformation about health is sponsored—through advertising—by the manufacturer of the leading causes of death.

The science of disease causation and prevention—epidemiology—is neither new nor mysterious. Medical books state that about two million Americans die each year, and some one million of those deaths are preventable (that is, premature). Half of the preventable deaths (500,000) are caused by cigarette smoking and an additional 100,000 or so are the result of alcohol misuse and abuse. Most of the rest of the preventable deaths were caused by violence, drug abuse or failure to use life-saving technologies like seat belts, smoke detectors or tests for the early detection of disease.

The role that diet plays in shortening life—other than engendering the complications of obesity—is speculative and controversial.

Yet the issues of popular magazines I examined focused not on smoking and other life-style factors but on the alleged ill effects of trace level chemicals and other hypothetical causes: *Redbook* and *Glamour* tell us of the hazards of methyl mercury and "potentially carcinogenic" PCB's in fish; *Self* writes of the alleged dangers of food additives like sodium nitrite, BHA and BHT. *Glamour* warns of the risks of eating imported fresh fruit which might be contaminated with surface bacteria.

Other publications raise red flags about salt; "carcinogens" in barbecued meat; electromagnetic fields emanating from refrigerators, stoves and alarm clocks (to reduce the risk of cancer, *Family Circle* cautions to "keep dial face clocks 5 feet and digitals 3 feet from your bed"); radiation emissions from computers; breast implants; toilet seats and hot tubs; lead wrappers on wine bottles; lead in dinnerware; halogen lights (*Harper's Bazaar* recommends using a plastic cover to block potentially harmful UV rays); and even thrill rides at amusement parks ("your life may be in your own hands," *Glamour* warns). *Self* says that smiles can be dangerous if they repress inner feelings. *New Woman* admonishes that "toxic relationships" can also bring on illness (beware the dangers of a "lethal lover") and deplores the "toxic" effects of television.

So what advice do the magazines offer on how to stay healthy? Here is a sampling: eat lots of broccoli to ward off cancer (*Redbook* and *New Woman*); take vitamins E and C and beta carotene (*Glamour*); eat garlic to fight colds and flu (*McCall's*); get a pet to lower blood pressure and cholesterol (*Self*); and eat active-culture yogurt to live longer (*Harper's Bazaar*).

One might argue that these magazines ignore the real health risks because their business is to entertain, not inform, and to refer regularly to the pervasive negative effects of smoking would put them in the undesirable role of nanny. But can the role of cigarette advertising revenues in discouraging stories about smoking be underestimated?

The magazines examined carried just under 200 cigarette advertisements—characterizing their product as glamorous, sexy, and, most of all, feminine. An ad for Misty cigarettes offers "the Misty Look Book" promising "fashions that fit your face, figure and coloring." Cigarettes showed up not only in ads, but in editorial copy (*Redbook* editors welcomed new advertisers, "Ligget & Meyers/Lark and R. J. Reynolds/Camels").

July's *Vanity Fair* carried seven photos of people smoking or carrying cigarettes. In one photo, the teen idols Luke Perry and Jason Priestly have cigarettes in their mouths; in another, Mr. Priestly, surrounded by teen-age girls, performs the function of model for Marlboro Lights, the pack placed carefully in his pants pocket.

Clearly cigarette advertising revenue places a chill on free discussion of the dangers of smoking, a topic only rarely even touched on by these publications. (*Redbook* in August did note that 90 percent of kids worry about the health effects of smoking on their parents, and the September *Glamour* did cover the nicotine patch.)

If historians ever puzzle about our nation's inverted health priorities—policies that draw attention to the alleged dangers of everything from apples to electric blankets, yet ignore the significance of nearly $4 billion in advertisements for the leading cause of death—then they will need to look no further than today's newsstands.[21]

15
"Let Women Fly in Combat"

• Jamie Ann Conway •

THE PENTAGON IS FREE TO ASSIGN women aviators to fighter jets, attack aircraft and bombers in combat missions. But it seems unwilling to move quickly enough to act on permission granted by Congress to do so.

The permission was granted by the 1992 Defense Authorization Act, which repealed portions of 1948 statutes that barred women from combat and was signed into law in November.

The Pentagon announced late last year [1991] that it would not allow women into combat aviation until the Presidential Commission on the Assignment of Women in the Armed Forces completed its work. The report is due Nov. 15, but creation of the commission was delayed for months and no one expects the deadline to be met.

The decision to carry out changes in the law rests with the Navy and Air Force Secretaries. No one has made a responsible case for keeping combat cockpits closed to women officers.

Given the military's unwillingness to let women engage the enemy in direct combat, the Pentagon apparently is using the commission as an excuse to delay action to give women a chance to compete for combat aviation duty. (Maj. Marie Rossi, killed in a Gulf War accident, was not a combat but a transport pilot.)

The "reasoning" and bureaucratic lethargy preventing progress today mirrors the policy toward black aviators from 1935 to 1941, when the Army Air Corps rejected every measure to train blacks as pilots.

Despite the exemplary performance of women aviators in noncombat aviation, and medical data showing women can handle the cockpit as well as men, Christopher Jehn, an assistant Secretary of Defense, testified last year at a Senate hearing that changes must "evolve deliberately." No, let's change this year, not in the vague future.

The mindset of some officials was illustrated by Gen. Merrill A. McPeak, the Air Force chief of staff, who testified that he would choose a male pilot vying for a combat position over a woman even if she were a person of superior intelligence and in every way more qualified. He admitted his remark "doesn't make much sense," but said "That's the way I feel." This and other testimony suggested rationalized emotional decisions, even at the expense of effectiveness. Perhaps the officials are being protective of women; yes, a captured woman soldier was molested during the Gulf War, but that is a combat risk women assume upon being commissioned.

Those who don't want to put women in combat roles argue readiness. But Pentagon statistics show women miss far less duty time than men. In 1980, its data showed that even with servicewomen's loss of time because of childbearing, absenteeism among men was twice as high because of alcoholism, misconduct and routine medical problems. In 1990, the Navy reached the same findings after a four-year study of 7,700 people of each gender.

Some critics make pregnancy an issue. A Navy study issued in 1989 showed that pregnancy was a problem only in the lower enlisted ranks and only in the first tour of duty. Senior Navy officials say pregnancy is negligible among officers. In any case, women aviators tend to schedule pregnancy to coincide with nonflying assignments or service schools.

The bottom line is that when I command a deployed unit, the survival of my soldiers will depend on a combat pilot's skill at air support. My concern will not be gender but the pilot's ability to put steel on target.[22]

16
"'Sex Work'?"

• Tracy Quan, Letter to the Editor, *New York Review of Books* •

TO THE EDITORS:

As Francine du Plessix Gray points out ["Splendor and Miseries," *New York Review of Books*, July 16], *sex work* is now fashionable terminology for *prostitution*. A "sex worker" myself for over a decade, I am skeptical about a trend which puts more picturesque language out of business.

In the '80s, *sex work* was coined by activists in the prostitutes' movement to describe a range of commercial sex. Porn stars, erotic dancers, peep show performers, sex writers, and others in the trade made it obvious that the prostitutes' movement should broaden its language. Thus the inclusive *sex worker*. But *sex work* is also code. In two words, "selling sex is just another occupation." *Sex work* sidesteps any pejorative meanings associated with *to prostitute* (the verb) and *prostitute* (the person).

As an activist hooker, I have helped to promote the fashionable status of the term *sex work* (and, apparently, of actual sex workers). Sometimes I have my regrets. *Sex work* doesn't sound immoral, but it doesn't sound like fun, either. *Sex worker* is to *prostitute* what *gender* is to *sex*: a usage (with some practical value) which is also identified with political rectitude.

Sex worker is "gender-free." It's true that males, females, and transsexuals can sell sex. But "genderless" lingo enables feminists to ignore the fact that differences between men and women are *accepted* in our industry—rather than neurotically denied, as is often the case in other fields.

Many indoor hookers complain that the word *prostitute* conjures up the image of a too-explicit street hussy. But I am alarmed to note that *sex worker* conjures up no image at all! Prostitutes, go-go dancers, porn stars *are* their images. The erotic image is our bread and butter—and the thing which makes us different from people in more prosaic occupations. Many of our feminist supporters have been using language to diminish the whore's sensationalistic image—hoping to claim her as one of their mundane "sisters." This is the price, it seems, of feminist support.

Sex work connotes that prostitutes are engaged in labor rather than business, making us acceptable to those who abhor the very thing we represent: a free market. In the old days, when the left was consistent, the only good whore was a "down-trodden" or reformed whore. In the 70s, when Vietnamese prostitutes were sent to camps for their political "re-education," many a socialist-feminist in the West took heart. In the 90s, unrepented harlots have been featured on [independent radio station] WBAI, courted by ACT-UP, praised in the pages of the *Village Voice* and *The Nation*. Politics makes for bedfellows even a prostitute would consider strange, and our new terminology has served as a political mating call to the left.

Sex work—a term once employed for practical reasons—has taken on a political life of its own, and we who purvey erotic pleasure are increasingly desexualized by political correct language. But this is not surprising, given the tendency of the prostitutes' movement to entertain the ideological fads of our various supporters.

Tracy Quan
PONY (Prostitutes of New York)
New York City[23]

APPENDIX:
RESOURCES FOR
CRITICAL READING

APPENDIX

Outlining

Analysis identifies structure—parts and their relationships. An **outline** is a visible display of that structure and can be displayed in various ways:

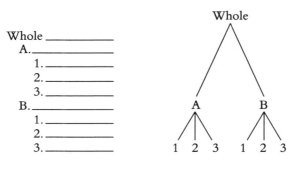

Outline   **Tree Diagram**

In each representation, the whole is divided initially into two parts (A and B). Each part is then subdivided into three parts at a lower level of analysis. The type of visual representation does not matter; what's important is that the parts and their respective levels are identified and shown. Notice that outlining does not encompass synthesis, the relationships of the parts (see Chapter 1).

RULES FOR OUTLINING

Five basic rules must be followed when outlining a text:

- **All parts should be included**. Put another way, the outline of a text must cover all of the text.

- **The parts at any level can vary in length**. A section of the outline may consist of a quarter, or even three-quarters, of the text. Length does not matter. The key consideration is how real the divisions are and how meaningfully they reflect the whole.

- **Each sublevel must contain ot least two items**. Otherwise, there would be no need to distinguish that level. Consider the following brief outline:

    Modes of Transportation
    A. Motor-powered
        1. cars
    B. Person-powered
        1. bicycles
        2. canoes

Here, there is no need to distinguish cars as a sublevel of motor-powered modes of transportation. A more sensible outline might be:

Modes of Transportation
A. Motor-powered, such as cars
B. Person-powered
    1. bicycles
    2. canoes

Alternatively, we might add another example of motor-powered modes of transportation:

Modes of Transportation

A. Motor-powered
    1. cars
    2. buses
B. Person-powered
    1. bicycles
    2. canoes

- **If any level of analysis contains more than five or six parts, another level of division is probably warranted**. Consider this tree diagram:

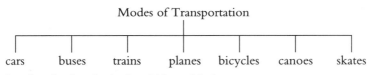

Another level of analysis should be added:

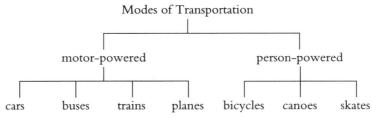

Adding an additional level forces the recognition of additional aspects to the discussion—here, the distinction between motor- and person-powered vehicles.

- **The headings at any particular level should be grammatically similar**. For example, at the second level of the diagram above, the headings "motor-powered" and "person-powered" might be replaced with "group travel/individual travel" depending on the point being made, but not with "motor-powered/using someone's muscles" or "group travel/by the sweat of one's brow."

Similar grammatical forms indicate divisions at the same level of analysis.

OUTLINING TEXTS

To outline is to analyze. Thus, the first step in outlining is to divide the text into major divisions. All texts might initially be divided into three major sections: a beginning, a middle, and an end.

Complete Text
A. Beginning
B. Middle
C. End

These sections will take different form with different texts. One text might raise a topic, consider possibilities, and reach a conclusion. Another might present one side of an issue, present another side, and make a decision. A third text might discuss the past, the present, and the future.

A. Raise a topic	A. One side of an issue	A. Past
B. Consider possibilities	B. Another side of an issue	B. Present
C. Reach a conclusion	C. A decision	C. Future

Each of these main sections can then be broken down into smaller units as needed. The level of analysis will depend on the time allotted, the complexity of the text, and the depth of analysis desired.

Most outlining involves a **sequential analysis**—presenting one part after another. Interpretative outlining is based on **thematic analysis**—presenting patterns of elements occurring throughout the whole.

Many books use headings to indicate main topics covered, as well as subheadings to indicate subtopics at even lower levels of analysis. Such headings, whether within the text or collected in a table of contents, offer a useful study guide for recalling the main areas of discussion. Readers should verify, however, that a text does what it claims to be doing. If, for example, a text says it will consider four views on a topic, number the views as you find them to ensure both their existence and your recognition of them. By creating your own outline, you reinforce the structure of the text in your own mind.

EXAMPLE: The Gettysburg Address

In 1863, in the middle of the Civil War, President Lincoln traveled to Gettysburg, Pennsylvania, to dedicate a cemetery for Union soldiers who had died in the war [Texts for Analysis 5].

The most obvious outline for this text is on the basis of the time periods discussed:

[**past**:] Fourscore and seven years ago our fathers brought forth on this continent a new nation, conceived in liberty, and dedicated to the proposition that all men are created equal.

[**present**:] Now we are engaged in a great civil war, testing whether that nation, or any nation so conceived and so dedicated, can long endure. We are met on a great battlefield of that war. We have come to dedicate a portion of that field, as a final resting place for those who here gave their lives that that nation might live. It is altogether fitting and proper that we should do this. But, in a larger sense, we cannot dedicate—we cannot consecrate—we cannot hallow—this ground. The brave men, living and dead, who struggled here, have consecrated it, far above our poor power to add or detract.

[**future**:] The world will little note, nor long remember, what we say here, but it can never forget what they did here. It is for us, the living, rather, to be dedicated here to the unfinished work which they who fought here have thus far so nobly advanced. It is rather for us to be here dedicated to the great task remaining before us,—that from these honored dead we take increased devotion to that cause for which they gave the last full measure of devotion—that we here highly resolve that these dead shall not have died in vain—that this nation, under God, shall have a new birth of freedom—and that government of the people, by the people, for the people, shall not perish from the earth.

Further examination on the basis of this chronological outline would describe what the text claims has been or should be done during each time.

The outline above follows the sequential development of the text. Other outlines might reflect themes interwoven throughout the text, such as the distinction between acts and proclamations or of who is being discussed (our forefathers, the dead, the living). Analyses such as these might still mirror the earlier sequential analysis, but from a different perspective.

The General/Specific Relationship

THINGS, CONCEPTS, AND WORDS

In our daily life, we confront many **things**: shoes and telephones, flowers and farmers. We can point to things and say, "There's one!" One what? To make sense of our experiences, we develop **concepts**, or ideas. For example, rather than pointing to all shoes, one by one, we develop a concept of shoes as a certain kind of protective footwear. Thus, whereas the thing we call a "shoe" exists in the physical sense, the notion of what is, or is not, a shoe exists only as an abstract concept. Finally, we name concepts by assigning **words** to them. Words are combinations of letters (or in speech, sounds) that have, through general usage, come to stand for particular concepts. Words are linguistic symbols for concepts.

To summarize:

- **Thing**—a physical object, event, property, or behavior in the world
- **Concept**—an idea in our mind
- **Word**—a written or spoken symbol

We kick the metal object, a can, with our foot. We think of such objects with the concept of "can." We refer to each such object with the word *can*.

•••••••••••••• DISTINGUISHING AMONG THINGS, ••••••••••••• CONCEPTS, AND WORDS

Indicate whether the terms in italics refer to a thing, concept, or word.

1. More often than not, *as is* means "broken."
2. *They* longed for a *romantic love* found only in *story books*.

•••

General and Specific Terms

Just as we examine a text at various levels of analysis, so we can organize thoughts and words at various levels of analysis. The primary scale for organizing such thoughts is the general/specific relationship.

Concepts are discussed on a sliding scale from those with the broadest meaning to the most limited of notions, or from general to specific:

general (broad meaning) — **specific** (limited notion)

"Specific" refers to individual or concrete references, while "general" refers to broader or more abstract notions. For example:

> actresses — Cher
>
> **general** cities   — Chicago   **specific**
>
> animals — my sister's dog Emma

When we offer an example of something, we **specify**:

> **general** cars — Buicks **specific**

When we classify an example or illustration, we generalize:

> **specific** giving a poor man money — an act of charity **general**

The Relativity of Terms

No concept is, by itself, general or specific. All such labels are **relative**. As with the notions of near and far, big and little, or hot and cold, one notion cannot exist without the other. Any decision as to whether a single item is general or specific must be based on a comparison with another. For example, "dogs" is general in comparison to "collies," but specific in relationship to "mammals":*

> **general** mammals — dogs — collies — Lassie **specific**

Likewise, the concept of a fork is general in comparison to a particular fork on a table, but specific in relationship to all types of silverware:

> **general** silverware — fork — particular fork **specific**

We get more specific as we move toward individual cases:

> **general** all — most — many — some — few — one **specific**

Some concepts, by their very nature, may seem fairly general, and others more specific. "Excuses" seems general; "tap shoes, size 8" seems specific. Yet "excuses" is specific relative to "all statements," since only some statements are excuses. "Tap shoes, size 8" is specific relative to "all shoes," but general relative to "the two size-8 tap shoes on the bench." Again, no concept is by nature general or specific—only *more* general or *more* specific than another.

---

*Actually, of course, the concepts referred to are being compared, not the words or things themselves.

•••••••••• ORDERING FROM SPECIFIC TO GENERAL ••••••••••

Put the items in each set in order from the most specific to the most general.

1. table / furniture / household items / desk
2. cow / mammal / animal / heifer
3. emotions / love / affection / feelings
4. music / performing arts / rap / vocal music
5. Sumo wrestlers / people / Asians / Japanese

General and Specific Statements

Statements, like words, can be relatively general or specific, depending on how broad or inclusive one remark is in comparison to another. Any two sentences might:

- **Exist on the same level:**

    The team lost yesterday. It also lost the day before.

    The two statements are equally general—or equally specific.

- **Move from general to specific:**

    The team lost yesterday. It was outscored 14 to 3.

    The second sentence provides specific details about the loss.

- **Move from specific to general:**

    The team lost yesterday. It is on a losing streak.

    The second sentence offers a more general observation on the team's record.

general   on a losing streak — lost a game — lost 14 to 3   **specific**

Notice that the sentence "The team lost yesterday" can be more general or specific than, or on the same level as, another sentence. As with the classification of words, any classification of the specificity (or generality) of a statement is relative—that is, based on its relationship to another statement.

Discussion at the different levels of generality can be compared to a camera lens zooming in on, and then back from, an object. Much of the movement of ideas in texts reflects such shifts in the levels of generality or specificity. As a result, much of the reading process is a matter of trying to recognize the relationships between relatively general and specific statements.

Facts and Opinions

The distinction between fact and opinion closely parallels the distinction between general and specific remarks. **Facts** tends to refer to specific items or events. **Opinions** tend to express generalizations based on facts. We reach general conclusions or make interpretations (opinions) on the basis of relatively specific evidence (facts). Drawing on general assumptions or ideas, we assume certain specific facts to be true.

TRACING SHIFTS IN THE LEVEL OF GENERALITY

The movement between general and specific statements usually can be traced by following shifts in reference. Consider the following sentence pairs:

> Crime is rising in America. More crime is also reported in Russia.
> Crime is rising in America. More robberies are reported each year.
> Crime is rising in America. The social fabric is coming apart.

In the first pair, both statements are about the rising crime rate and both specify a single country, so they are on the same level of generality. In the second pair, the shift in reference from a general category (crime) to an example of that category (robbery) indicates a shift to a relatively specific assertion. In the third pair, the shift in focus from a single aspect of social life (crime) to all social life (the social fabric) indicates a shift to a relatively general assertion.

general   social fabric — crime — robberies   **specific**

Clearly, reading involves more than simply recognizing words. To make sense of a text, readers must read *ideas* as well as *words*. They must recognize how seemingly different concepts are related to one another.

The Same Level of Generality

Statements at the same level of generality commonly occur in texts that clarify ideas, report observations, recount events, or describe or compare things.

- **Restating an idea for clarity or emphasis** [from Charles R. Hoffer's *A Concise Introduction to Music Listening*]:

  > Recording cannot reproduce fully the sound of an instrument or voice. There is always some loss or "fall off" between the original sound and its reproduction.[1]

  > The strings are the backbone of the orchestra. They constitute about half its membership.[2]

- **Presenting a series of observations** [from Serena Nanda's *Cultural Anthropology*]:

  > The Rastafari subculture has a value system that emphasizes economic communalism, solidarity within the group, and a rejection of the economic values of the culture that surrounds them. Also, the Rastafari subculture values the beliefs and visible markers of identity, such as clothing, hair style, and special linguistic usages, that set them apart from the larger society. In addition, the Rastafari are often in trouble with the law, particularly because of their use and distribution of marijuana, and this negatively affects the way in which they are viewed by the outside world.[3]

- **Narrating a sequence of events** [from R. Jackson Wilson et al.'s *The Pursuit of Liberty: A History of the American People*]:

  > Shortly after Burr left for the West, Wilkinson started downriver from St. Louis. He reached Natchez early in September and started up the Red River to the main American fort at Natchitoches. He arrived there September 22 to find a small, unprepared garrison, with no cannon or horses ready for duty.[4]

- **Describing different qualities or characteristics of something** [from William K. Hartmann's *The Cosmic Voyage: Through Time and Space*]:

  > The Viking probes landed during the Martian summer, but air temperatures at the two sites ranged from nighttime lows around 187 K (–123°F) to afternoon highs around 224 K (–20°F). Temperatures of the soil, which absorbs more sunlight than the air, exceeded freezing (273 K, or 32°F) on some summer afternoons, so that any frost formed at night near the surface can melt and produce moisture or water vapor. Winds at the two sites were usually less than 17 kph, with gusts exceeding 50 kph.[5]

- **Comparing or contrasting things** [from Mary Ann Lamanna and Agnes Riedmann's *Marriages and Families: Making Choices and Facing Change*]:

  > Monahan (1970) found in Iowa that black–white marriages were more stable than those between blacks and, furthermore, that couples in which a black man was married to a white woman had a lower divorce rate than did white couples. However, Heer (1974) found that intermarried couples (married in the 1950s and 1960s and surveyed in 1970) were less likely to remain married than homogamous couples of either race.[6]

Throughout these excerpts, various terms and phrases signal the relationship between statements, whether for a series of observations (*also, in addition*) or contrasting observations (*however*).

Different Levels of Generality

Statements at different levels of generality often occur in texts dealing with parts and divisions, examples and illustrations, or logical arguments (deduction and induction).

Parts and divisions

In the following passage, from Hartmann's *The Cosmic Voyage*, note how the text moves from general to specific:

> Two basic designs have been used for telescopes. The first to be built, the **refractor**, uses a lens to bend, or refract, light rays to a focus, as in Figure 5-12. Galileo first used this type astronomically in 1609. The second type, the **reflector**, uses a curved mirror to reflect light rays to a focus, as in Figure 5-13. Isaac Newton built the first reflector in 1668.[7]

The general notion of telescopes is divided into two types: refractor and reflector, and each is described.

Examples and illustrations

There is a difference between simply making a series of statements and developing an argument. Here, the term *argument* isn't meant to suggest a conflict, but rather to indicate an extended discussion leading to a conclusion.

To prove a point, one needs to offer **evidence**—examples or illustrations in the service of the argument. One presents **examples** to make a case or support an assertion; one offers **illustrations** to document the case once it is made. Examples or illustrations may be offered for all major divisions of the overall topic or selected, individual cases or groups of cases.

In the following excerpt from Michael Milburn's *Persuasion and Politics*, the examples encompass all major divisions of the initial topic. The discussion moves from the general group to relatively specific segments of the whole (indicated by boldface).

> **People** vary considerably in the type of reasoning they apply to political issues. **Some people** reason at only a very low level. They observe events and either are unable to explain them or offer only the simplest or inaccurate kinds of explanations. **Others** see events as causally related, but the relationships they see involve one factor causing another, without the possibility of interactions or combinations of factors. Finally, there are **those individuals**, whom Piaget would say have reached the stage of formal operations, who are aware of complex systems of interrelated factors that combine and interact to influence political events.[8]

In the next excerpt, from Nanda's *Cultural Anthropology*, the examples offer selected illustrative examples:

> Although anthropology as an academic discipline is mainly concerned with basic research—that is, asking the "big" questions about the origins of our species, the development of culture and civilization, and the functions of human social institutions such as the family or religion—anthropologists are also putting their knowledge to work to solve human problems. **Biological anthropologists**, for example, can

shed light on some of the major diseases of the modern, industrial world by comparing our diet and life style with those of prehistoric and contemporary hunter-gatherer societies who do not suffer from heart disease, high blood pressure and diabetes (Eaton and Konner, 1989). **Forensic anthropologists**, specialists in analyzing bones, identify remains from airplane crashes and in criminal investigations. **Archaeologists'** research about what people in our contemporary society throw into the garbage is being used to help solve our nation's "garbage crisis"—a problem partly caused by our consumerism—and also to address more theoretical problems, such as how eating habits differ in different social classes (Rathje, 1974).[9]

Three different types of anthropologists are offered as examples for the initial generalization.

Logical arguments

Logical arguments generally are either inductive or deductive. In **deduction**, a conclusion is reached with mathematical precision on the basis of specific rules of logic. If the initial assumptions (statements) are true and the reasoning is carried out correctly, the conclusion will be true. In **induction**, a more tentative conclusion is reached based on prior experience or incomplete knowledge. For a more complete discussion of forms of logical argument, see Appendix F, "Logic and Statistics."

APPLYING THE GENERAL/SPECIFIC MODEL

To understand what is going on in a text, readers must go back after completing a paragraph to consider how the sentences fit together. They must look not only at what individual sentences say, but at how they fit into the larger whole.

The general/specific model is a tool for following shifts in the text. The model helps identify which statements are examples or illustrations and which are broader assertions. The model also suggests ways in which a broad topic can be broken down into more specific aspects, parts, or qualities for closer examination.

Finally, we should note that readers do not consciously analyze levels of generality as they read. Here, as elsewhere, the model is a tool to be invoked when you cannot make immediate sense of a text or wish to obtain a better understanding of how a text is constructed. The more you understand the model, the more you will unconsciously employ its insights. What might otherwise have appeared complex will, on first or second reading, appear obvious.

The Role Model of Paragraph Structure

When someone speaks, we attend to both what they say and how they develop their thoughts. We recognize when they are boasting or pontificating, pleading or announcing, questioning or approving. We demonstrate an understanding not simply by repeating their statements, but by describing how they have made their case.

Texts can do most everything one can do in speech. A text can focus on a single topic or change topics midway through. A text can make an argument, tell a story, or describe something. A text can introduce a topic for discussion or reach a conclusion; it can plead, proclaim, or whine. These are everyday activities of communication. Often, one has only to think of a text as spoken to recognize the role of different assertions.

DESCRIBING THE STRUCTURE OF A TEXT

Our focus here is on the roles that statements can play in the development of ideas within a text. The sentences in a given paragraph might fulfill these roles:

- Raise an initial idea, topic, or question
- Shape the direction or scope of the discussion
- Discuss an idea
- Conclude an idea
- Add material for emphasis, clarification, or persuasion

Raising an Initial Idea, Topic, or Question

A text can raise a topic by asking a question, suggesting a possibility, asserting an idea, making an observation, or offering an anecdote or quotation. There have been many classic opening lines, from Herman Melville's "Call me Ishmael" in *Moby Dick* to the following from Henry David Thoreau's *Civil Disobedience*:

> I heartily accept the motto,—"That government is best which governs least"; and I should like to see it acted up to more rapidly and systematically. Carried out, it finally amounts to this, which also I believe,—"That government is best which governs not at all"; and when men are prepared for it, that will be the kind of government which they will have.

The initial mention of the topic may be a teaser to invoke interest, a statement of the ultimate conclusion, or a specific example to be considered. Only by reading on can you determine at what level the discussion has begun.

Shaping the Direction or Scope of the Discussion

The topic can be shaped by specifically indicating what ideas are to be included or excluded, by defining terms, or by breaking up or limiting the scope of a discussion. In the following excerpt from Joan Ferrante's *Sociology: A Global Perspective*, notice how the final sentence tells precisely where the discussion is headed:

> In addition to discipline problems, teachers must deal with students from diverse family and ethnic backgrounds and with a student subculture that values and rewards athletic achievement, popularity, social activities, jobs, cars, and appearance at the expense of academic achievement. **We turn to the work of a sociologist James Coleman (the 1991 president of the American Sociological Association), who has studied both family background and the adolescent student subculture.**[1]

Discussing an Idea

The discussion of an idea may involve providing evidence or reasons in support of a conclusion, offering background information or documentation, or comparing or contrasting events or ideas. Consider these two excerpts:

> At first, movies were a sideshow. **Penny arcade owners showed movies behind a black screen at the rear of the arcade for an extra nickel.**[2]

> Psychoanalysis, Sigmund Freud's method of treating psychological disorders, continues to exercise a strong influence on many psychologists. **Psychoanalysts assume that people have unconscious thoughts and motives as well as conscious ones.**[3]

In the first excerpt, from Shirley Biagi's *Media/Impact: An Introduction to Mass Media*, the final sentence explains how movies were a sideshow. In the second, from James Kalat's *Introduction to Psychology*, the final sentence explains exactly what "Freud's method" was. Notice how, in both examples, an initial idea is discussed further, a pattern common to most texts. Notice also how we must follow the idea, not just the words, to recognize the connection between one sentence and another.

Concluding an Idea

A text can conclude a discussion by resolving a question or stating a main idea, as in this passage from Charles Hoffer's *A Concise Introduction to Music Listening*:

> Certainly much singing in jazz, rock, and art songs sheds "crocodile tears" over lost love and expresses exuberant joy over found ones (although for some reason there

seem to be more songs about unhappy events than happy ones). **But contrived or not, natural or trained, folk, popular, or art—singing has an expressiveness about it that is fascinating.**[4]

Notice that "concluding an idea" can mean two things. It can refer to a focus on the end of a document—the conclusion of the written text. Or it can encompass the overall thought or final argument—the conclusion of the reasoning process—which can appear anywhere within the text. In the first case, we might speak of "concluding the discussion"; in the second, of "reaching the conclusion of an argument."

Additional Comments for Emphasis, Clarification, or Persuasion

At various points in a discussion, a text may emphasize an idea by repeating or amplifying it, or otherwise proclaiming its significance. Note in this excerpt from *Introduction to Psychology* how Kalat restates the main idea to clarify it:

> Unmarried men are more likely than married men are to wind up in a mental hospital or prison. **So we can say that, for men, marriage is negatively correlated with mental illness and criminal activity.**[5]

Such comments do not develop the discussion so much as clarify remarks already made. We can also distinguish elements that are there essentially to persuade the reader to accept the arguments or evidence (see Chapter 10, "Invoking Belief and Acceptance"). This can be done by appealing to emotions, by belittling or praising, by exaggerating, or by appealing to authority. In this excerpt from his famous *Letter from the Birmingham Jail*, Rev. Martin Luther King, Jr., seeks to convince readers of the appropriateness of his actions by questioning the reasoning of others:

> In your statement you assert that our actions, even though peaceful, must be condemned because they precipitate violence. **But is this a logical assertion?**[6]

The Relativity of Roles

Like the notions of general and specific, the roles sentences play are, for the most part, relative. They describe the relationships *between* statements. A single statement may appear to raise an initial idea in relationship to one sentence and offer a conclusion in relationship to another. Understanding a text involves sensing how any single sentence is related to both the preceding and following sentences. Finally, these categories can be applied to describe not only the roles of sentences themselves, but also the roles of portions of sentences or collections of sentences.

APPLYING THE MODEL

EXAMPLE: **Economics Textbook**

The following is a continuation of the excerpt from Samuelson's *Economics* text discussed in Chapter 1. Specific roles are highlighted in boldface within brackets.

> Journalists ask why workers go out on strike just because of a 10-cent disagreement. [**raises question of motive**] They point out that it might take two or three years for the workers to recover—at 10 cents an hour—their loss of earning during the strike. [**emphasizes and discusses**] But workers look at it differently. [**discusses by presenting alternative view**] To them the employer caused the strike by stubbornness. [**discusses by offering other view**] They point out that the amount the employer will also lose by the strike is greater than what would be saved by refusing to pay the extra 10 cents. [**emphasizes with further discussion**]
>
> Actually, a strike is not over just the last 10 cents of wage disagreement! [**clarifies**] The workers believe that the employer would not have been forced from $9 up even to $9.50 except for the threat of a strike, which hangs over the negotiations like a time bomb. [**offers example/illustration**] To keep the bomb from going off, both sides must agree. [**emphasizes**]
>
> Threats become hollow unless occasionally carried out. [**discusses**] Both parties must show that they are truly prepared to incur at some point the costs of a strike. [**emphasizes previous idea**] Thus, suppose the employer was deprived, voluntarily or by law, of the right to refuse any wage demand if it would bring on a strike. [**continues discussion of illustration**] Would this cost the employer only 10 cents an hour? [**discusses by raising rhetorical question**] Obviously not. [**emphasis**] There would then be no reason why the union might not hold out for a 90- rather than a 55-cent wage increase. [**discusses with explanation**] Similarly, if the union could never exercise the right to strike, why should not the employer offer $7 rather than $9? [**continues discussion by illustration/explanation**][7]

The exact labels assigned may vary from reader to reader; various categories (discussing, shaping, concluding) might mean much the same thing when describing sentences within a short text. This should not, however, detract from the overall usefulness of attempting to describe roles sentences play within the text.

EXAMPLE: **George Washington**

Consider one more example illustrating the role model of paragraph structure, from R. Jackson Wilson et al.'s *The Pursuit of Liberty, A History of the American People*:

> [George] Washington's concern, at this point [1776] and throughout the [Revolutionary] war, was to keep his army together and supplied. [**raises initial**

topic] Many of the militiamen signed up for short periods, and even the regulars tended to drift away. **[discussion of question of commitment]** Men would sign on to defend their homes, but might stay behind if the army moved on. **[further discussion]** Discipline was the heart of the British regime. **[further discussion; shapes discussion by shifting to British]** The men were trained to behave like automatons under fire. **[discussion; restatement for emphasis]** Such unquestioning discipline could not be achieved in the citizen army of the American forces. **[discussion; conclusion]** When Baron von Steuben, a Prussian soldier who volunteered to work with Washington, trained the troops in the Valley Forge winter of 1777–78, he wrote to a European friend: "You say to your soldier, 'Do this,' and he does it, but I am obliged to say, 'This is the reason why you ought to do that,' and he does it." **[further discussion of discipline]**[8]

Based on the roles identified for various sentences, we can describe this paragraph as a discussion of Washington's problems maintaining discipline in a sometimes partially motivated citizen army that demanded explanations for orders, as contrasted with the strict obedience adhered to by British and European troops.

The Descriptive Model
of Paragraph Structure

As noted in Appendix C, texts can do just about everything one can do in speech. Texts can:

- **analyze:** break into sections or parts for discussion or examination
- **argue:** make a case or offer evidence or reasons for
- **classify:** divide, distinguish, and label
- **compare:** present similarities
- **contrast:** present differences
- **define:** indicate the meaning of
- **describe:** indicate basic characteristics or qualities
- **discuss:** talk or provide information about
- **endorse:** show approval for
- **evaluate:** appraise or judge
- **explain:** interpret or discuss to clarify
- **illustrate:** provide an example of
- **instruct:** explain how to do something
- **narrate:** tell a story or recount an event
- **persuade:** argue based more on feelings than reason

CLASSIFYING TEXTS BY RHETORICAL CATEGORY

Traditionally, texts are classified according to rhetorical categories that include the following:

argument: developing a conclusion based on evidence, reason, appeal, or other persuasive devices. This category includes *evaluation*, *proposal*, *refutation*, and *analysis*.

comparison/contrast: discussing two objects, ideas, events, or other topics based on whether features are shared in common or are different.

definition: indicating the meaning of a term or phrase; distinguishing one idea from another.

description: relating the characteristics or features of an event, process, place, or the like.

narration: relating events; telling a story.

Each of the rhetorical categories above has required elements or ingredients. To argue, for instance, one must present a conclusion, give reasons, and show how the reasons justify the conclusion. To narrate, one must indicate who did what, when and where, and maybe why. In each case, the reader should ask: What is the nature of this category and what must one do to achieve it? For review, the central concerns of each rhetorical category are outlined here.

- **argument**: What is to be believed and why? On the basis of what evidence, reasons, needs, values, or assumptions? Argument can be inductive (a generalization based on specific examples), deductive (a specific conclusion from certain assumptions or statements), or analogous (implications based on similarities). Arguments can investigate the logical connection of ideas (reason and conclusion) or the physical interconnection of events (cause and effect).

- **comparison/contrast**: In what ways are the objects or ideas similar and/or different? On what basis? What difference do the differences make? Comparison generally moves from one quality or concern to another. It might also present both similarities and differences so as to highlight one or the other.

- **definition**: What is it? How should one look at something, and how should it be distinguished from otherwise similar things? Definition must indicate what kind of thing is being discussed and how the particular item differs from other items in that general category. Definition might also address why one would want to isolate the particular idea, how it is a useful idea for discussion.

- **description**: What is being described? For an object, what qualities, features, or characteristics are present? For an idea, what does it mean or what is involved? Description can move in various directions: from the obvious to the less obvious, left to right, top to bottom, then to now, the most interesting to the most boring, inside to outside, the conventional to the radical.

- **narration**: Who or what did what, when and where, and why or how did it happen? Narration generally follows a chronological order, but it can also focus on different individuals or different locales. In general we narrate the actions of people but describe the actions of animals.

APPLYING THE MODEL

EXAMPLE: **Public Statement by Eight Alabama Clergymen**

The following analysis of the Public Statement by Eight Alabama Clergymen [Texts for Analysis 6] uses the rhetorical categories of the descriptive model to identify the role of each paragraph within the text as a whole.

(1) We the undersigned clergymen are among those who, in January, issued "An Appeal for Law and Order and Common Sense," in dealing with racial problems in Alabama. We expressed understanding that honest convictions in racial matters could properly be pursued in the courts, but urged that decisions of those courts should in the meantime be peacefully obeyed. [**narrating events**; **offering evidence of previous position**]

(2) Since that time there has been some evidence of increased forbearance and a willingness to face facts. Responsible citizens have undertaken to work on various problems which cause racial friction and unrest. In Birmingham, recent public events have given indication that we all have opportunity for a new constructive and realistic approach to racial problems. [**narrating of the events leading to description of the present situation**]

(3) However, we are now confronted by a series of demonstrations by some of our Negro citizens, directed and led in part by outsiders. We recognize the natural impatience of people who feel that their hopes are slow in being realized. But we are convinced that these demonstrations are unwise and untimely. [**describing present situation; asserting position**]

(4) We agree rather with certain local Negro leadership which has called for honest and open negotiation of racial issues in our area. And we believe this kind of facing of issues can best be accomplished by citizens of our own metropolitan area, white and Negro, meeting with their knowledge and experience of the local situation. All of us need to face that responsibility and find proper channels for its accomplishment. [**asserting belief and arguing for that position**]

(5) Just as we formerly pointed out that "hatred and violence have no sanction in our religious and political traditions," we also point out that such actions as incite to hatred and violence, however technically peaceful those actions may be, have not contributed to the resolution of our local problems. We do not believe that these days of new hope are days when extreme measures are justified in Birmingham. [**arguing based on comparison (similarity)**]

(6) We commend the community as a whole, and the local news media and law enforcement officials in particular, on the calm manner in which these demonstrations have been handled. We urge the public to continue to show restraint should the demonstrations continue, and the law enforcement officials to remain calm and continue to protect our city from violence. [**arguing for certain behaviors**]

(7)   We further strongly urge our own Negro community to withdraw support from these demonstrations, and to unite locally in working peacefully for a better Birmingham. When rights are consistently denied, a cause should be pressed in the courts and in negotiations among local leaders, and not in the streets. We appeal to both our white and Negro citizenry to observe the principles of law and order and common sense. [**arguing for actions based on the assertion of certain principles of conduct**]

Analyzed this way, we can say that, overall, the statement is a plea for certain behavior. It *argues* for further court action and against Martin Luther King's protest activities. Along the way, it *narrates* past events, *describes* the present situation, and *argues* for and *urges* particular behaviors. Again, notice also that we talk of the text or elements of the text, and *not* the authors, engaging in these activities.

A short description of the letter of the Birmingham clergy might contain only a few sentences indicating the overall conclusion and a general description of how that message is conveyed. For example:

The Birmingham clergy argue against the confrontational tactics of civil rights demonstrators by contrasting what they take to be the patient virtue of those who have refrained from public protest with confrontational tactics that they describe as ineffective.

Here, general statements about the overall direction of the text are supported with more specific descriptions of the discussion. Further description would go into greater detail of precisely how the Birmingham clergy portray each of these sides. Indeed, one could go through the document paragraph by paragraph indicating how each one contributes to the effort described above.

EXAMPLE: **George Washington**

The excerpt from *The Pursuit of Liberty* is repeated here to indicate different observations possible with an alternative model.

[George] Washington's concern, at this point [1776] and throughout the [Revolutionary] war, was to keep his army together and supplied. [**argument**] Many of the militiamen signed up for short periods, and even the regulars tended to drift away. [**narrates events**] Men would sign on to defend their homes, but might stay behind if the army moved on. [**continued narration**] Discipline was the heart of the British regime. [**comparison; description of British**] The men were trained to behave like automatons under fire. [**description**] Such unquestioning discipline could not be achieved in the citizen army of the American forces. [**argument**] When Baron von Steuben, a Prussian soldier who volunteered to work with Washington, trained the troops in the Valley Forge winter of 1777–78, he wrote to a European friend: "You say to your soldier, 'Do this,' and he does it, but I am obliged to say, 'This is the reason why you ought to do that,' and he does it." [**further description/narration**][1]

With the above observations, we can describe this as a paragraph that argues that Washington's main problem was maintaining discipline and that compares the behavior of Washington's army to the strict obedience adhered to by British and European troops. The American soldiers are described as a partially motivated citizen army demanding explanations for orders.

The Relationship Model of Paragraph Structure

Like the role model and the descriptive model, the relationship model offers categories and terminology with which to describe the development of a text. These categories are particularly useful for inferring meaning from the relationships of patterns of content and language within a text (see Chapter 8, "Inferring Meaning from Relationships").

CLASSIFYING RELATIONSHIPS

The major categories of the relationship model include the following:

series: presenting a sequence of similar remarks, often in description (a series of different characteristics) or narration (a series of events). This category includes *progression* and *repetition*.

time/chronological order: developing a series according to a time framework.

general/specific: making generalizations and then giving specific examples or illustrations.

comparison/contrast: noting similarities or differences between objects, events, or ideas.

logic: asserting a conclusion based on evidence and/or reasoning. This group includes three subgroups: *reason/conclusion, cause/effect,* and *conditional.*

EXAMPLE: **The Witches of Salem**

The following excerpt from R. Jackson Wilson et al.'s *The Pursuit of Liberty* illustrates several relationships between elements within the text.

In 1692, one of the most remarkable events in American history took place. It began in a small village just outside the town of Salem in the British colony of Massachusetts. A group of young people, most of them female, began to have what their elders called "fits." Then they started to accuse adults of being witches, tormenting them in league with the Devil. The little community was terrified. Almost everyone believed the Devil was real and that he could visit the earth and take possession of people's souls if they agreed to make a covenant with him. So the people of Salem Village set out to combat what they believed was a conspiracy, set afoot by the Devil himself. Within a few weeks, hundreds of women and men had been accused of being witches. Soon the highest authorities in the colony intervened, not to restore calm but to stamp out the Satanic conspiracy. Dozens of people were put on trial, and several "confessed." By the time the hysteria and the trials ended, nineteen supposed witches had been hanged.[1]

The organizing principle here—the link between the sentences within the paragraph—is the notion that these events occurred one after the other (chronological relationship) and that they influenced one another (cause and effect). The sole deviations from this pattern are the initial judgment about the significance of the events in the first sentence and the inserted information about peoples' belief in the devil.

Signal Words

Each of these categories is associated with a variety of terms that signal the relationship.

- **series**: *and, also, in addition, then, another, finally, moreover, besides, next, first, furthermore, many, some, other, several, lastly, as well as*
- **general/specific**: *in general, for example, overall*
- **time/chronological order**: *then, after, before, soon, immediately, at that time, until, when, during, later, next, prior*
- **comparison/contrast**:

    similarity: *like, both, similarly, in the same way, comparatively, equally*

    difference: *yet, except, but, although, or, rather, on the contrary, however, in contrast, even though, otherwise, not, in spite of, whereas*
- **logic**

    cause or reason: *because, if, since*

    effect or conclusion: *thus, hence, therefore, then, consequently, so, after all*

    conditional: *if, then*

Notice that some terms (such as *since* and *if*) can signal more than one relationship. They must be analyzed within the context to determine which relationship is indicated.

EXAMPLE: **UN Peacekeepng Costs**

Signal words occur throughout the following excerpt from a speech by Brian Urquhart, former Undersecretary General of the United Nations. Actual signal words appear in boldface; *implied* signal words have been added in square brackets.

(1) There is an extraordinary double standard in the public and government perception of the financial problems of the United Nations. (2) **[For example]** The cost of two days of Operation Desert Storm, **at about** a billion dollars a day, would have easily covered all the UN's expenses, including peace-keeping and emergency operations, for a whole year. (3) **Yet** nobody ever questioned the costs of Desert Storm,

whereas governments never cease to bemoan the costs of UN peace-keeping. (4) **At the moment** there are complaints that the operation to try to rebuild Cambodia as a peaceful state may cost up to $2 billion. (5) There is **also** much concern at the projected cost of about $650 million for a UN peace-keeping force in Yugoslavia. (6) It is worth recalling that this sum is to be used to create a peaceful future for large numbers of people in several countries, while one B-2 bomber costs $880 million.

(7) **If** governments really find it difficult to pay their assessment for peace-keeping, which is true at the moment of the United States and a number of other countries, **maybe** the cost of peace-keeping should be shifted to defense budgets, which are infinitely larger than diplomatic or foreign aid budgets. (8) **After all**, an effective system of peace-keeping should have the result of reducing defense costs worldwide. (9) **Other** possibilities would be to have some kind of levy on the parts of the private sector, such as shipping or airlines, which profit greatly from peace-keeping activities—or perhaps to have 1 percent levy on all international arms transactions. (10) [**Overall**] Peace-keeping has proved itself to be a bargain by comparison with its alternative, war. (11) It **therefore** makes no sense to complain that it is too expensive.[2]

APPLYING THE MODEL

Drawing on the relationship model, as well as other models, this text can be analyzed as follows:

(1) There is [**introductory main idea or initial evidence**] an extraordinary double standard in the public and government perception of the financial problems of the United Nations. (2) The cost of two days [**example of financial problem**] of Operation Desert Storm, at about [**general/specific—example**] a billion dollars a day, would have easily covered [**contrast**] all the UN's expenses, including [**series—emphasis**] peace-keeping and emergency operations, for a whole year. [**further emphasis**] (3) Yet [**contrast**] nobody ever questioned the costs of Desert Storm, whereas [**contrast**] governments never cease to bemoan the costs of UN peace-keeping. (4) At the moment there are complaints [**illustration**] that the operation to try to rebuild Cambodia as a peaceful state may cost up to $2 billion. [**comparison with earlier costs**] (5) There is also [**series—further illustration/contrast**] much concern at the projected cost of about $650 million [**further series of costs—contrast**] for a UN peace-keeping force in Yugoslavia. (6) It is worth recalling [**series—emphasis**] that this sum is to be used to create a peaceful future for large numbers of people in several countries, [**contrast—more countries**] while one B-2 bomber costs $880 million. [**comparison—cost**]

(7) If [**reason/conditional**] governments really find it difficult to pay their assessment for peace-keeping, [**restatement of main idea**] which is true [**emphasis**] at the moment of the United States and a number of other countries, maybe [**conditional—conclusion**] the cost of peace-keeping should be shifted to defense budgets,

[**carrying to extreme**] which are infinitely larger than diplomatic or foreign aid budgets. [**comparison/satire—exaggeration**] (8) After all, [**conclusion**] an effective system of peace-keeping should have the result of reducing defense costs worldwide. [**justification**] (9) Other possibilities [**comparison—series**] would be to have some kind of levy on the parts of the private sector, such as [**specific—illustration**] shipping or airlines, which profit greatly from peace-keeping activities—or perhaps [**series—third example**] to have 1 percent levy on all international arms transactions. (10) Peace-keeping [**summing up**] has proved itself to be a bargain by comparison with its alternative, war. (11) It therefore [**conclusion**] makes no sense to complain that it is too expensive.

These observations lead to a description of the text as a plea for increased financial support of United Nations peace-keeping operations built on a positive comparison of peace-keeping versus war costs and on the contrast of countries' willingness to shoulder the burden of the latter and not the former. The argument is reinforced by a variety of persuasive techniques, including playing to the reader's reason and common sense while belittling alternative actions. (In the light of subsequent events in Yugoslavia, one can only lament that these remarks went unheeded.)

Logic and Statistics

Logic involves supporting assertions with reasoning. That reasoning may be based on evidence or other arguments to "back up" one's statements. Not all remarks, or course, are logical, nor do remarks have to be logical to be believed. Much thought and behavior is based on emotion, intuition, faith, superstition, or wishful thinking, and much of what we may think is logical actually reflects incorrect or simply poor reasoning.

The study of logic is usually broken into two major areas: deductive and inductive reasoning. The distinction often depends on whether the reasoning moves from general to specific (deduction) or specific to general (induction)—but this is not always the case. A better distinction can be made on the basis of the relative certainty of the conclusion.

INDUCTION

In the classic example of induction, apples are drawn at random from a barrel. If each apple drawn is rotten, one assumes that all of the apples in the barrel are rotten:

If each apple drawn from a barrel at random is rotten,	**specific statement**
all the apples in the barrel are rotten.	**general statement**

Inductive reasoning thus tends to extend an argument based on a particular instance to all such instances, from select experiences to all such experiences, from a pattern of evidence to all such cases. In so doing, induction requires a leap of faith, an assumption that the evidence considered actually represents all of the evidence. Whenever we see the terms *seems to be* or *appears to be*, the odds are we are dealing with induction. Much prediction involves induction, as in making projections based on political polls and other statistical surveys.

When supporting evidence precedes a conclusion, it functions as an *example* in support of the conclusion. When supporting evidence follows an assertion, it functions as an *illustration* explaining the earlier assertion. In this excerpt from Kalat's *Introduction to Psychology*, notice how the latter technique is used.

> According to social psychologists, one reason individuals behave differently is that other people *expect* them to behave differently. [**general assertion**] For example, suppose a first-grade teacher believes, rightly or wrongly, that Johny and Susy are particularly bright children who are likely to make good academic progress. [**supporting illustration**] The teacher gives a little more attention to those children than to the rest of the class. As a result, they may in fact make the progress the teacher expects (Rosenthal & Rubin, 1978).[1]

Here, the term "suppose" itself suggests an example is to follow.

DEDUCTION

Formal deduction usually proceeds from a general assumption, belief, or generalization (called a premise) to a relatively specific conclusion:

All men are mortal.	**initial premise**
Socrates is a man.	**secondary premise**
Therefore Socrates is mortal.	**conclusion**

The argument starts with an initial statement about all men and, based on a second assumption about a specific person, moves to a more specific conclusion about that man. The pattern of assumption-assumption-conclusion or assumption-fact-conclusion is known as a **syllogism**.

Deductive reasoning follows a strict mathematical logic. If the initial statements are true and the conclusion is reached according to specific rules, the conclusion must, of necessity, be true.

Syllogisms are fairly straightforward. In actual practice, however, the steps are not necessarily spelled out so clearly, nor are all assumptions necessarily present. Consider the following:

The "Star Spangled Banner" is difficult to sing. Therefore, we should find an alternative anthem.

Such an argument follows the syllogistic pattern of deductive argument, but the initial premise is missing: that a national anthem should not be difficult to sing:*

A national anthem should not be difficult to sing.	**premise**
The "Star Spangled Banner" is difficult to sing.	**premise**
Therefore, we should find an alternative anthem.	**conclusion**

Actually, the argument stops short at declaring that the "Star Spangled Banner" should not be the national anthem. To argue that we should find an alternative is to assume that we must have a national anthem in the first place:

We must have a national anthem.	**premise**
Our present anthem, the "Star Spangled Banner" should not be the national anthem.	**premise**
Therefore we should find an alternative anthem.	**conclusion**

*Deductive arguments in which one of the initial premises is implied are referred to as *enthymemes*.

The deductive format is typical with moral or ethical issues. From the assertion of a basic belief, we draw a conclusion that certain behavior should follow. For example, based on the principle that cruel and unusual punishment is prohibited by the Constitution, and the assertion that capital punishment is cruel and unusual, an editorial might argue that a scheduled execution should be halted. A value is asserted, an assertion made, and a conclusion drawn.

EXAMPLE: **Operation Desert Storm**

At the conclusion of Operation Desert Storm, the United Nations/United States military operation to liberate Kuwait from Sadam Hussein's Iraqi forces, U.S. pilots attacked lines of retreating Iraqi soldiers. One commentator justified such attacks with the following argument:*

> In my opinion, armed enemies who have not surrendered and who are capable of hostile actions are legitimate targets. [**premise**] Even if they are retreating they are subject to attack. [**clarification**] As the Riyadh [Saudi Arabia] briefing officer, Brigadier General Neale, explained, a "retreat" is different from a "withdrawal." [**premise**] Had Saddam Hussein announced that the Iraqi troops fleeing Kuwait City were being withdrawn to Iraq it might have been in order to permit them to do so unimpeded. [**assertion**] In fact, however, those troops simply retreated, carrying their loot with them, because the U.S./coalition ground offensive had defeated them. [**assertion**] In these circumstances I consider that the attacks on these retreating Iraqi along the highways back to Iraq were proportionate to the legitimate military objectives of destroying or incapacitating as much of the active armed forces as possible. [**conclusion**][2]

The paragraph argues both a general point (that attacks on retreating soldiers are justified) and the specific instance (that the attack on retreating Iraqi soldiers was justified). The first argument takes this basic form:

It is O.K. to destroy active enemy forces.

Retreating troops are active enemy forces.

Therefore, it is O.K. to attack retreating forces.

We can rephrase the argument in more precise terms:

[There is a] legitimate military objective of destroying or incapacitating as much of the active armed forces as possible.

As the Riyadh [Saudi Arabia] briefing officer, Brigadier General Neale, explained, a "retreat" is different from a "withdrawal" [retreating forces are active armed forces].

[Therefore] retreating soldiers are subject to attack.

---

*The structure of this excerpt was examined earlier in Chapter 1.

The second argument takes this form:

> [There is a] legitimate military objective of destroying or incapacitating as much of the active armed forces as possible . . . even if they are retreating.
>
> Those troops simply retreated.
>
> [Therefore] the attacks on these retreating Iraqi along the highways back to Iraq were [justified].

One might note that in the case cited, the forces are characterized not only as retreating, but as "defeated," thereby seemingly obviating the claim that they were "active."

EXAMPLE: **Western Civilization**

Consider the arguments inherent in the following excerpt from Ruth Benedict's *Patterns of Culture*:

> Western civilization, **because of** fortuitous historical circumstances, has spread itself more widely than any other local group that has so far been known. It has standardized itself over most of the globe, **and** we have been led, **therefore**, to accept a belief in the uniformity of human behavior that under other circumstances would not have arisen. **Even** very primitive peoples are sometimes far more conscious of the role of cultural traits than we are, and **for good reason**. They have had intimate experience of different cultures.[3]

This example offers a series of conclusions—as suggested by the phrases "because of," "therefore," and "for good reason."

The paragraph opens with an explanation (reason/conclusion) for the unusually wide spread of Western civilization, although it does not indicate exactly what the "fortuitous historical circumstances" have been. The concern is thus more for the fact of the expansion than for how it happened—as we see when the next sentence addresses the effect of that expansion:

> . . . we have been led . . . to accept a belief in the uniformity of human behavior that under other circumstances would not have arisen.

The conclusion derives from the preceding assertion:

> [Western civilization] has standardized itself over most of the globe . . .

The assumption is that we know only what we see, that we cannot recognize diverse cultural behaviors where we experience only one culture. This is spelled out further in reverse in the following illustration:

Even very primitive peoples are sometimes far more conscious of the role of cultural traits than we are, and **for good reason**. They have had intimate experience of different cultures.

One cannot recognize or appreciate cultural differences, the text argues, unless one has experienced them.

Happily, we do not often have to parse out the structure of a logical argument to make sense of the assertions. On the other hand, unless we do assure ourselves of the legitimacy of the argument, we can be suckered into a conclusion by smooth-flowing nonsense—hence the effectiveness of fallacies.

REASON/CONCLUSION VERSUS CAUSE/EFFECT

Deductive and inductive reasoning are distinguished by the *kind of reasoning* involved. Reasoning can also be classified according to the *kinds of assertions* involved. From this perspective, a distinction can be made between reason/conclusion and cause/effect reasoning. **Cause and effect** applies to **physical events**:

Cars skid on oil.	premise
There was oil on the street.	cause
The car skidded.	effect

For cause/effect reasoning to be valid, (1) the cause must come before the effect, (2) the cause must be capable, alone, of preciptiating the effect, and (3) all other possible causes must be eliminated.

Cause/effect reasoning is subject to various abuses. Indeed, each of the steps listed as a requirement is often abused. Just because something precedes something else does not mean that it caused it, and just because something is capable of a particular effect does not mean it caused it. In all such cases, a careful reader will reflect on the actual possibility of events occurring a certain way and not simply accept a text's assertions that they did occur that way.

Reason/Conclusion refers to mental activities, and hence to the process of human decision making. The following statement is an example of reason/conclusion:

Because it rained, we did not go to the beach.

Rain may cause grass to grow or rivers to flood, but it does not determine human actions.*

---

*As with other deductive arguments, the initial premise is assumed here. The statement "because it rained, we did not go to the beach" is based on the assumption that "one should not go to the beach if it rains" or, even more generally, that "one should not vacation outdoors in bad weather."

Human actions are often the result of the decision-making process; as such, they are examples of reasoned behavior. The 1993 Brady Bill for example, which enacted a waiting period in the purchase of handguns, was named after James Brady, President Reagan's press secretary who was severely injured during an assassination attempt on the president. While Brady did lobby for the bill, he did not cause it to be passed, nor was his experience alone reason for approving the bill. He did influence the debate and the voting, but that is quite different from asserting that the bill passed because of him. Apples fall because of gravity—that's cause/effect. People decide to think or do things based on mental calculations—that's reason/conclusion.

EXAMPLE: Cause and Effect or Coincidence?

When two events generally occur together, an attempt is often made to associate them in a cause/effect relationship. Determining cause and effect can be extremely tricky, as the following passage from Kalat's *Introduction to Psychology* demonstrates:

> Once in a while, we find a correlation in which one of the variables obviously causes change in the other. For example, meteorologists have discovered that there is a positive correlation between the number of sunspots and winter temperatures in the stratosphere over the North Pole. Although we are not sure just how sunspots could affect the weather on Earth, it is far more likely that they do affect the weather rather than that the weather on Earth affects the sunspots.
>
> Ordinarily, however, the direction of causation is far from obvious; for example:
>
> - Unmarried men are more likely than married men are to wind up in a mental hospital or prison. So we can say that, for men, marriage is negatively correlated with mental illness and criminal activity. Does the correlation mean that marriage leads to mental health and good social adjustment? Or does it mean that men who are confined to mental hospitals or prisons are unlikely to marry?
> - Most depressed people have trouble sleeping. Depression is negatively correlated with sleeping well. Does that mean depression causes poor sleep? Or does it mean that people who have difficulty sleeping become depressed? Or does something else, such as a dietary deficiency, lead to both depression and poor sleep?
>
> Determining the size and direction of a correlation between two variables is an important first step in a study. But a correlation does not tell us about causation. To determine causation, an investigator needs to manipulate one of the variables directly, through a research design known as an *experiment*. When an investigator manipulates one variable and then observes change in another variable, the causation is clear.[4]

Implied Signal Words

The terms signaling cause/effect and reason/conclusion are often implied. In the following excerpt from Gregory N. Connolly et al.'s "Snuffing Tobacco Out of Sport," signal words have been inserted for clarification:

> Use of oral snuff [chewing tobacco] has risen sharply among baseball players **[because of]** following a tobacco industry marketing campaign that linked smokeless tobacco with athletic performance and virility. Millions of adolescents have copied these professional role models and, today, **[as a result]** are at risk of developing oral cancer and other mouth disorders. **[therefore]** New policies and programs are needed to break the powerful grip that the tobacco industry has on professional sport. **[for example]** Health agencies, including the National Cancer Institute and the National Institute of Dental Research, have teamed up with major league baseball to help players quit and reduce public use of oral tobacco. **If** these efforts are successful, **[then]** our national pastime will once again become America's classroom for teaching health and fitness, not nicotine addiction.[5]

The proof of the validity of this analysis is that inserting these signal words does not alter the meaning of the passage.

In this text on snuff, someone reasons that ballplayers use more snuff because of the ad campaign. The ad campaign did not force it to happen; the players might have been more skeptical of advertising. There is no cause and effect here. The adolescents chose to use ballplayers as role models. Again, no cause and effect. The risk of cancer, however, has nothing to do with how people feel or reason. The use of snuff and an increased risk of cancer reflect a cause/effect relationship.

Analogy

Analogies combine elements of comparison and inductive reasoning, metaphor, and reference. In an analogy, things similar in one respect are assumed to be similar in another:

> If the state can legislate that motorcycle riders wear helmets, it can legislate that school bus riders wear seat belts.

Analogies are similar to metaphors insofar as the two things being compared are of a very different nature—here, motorcycle riders and school bus passengers. Analogies have the quality of references insofar as the reader must be familiar with both things for the analogy to make sense. Defending her policy of providing condoms to teenagers against charges that by doing so she encouraged teenage sex, Surgeon General Dr. Joycelyn Elders told a meeting of health officials, "There is not a person in this room that doesn't have car insurance, but you're not going to go out and have a wreck because of it."[6]

While analogies seem to draw a conclusion, they are not really a form of reasoning for they do not prove anything. They are more devices for suggesting something.

He runs with the stride of a deer.	**metaphor**
Since he runs with the stride of a deer, he must be fast.	**analogy**

But the dangers of the misuse of analogy must be evident by now, for we could just as easily say:

> Since he runs with the stride of a deer, he must be a vegetarian.

> If the state legislates that motorcycle riders wear helmets, it will next legislate that tractor drivers wear gimme caps.

Analogies break down when similarities in one respect have nothing to do with similarities in another respect. As noted previously, analogies do not prove anything; they simply help the reader/listener visualize an idea.

Evaluating an Argument

Logic is the science of *correct* reasoning. It examines whether statements are supported by the right amount and kinds of evidence. It provides tools for evaluating claims in an argument.

In general, for an argument to be logically valid, three conditions must be met:

- The initial evidence or assumptions must be true. Evidence must be **adequate** (the right kind), **sufficient** (the necessary amount), and **reliable** (itself unquestionable).
- All relevant information must be considered.
- The reasoning process must be in accordance with the rules of correct or valid reasoning.

If any one of the three conditions is violated, a false conclusion can result.

Deductive logic

A well-reasoned argument can result in a false conclusion if it is based on unjustified evidence or assumptions. For example, notice in the following how unreliable evidence leads to a false conclusion:

> All men are mortal.
> This table is a man.
> > Therefore this table is mortal.

In the next example, the premises are true, but the logic is faulty:

> All tigers have spots.
> My dog has spots.
> > Therefore my dog is a tiger.

Inductive logic

Induction, while not as exacting as deduction, is equally open to abuses. In most cases of induction, we do not have evidence of all possible cases; we must rely on a sampling of available evidence. This raises the question of how representative that sample is of the whole.

The evidence on which an inference is made must meet certain standards. First, it must be complete enough to be **representative** of the whole, not merely of some aspect of the whole. One cannot, for instance, predict the outcome of an election on the opinion of three voters! Second, the evidence must be **relevant**. The data on which the reasoning is based must directly affect the conclusion. Using the example of an election again, one cannot infer the results from the number of bumper stickers observed for each candidate, because one candidate may not have bumper stickers. Election predictions based on the opinions of registered voters are more accurate than those based on public opinion polls in general, and those based on registered voters intending to vote are more accurate than those based on all registered voters. Finally, the evidence on which the conclusion is based must be **accurate**. Again, conclusions can only be as good as the evidence on which they are based ("garbage in, garbage out").

STATISTICS

Statistics refers to the collection and analysis of numerical information. As such, statistics is concerned with how we obtain and explain measurements or other numerical data. As a scientific tool, statistics can be a powerful aid in investigating complicated phenomenon. Statistics are, however, subject to a wide variety of abuses and misunderstandings.

Statistics occur in two forms. The first, commonly associated with public opinion surveys, is **inferential statistics**. To judge popular feeling on an issue, we ask some people how they feel about that issue, and, from this sample, we *infer* group characteristics. The results of the poll approximate the answers that would result from asking the whole population the same question. Assuming that the people surveyed are truly representative of all people, we generalize about how all people feel. If, for example, three out of four people (75 percent) asked say the president is doing a good job, we say that the president has a 75 percent approval rating. In fact, the data measure only how the selected population responded. Only by an act of inference can the results be applied to a larger group.

Survey evidence, like all other evidence in a text, is selective. Someone has chosen what to measure and what not to, how to count responses, and how to process and interpret the data. Someone has decided whether a particular sample is representative or not. A picture based on true, but selected, data is not necessarily a true picture of the whole.

• PHRASING QUESTIONS •

The way in which a question is phrased can affect the answer. And getting an honest answer is often a problem. People respond to different interviewers differently; who is asking the question may be as important as what questions are asked.

In a textbook example of poll manipulation, would-be presidential candidate Ross Perot in March 1993 asked readers of a newspaper to respond to this question:

> Should laws be passed to eliminate all possibilities of special interests giving huge sums of money to contribute to candidates?

Ninety-nine percent of those responding—a self-selected group of interviewees—answered yes. But note what happened when the question was rephrased:

> Do groups have a right to contribute to the candidate they support?

Only forty percent favored contribution limitations.[7]

Even simple data collection can be troublesome. In the 1974 election of a junior senator from New Hampshire, the Republican candidate was the unofficial winner by 355 votes. A recount by the New Hampshire Secretary of State found the Democratic candidate to be the winner by 10 votes. The State Ballot Law Commission then found the Republican candidate the winner by 2 votes. And, until 1975, when a new election was called, the United States Senate was unable to resolve the election. No one would deny that there were just so many valid votes cast for each candidate. But the way in which valid votes were defined and the ballots subsequently counted varied from one standard to another.

The second form of statistical discussion, **descriptive statistics**, is exemplified by baseball batting averages or the median cost of a house in a certain neighborhood. From information about all cases, we compute numbers that describe group tendencies. The most common quantities computed in this format are central tendencies (for example, mean, median, and mode) and measures of how actual values diverge from these central tendencies (for example, range, variability, and standard deviation). Such numbers are not, in themselves, direct measurements; they are mathematical ways of summing up complex measurements.

Measures of group tendencies, as such, do not provide information on individual cases. "Nine out of ten" is not always "nine out of *every* ten"; and there is no way to tell whether a particular instance is the ninth or the tenth. Batting averages indicate how a batter has hit *on average* so far; they do not tell us whether the batter will get a hit next time. A baseball manager may "play the averages" when he puts in a right-handed hitter to bat against a left-handed pitcher, but the outcome in any given situation is by no means a foregone conclusion.

The commonly quoted Dow Jones Average of the daily stock market behavior is a combination of these two forms of statistics. As a single number, a Dow Jones average mathematically describes the rise or fall of the stock market as a whole. And rather than being based on all stocks, it is based on a selected survey of stocks chosen to represent the behavior of all.*

In all cases, problems can occur in the movement from statistical data to inferences based on that data. Numbers cannot show how people think, how one event influences another, what values people hold, or why a government takes a certain action or follows certain priorities. Statistics portray a situation, but they do not explain—"statistical analysis is not concept analysis; it is *data* analysis."[8] (The "inference" in inferential statistics is really more a generalization than a new thought. To that extent, inferential statistics is also essentially descriptive in the broad sense of that term.) The arithmetic of statistical analysis may be exact, but the interpretation will remain subject to question. Have all significant factors been considered? Have all alternative explanations been investigated and rejected? Statistics alone cannot answer these questions. As the old saying goes: "There are lies, damn lies, and statistics."

Above all, one must be quite sure of exactly what is being measured. For example, a foreign car company recently advertised that 90 percent of their cars sold in the past twenty years were still on the road. This seemed to be strong evidence of the reliability of their cars. The ad did not point out, however, that 90 percent of the cars sold by that company in the last twenty years may have been sold in the previous year. And when a sportswriter says that a ballplayer's batting average has risen sharply, we cannot necessarily assume that the player is hitting well—only better than before.

The discussion here can only suggest the pitfalls of the misuse of statistical evidence. For the purposes of critical reading, it is not essential that you immediately discover any potential distortion. The main concern is to recognize how the text wishes you to perceive the topic—as with the attempt to portray a brand of car as extremely reliable.

For a more complete discussion of logic and logical fallacies, consult a logic textbook. Classic works particularly useful for critical reading include:

- Howard Kahane, *Logic and Contemporary Rhetoric: The Use of Reason in Everyday Life*, 6th ed. (Belmont, CA: Wadsworth, 1992)

---

*The two forms of statistics mirror the two forms of reasoning. Inferential statistics, like inductive reasoning, asserts a general statement based on specific instances. Descriptive statistics, like deductive reasoning, makes a relatively specific assertion that follows with logical or mathematical precision.

- Monroe Beardsley, *Thinking Straight: Principles of Reasoning for Readers and Writers* (Englewood Cliffs, NJ: Prentice-Hall, 1966)
- Darrell Huff, *How to Lie with Statistics* (New York: Norton, 1954)
- Stephen Campbell, *Flaws and Fallacies in Statistical Thinking* (Englewood Cliffs, NJ: Prentice-Hall, 1974)

Notes

Introduction

1. M. A. Just and P. A. Carpenter, *The Psychology of Reading and Language Comprehension* (Boston: Allyn & Bacon, 1987).

2. "A Graduation Gift from Uncle Sam," in "Grapevine," by Guy Garcia, reported by Sidney Urquhart, *Time*, February 11, 1991, p. 17. Copyright © 1991 by Time Inc. Reprinted by permission.

3. Richard D. Altick, *Preface to Critical Reading*, 5th ed. (New York: Holt, Rinehart & Winston, 1969), p. 57.

4. Bertrand Russell, as cited in a transcript of a conversation between Neil Postman and Camille Paglia in which Postman recalls that "[the philosopher] Bertrand Russell used to utter a lovely phrase . . . that the purpose of education was to teach each of us to defend ourselves against the 'seductions of eloquence.'" "She Wants Her TV! He Wants His Book," *Harper's Magazine*, March 1991, p. 47. Copyright © 1991 by *Harper's Magazine*. All rights reserved. Reprinted by special permission.

Chapter 1

1. Mortimer Adler, *How to Read a Book* (New York: Simon & Schuster, 1940), p. 14.

2. Neil Postman and Charles Weingartner, *Linguistics: A Revolution in Teaching* (New York: Dell, 1966; Delta edition), p. 176.

3. "Always Two Possibilities," from *A Treasury of Jewish Folklore*, ed. Nathan Ausubel, abridged and with a new introduction by Alan Mintz (New York: Bantam, 1980), p. 63. Copyright © 1948, 1976 by Crown Publishers, Inc. Reprinted by permission of Crown Publishers, Inc.

4. Charles R. Hoffer, *A Concise Introduction to Music Listening*, 5th ed. (Belmont, CA: Wadsworth, 1992), p. 46.

5. Rodney Stark, *Sociology*, 4th ed. (Belmont, CA: Wadsworth, 1992), p. 39.

6. Robert L. Allen, *English Grammars and English Grammar* (New York: Scribner, 1972), p. 99.

7. Shirley Biagi, *Media/Impact: An Introduction to Mass Media*, 2nd ed. (Belmont, CA: Wadsworth, 1992), p. 168.

8. Michael A. Milburn, *Persuasion and Politics: The Social Psychology of Public Opinion* (Pacific Grove, CA: Brooks/Cole, 1991), p. 63.

9. Paul A. Samuelson, *Economics*, 11th ed. (New York: McGraw-Hill, 1980), p. 551.

10. Stark, *Sociology*, p. 189.

11. William V. O'Brien, "The Gulf War and Just War Doctrine," *Freedom Review*, May-June 1991, p. 17. Reprinted by permission of *Freedom Review*.

12. Joseph F. Sheley, *Criminology: A Contemporary Handbook* (Belmont, CA: Wadsworth, 1991), p. 14.

13. R. Farr, "Keynote Address," Virginia State Reading Association Annual Conference, Roanoke, VA, April 1977, cited in Edward V. Jones, *Reading Instruction for the Adult Illiterate* (Chicago: American Library Association, 1981), p. 55.

14. Esther B. Fein, "Book Notes: Women and Wolves," *The New York Times*, January 20, 1993, p. B8. Copyright ©1993 by The New York Times Company. Reprinted by permission.

15. Robert E. O'Connor, Thomas G. Ingersoll, and Robert F. Pecorella, *Politics and Structure: Essentials of American National Government*, 5th ed. (Belmont, CA: Wadsworth, 1990), p. 47.

16. Youssef M. Ibrahim, "Criticism of Raids on Iraq Spreads Among Arabs," *The New York Times*, January 20, 1993, p. A6. Copyright ©1993 by The New York Times Company. Reprinted by permission.

17. Stark, *Sociology*, p. 353.

18. James W. Kalat, *Introduction to Psychology*, 2nd ed. (Belmont, CA: Wadsworth, 1990), p. 14.

19. Milburn, *Persuasion and Politics,* p. 63.

20. Erving Goffman, *Asylums: Essays on the Social Situation of Mental Patients and Other Inmates* (Garden City, NJ: Anchor Books, 1961), p. 325.

21. Stark, *Sociology*, p. 163.

22. H. Thorne Compton, "The Liberal Arts and Critical Thinking: Building Blocks of the Educated Person," in John N. Gardner and A. Jerome Jewler, eds., *College Is Only the Beginning: A Student Guide to Higher Education*, 2nd ed. (Belmont, CA: Wadsworth, 1989), p. 115.

23. Joan Ferrante, *Sociology: A Global Perspective* (Belmont, CA: Wadsworth, 1992), p. 68.

Chapter 2

1. W. Ross Winterowd, *The Culture and Politics of Literacy* (New York: Oxford, 1989), pp. 62–63.

2. Sir Arthur Conan Doyle, "A Case of Identity," in *The Complete Sherlock Holmes Short Stories* (London: John Murray and Jonathan Cape, 1928), p. 67.

3. John N. Gardner, "Decoding Your Professors," in John N. Gardner and A. Jerome Jewler, eds., *College Is Only the Beginning* (Belmont, CA: Wadsworth, 1989), p. 63.

4. Howard Kahane, *Logic and Contemporary Rhetoric: The Use of Reason in Everyday Life*, 6th ed. (Belmont, CA: Wadsworth, 1992), p. 220.

5. William Dwight Whitney, "Figurative Language," in *Reading About Language*, Charlton Laird and Robert M. Gorrell, eds. (New York: Harcourt Brace Jovanovich, 1971),p. 138.

6. Winterowd, *The Culture and Politics of Literacy*, p. 58.

7. Richard Corliss, "Sea Shepherd from Outer Space," *Time*, December 8, 1986.

8. H. Thorne Compton, "The Liberal Arts and Critical Thinking: Building Blocks of the Educated Person," in Gardner and Jewler, eds., *College Is Only the Beginning*, p. 15.

9. Rodney Stark, *Sociology*, 4th ed. (Belmont, CA: Wadsworth, 1992), p. 256.

10. Patricia Leigh Brown, "America, in High-Tech Sneakers, Is Wearing Its Heart on Its Feet," *The New York Times*, May 28, 1992, p. B1. Copyright © 1992 by The New York Times Company. Reprinted by permission.

11. "Heart of the Country," *The New Yorker*, December 28, 1992/January 4, 1993, p. 58.

12. Todd Barrett, "The Cradle Will Rock (and Roll)," *Newsweek*, January 4, 1993, p. 47.

13. Ted Solotaroff, "The Paperbacking of Publishing," *The Nation*, October 7, 1991, p. 399.

14. Reverend Martin Luther King, Jr., "I Have A Dream," speech given in Washington, DC, August 28, 1963. Cf. *Journal of Negro History*, United Publishing Company.

15. Allen R. Myerson, "Are Fallen Barons Victims of Their Press Clippings?" *The New York Times*, February 7, 1993, p. E7. Copyright © 1993 by The New York Times Company. Reprinted by permission.

16. Senator Bill Bradley, "The Real Lesson of L.A.," an adaptation of a speech on the Senate floor, March 26, 1992, in *Harper's Magazine*, July, 1992, p. 11. Copyright © 1992 by *Harper's Magazine*. All rights reserved. Reprinted from the July issue by special permission.

17. Lewis Thomas, "On Societies as Organisms," in *Lives of a Cell: Notes of a Biology Watcher* (New York: Viking Press, 1974; Penguin edition), pp. 11–12.

Chapter 3

1. Neil Postman and Charles Weingartner, *Linguistics: A Revolution in Teaching* (New York: Dell, 1966; Delta Edition), p. 184.

2. Rev. Jesse Jackson, as quoted in *Newsweek*, December 13, 1993, p. 17.

3. Elizabeth Cady Stanton, "The Seneca Falls Declaration," 1848.

4. Tom Reagan, "Religion and Animal Rights," a presentation before the Conference on Creation Theology and Environmental Ethics, World Council of Churches in Annecy, France, 1988, reprinted in *Animal's Voice Magazine*.

5. Kurt Schmoke, "A War for the Surgeon General, Not the Attorney General," *New Perspective Quarterly*, vol. 6, no. 2 (Summer 1989), p. 15.

6. Dalton Trumbo, Introduction, March 25, 1959, to *Johnny Got His Gun* (New York: Bantam, 1959), p. iv.

7. Editorial, *Free Student* (May 2nd Movement, New York, NY), no. 4 (July 1965), p. 11.

8. Northrop Frye, "Literary Criticism," in James Thorpe, ed., *The Aims and Methods of Scholarship in Modern Languages and Literature*, 2nd ed. (New York: Modern Language Association, 1970), p. 71.

9. *AAA Texas Tourbook* (Heathrow, FL: American Automobile Association, 1991), p. A80.

10. Hans Kraus, *Backache, Stress and Tension* (New York: Pocket Books, 1965), p. 107.

11. Phil Richards and John J. Banigan, *How to Abandon Ship* (New York: Cornell Maritime Press, 1943), p. 112.

12. Mary Gloyne Byler, Preface to *American Indian and Eskimo Authors: A Comprehensive Bibliography*, compiled by Arlene B. Hirschfelder (New York: Association on American Indian Affairs, 1973), p. 2.

13. Nathan Glazer, "Some Very Modest Proposals for the Improvement of American Education," *Daedalus, Journal of the American Academy of Arts and Sciences*, Fall 1984, p. 169.

14. *Report of the National Advisory Commission on Civil Disorders* (New York: Bantam Books, 1968), p. 33.

15. Paul Postal, *Constituent Structure: A Study of Contemporary Models of Syntactic Description* (Bloomington, IN: Research Center for the Language Sciences, Indiana University, 1967), p. 6.

16. Ralph Reed, "A Strategy for Evangelicals," *Christian America, A Christian Review of the News*, January 1993, p. 15.

Chapter 4

1. Edmund Burke Huey, *The Psychology and Pedagogy of Reading* (New York: Macmillan, 1908), p. 349.

2. Harry Austryn Wolfson, "The Philonic God of Revelation and His Latter-Day Deniers," in *Religious Philosophy: A Group of Essays* (Cambridge, MA: Belknap Press, 1960), p. 1.

3. *Walker's Britain* (London: Pan Books/Ordnance Survey, 1982), back cover.

4. Milton Friedman, "Prohibition and Drugs," *Newsweek*, May 1, 1972, p. 104.

Chapter 5

1. Neil Postman and Charles Weingartner, *Linguistics: A Revolution in Teaching* (New York: Dell, 1966; Delta edition), p. 39.

2. Mao Tsetung, "Oppose Book Worship," in *Selected Readings from the Works of Mao Tsetung* (Peking: Foreign Language Press, 1971), pp. 42–43.

3. Richard W. Stevenson, "Magic: 'It Can Happen to Anybody,'" *Austin American-Statesman*, November 8, 1991, p. A1. © 1991 by The New York Times Company. Reprinted by permission.

4. Roger Phillips, *Austin American-Statesman*, November 4, 1992, p. C1. Reprinted by permission: Tribune Media Services.

5. A. Phillips Brooks and Scott W. Wright, "Johnson's Case May Raise AIDS Awareness," © *Austin American Statesman*, November 8, 1991, P. A1. Reprinted by permission.

6. S. L. Price, *Miami Herald*, as cited in *Austin American-Statesman*, November 4, 1992, p. C3. Used by permission.

7. David L. Cohen, MD, et al., "Denver's Increase in HIV Counseling After Magic Johnson's HIV Disclosure," letter to the editor, *American Journal of Public Health*, vol. 82, no. 12, p. 1692. Used by permission.

8. Charles Beard, "Written History as an Act of Faith," *American Historical Review*, vol. 39, no.2, p. 220.

9. Ruth A. Wallace and Alison Wolf, *Contemporary Sociological Theory* (Englewood Cliffs, NJ: Prentice-Hall, 1980), p. 3.

10. Earl Babbie, *The Practice of Social Research*, 6th ed. (Belmont, CA: Wadsworth, 1992), p. G6.

11. S. I. Hayakawa, "General Semantics: Where Is It Now?" summarizing Edith Efron's observations in *The News Twisters*, transcript of a speech before the National Council of Teachers of English convention, Minneapolis, November 1972, in Hugh Rank, ed., *Language and Public Policy* (Urbana, IL: National Council of Teachers of English, 1974), pp. 153–154.

12. As cited by Rick Du Brow in "TV and the Gulf War," *Los Angeles Times*, February 21, 1991, p. 18.

13. George Wood, in "Novel History," a review of *Dead Certainties (Unwarranted Speculations)* by Simon Schama, in *The New York Review of Books* 38(12), July 27, 1991, p. 16.

14. Introduction to Toni Morrison, ed., *Race-ing Justice, En-gendering Power: Essays on Anita Hill, Clarence Thomas, and the Construction of Social Reality* (New York: Pantheon, 1992).

15. In *The New Yorker*, December 28, 1992/January 4, 1993, p. 62.

16. Bernard Wasserstein, "Little White Lies, and Others: The Art and Craft of Mendacity," review of *The Penguin Book of Lies* (New York: Viking, 1990), in *Bostonia Magazine*, July/August 1991, p. 23.

17. Michael Olesker, "Playing It down the Middle," *Baltimore Sun*, September 11, 1983, p. B1.

18. Lewis H. Lapham, "Gilding the News," *Harper's Magazine*, July 1981, p. 35. Copyright © 1981 by *Harper's Magazine*. All rights reserved. Reprinted from the July issue by special permission.

19. Ellen K. Coughlin, "Finding the Message in the Medium: The Rhetoric of Scholarly Research," *The Chronicle of Higher Education*, April 11, 1984, pp. 7, 9, a report on a scholarly conference, "The Rhetoric of the Human Sciences," sponsored by, among others, The National Endowment for the Humanities and the University of Iowa.

20. Edward Hallett Carr, *What Is History?* (New York: Knopf, 1962).

21. Michael B. Rosen, "What the Jury Saw: Does the Videotape Lie?" *Bostonia Magazine*, Winter 1992/1993, p. 30.

Chapter 6

1. James W. Kalat, *Introduction to Psychology*, 2nd ed. (Belmont, CA: Wadsworth, 1990), p. 355.

2. Rodney Stark, *Sociology*, 4th ed. (Belmont, CA: Wadsworth, 1992), p. 478.

3. Barbara Tuchman, "History by the Ounce," *Harper's Magazine*, July 1965. Copyright © 1965 by *Harper's Magazine*. All rights reserved. Reprinted from the July issue by special permission.

4. Petition of the Inmates of Rahway State Prison, *The New York Times*, November 27, 1965, p. 18.

5. E. B. White, editorial from *The New Yorker*, July 3, 1944, in E. B. White, *The Wild Flag* (Boston: Houghton Mifflin, 1946), p. 31. Reprinted by permission of the Estate of E. B. White.

6. From materials developed by Christopher Waldrep, cited in Thomas J. DeLoughry, "History, Post-Print," *Chronicle of Higher Education*, January 12, 1994, p. A20.

7. *The Wall Street Journal,* May 13, 1983, as cited in Joyce Bermel and Carol Levine, "On Tongan Chic and Cultural Relativism," *The Hastings Center Report*, vol. 13, no. 4, p. 3.

8. Jeane Ann Grisso, quoted in "High Injury Rate Found," *The Nation's Health* (American Public Health Association), vol. 21, no. 10, p. 2., a report of Jeane Grisso et al., "A Population-based Study of Injuries in Inner-City Women," *American Journal of Epidemiology*, vol. 134, no. 1, pp. 59–66.

9. Anna Quindlen, "The Standard Bearers," *The New York Times*, July 12, 1992, p. 21. Copyright © 1992 by The New York Times Company. Reprinted by permission.

10. Shirley Biagi, *Media/Impact: An Introduction to Mass Media*, 2nd ed. (Belmont, CA: Wadsworth, 1992), p. 98.

11. "Harper's Index," *Harper's Magazine*, July 1991, p. 15. Copyright © 1991 by *Harper's Magazine*. All rights reserved. Reprinted from the July issue by special permission.

12. Jean Dresden Grambs, *Women over Forty: Visions and Realities*, rev. ed. (New York: Springer, 1989), p.1.

Chapter 7

1. Thomas E. Porter, Charles Kneupper, and Harry Reeder, *The Literate Mind: Reading, Writing, Critical Thinking* (Dubuque, IA: Kendall/Hunt, 1987), p. 13.

2. Ronald Walters and T. H. Kern, "How to Eschew Weasel Words . . . ," *Johns Hopkins Magazine*, December 1991, p. 28.

3. Thomas Love Peacock (1785–1866), *Gryll Grange* (1861).

4. Amerigo Vespucci, *Amerigo Vespucci: Letter to Piero Soderini, Gonfaloniere*, trans. and ed. George Tyler Northup (Princeton, NJ: Princeton University Press, 1916), p.7.

5. All figures from "Directory of Colleges and Universities," in *America's Best Colleges, 1992,* published by *U.S. News & World Report*.

6. Robert S. Lynd, *Knowledge for What? The Place of Social Science in American Culture* (Princeton, NJ: Princeton University Press, 1939), pp. 59–64.

Chapter 8

1. Lev Semenovich Vygotsky, *Language and Thought*, ed. and trans. Eugenia Hanfmann and Gertrude Vakar (Cambridge, MA: MIT Press, 1962), p. 125.

2. *What Your 1st Grader Needs to Know: Fundamentals of a Good First-Grade Education*, ed. E. D. Hirsch, Jr. (New York: Doubleday, 1991), pp. 232–233.

3. Susan Altman, *Extraordinary Black Americans* (Chicago: Children's Press, 1989), p. 163.

4. Richard Hofstadter, *Great Issues in American History, from the Revolution to the Civil War, 1765–1865* (New York: Random House, 1953), pp. 384–385.

Chapter 9

1. Bergen Evans, *The Word-a-Day Vocabulary Builder* (New York: Random House, 1963).

2. Thomas Szasz, *The Second Sin* (New York: Doubleday, 1973), p. 20.

3. Thomas L. Beauchamp and James F. Childress, *Principles of Biomedical Ethics* (New York: Oxford, 1979), p. 86.

4. Francis X. Clines, "What's 3 Letters and Zoologically Correct?" *The New York Times*, February 4, 1993, p. A1. Copyright © 1993 by The New York Times Company. Reprinted by permission.

5. Richard Harwood, "We Hang Our Labels on the Totem Pole of What's Handy," *Austin American-Statesman*, December 6, 1990, p. A23. Reprinted by permission of *The Washington Post*.

6. David Herbert Donald, "A People's Experience," review of *Black Odyssey: The Afro-American Ordeal in Slavery* by Nathan Irvin Huggins (New York: Pantheon, 1977), in *The New York Times Book Review,* December 11, 1977, p. 10. Copyright © 1977 by The New York Times Company. Reprinted by permission.

7. Jim Fain, "Earth's Warming Draws a Cold Stare," *Austin American-Statesman*, March 13, 1991, p. A11. Reprinted by permission of the Cox News Service.

8. Rachel Carson, *Silent Spring* (Boston: Houghton Mifflin, 1962), p. 6.

9. Otto Freidrich, "A Vivacious Blonde Was Fatally Shot Today or How to Read a Tabloid," *American Scholar* 28(4), p. 467.

10. Speech at the Southeast Fairgrounds, Atlanta, Georgia. Governors' Administrative Files (Wallace): Speeches, Alabama State Archives.

11. Malcolm X, "After the Bombing," *Malcolm X Speaks: Selected Speeches and Statements,* ed. George Breitman (New York: Pathfinder, 1965), p. 166.

12. Szasz, *The Second Sin*, p. 21.

13. Editorial, "Clinton Express?" *The Nation*, March 30, 1992, p. 399.

14. Martin Luther King, Jr., *Letter from the Birmingham Jail*, in *Why We Can't Wait* (New York: Harper & Row, 1963).

15. Senate Judiciary Hearings, July 21, 1993, unedited transcript, p. 7.

Chapter 10

1. D. G. Kehl, "The Electric Carrot: The Rhetoric of Advertisement and the Art of Persuasion," first delivered at the 1974 Conference on College Composition and Communication, Anaheim, CA, in *Language and Public Policy*, ed. Hugh Rank (Urbana, IL: National Council of Teachers of English,1974), p. 53. Kehl cites as the source of the Stevenson Quotation, "Beggars," *Across the Plains* (London: Chatto and Windus, 1892), p. 263.

2. Barry Meier, "Dubious Theory: Chocolate a Cavity Fighter," *The New York Times*, April 15, 1992, p. A1. Copyright © 1992 by The New York Times Company. Reprinted by permission.

3. Judith Martin, "Euphemisms Are a Delicate Way to Spare Other People's Feelings," *Austin American-Statesman*, March 1, 1992, p. G15.

4. "Typing Pain: British Judge Dismisses It," *The New York Times*, October 29, 1993, p. B10.

5. Michiko Kakutani, "The Word Police Are Listening for 'Incorrect' Language," *The New York Times*, February 1, 1993, p. B4. Copyright © 1993 by The New York Times Company. Reprinted by permission.

6. Gordon Allport, *The Nature of Prejudice* (Cambridge, MA: Addison-Wesley, 1954), p. 179.

7. S. I. Hayakawa, *Through the Communication Barrier: On Speaking, Listening and Understanding* (New York: Harper & Row, 1979), p. 80.

8. Julian L. Simon and Aaron Wildavsky, "Facts, Not Species, Are Periled," *The New York Times*, May 13, 1993, p. A11. Copyright © 1993 by The New York Times Company. Reprinted by permission.

9. Sally Mcdonald, "Defense Department Cited for Strategic Mangling of Language," *Austin American-Statesman*, November 23, 1991, p. A6.

10. Hugh Rank, "The Teacher-Heal-Thyself Myth," in *Language and Public Policy*, ed. Hugh Rank (Urbana IL: National Council of Teachers of English, 1974), p. 219.

11. Joseph Sobran, "New Military Way of Life and Strife," *Washington Times*, January 1, 1993.

12. David B. Kopel, "Kids and Guns," *American Rifleman* 141(8), p. 42.

13. George Will, "Term Limits: The Political Version of Antitrust," *Austin American-Statesman*, November 3, 1991, p. E3.

14. *Masson v. New Yorker Magazine, Inc.*, cited by Michael Kinsley, "Please Don't Quote Me" in *Time*, May 13, 1991, p. 82, a commentary on the media's fascination with the use of quotations. The perceptive reader will notice that the use of Judge Kozinsky's quotation reflects his point.

15. M. J. Moroney, *Facts from Figures*, 3rd ed. (Baltimore: Penguin, 1956), p. 3.

16. Mark Green and Gail McColl, "R.R.—Found In 'Error'," *The New York Times*, December 20, 1983, p. A31. Copyright © 1983 by The New York Times Company. Reprinted by permission. Cf. the authors *There He Goes Again: Ronald Reagan's Reign of Error* (New York: Pantheon, 1983).

17. For a complete discussion of the NCTE Committee on Public Doublespeak, see the first of their volumes, *Language and Public Policy*, ed. Hugh Rank (Urbana, IL: National Council of Teachers of English, 1974).

18. Mcdonald, "Defense Department Cited," p. A6.

19. (1) standing still, (2) flunking out, (3) removing books from a school library for purposes of censorship, (4) a farmer's market, (5) plastic, (6) an electric fan, (7) death.

Chapter 11

1. Hugh Rank, *The Pep Talk: How to Analyze Political Language* (Park Forest, IL: Counter-Propaganda Press, 1984), p. 204.

2. Rev. Doug Carpenter, "Thirty Years of Hindsight," *The Apostle*, publication of the Diocese of Alabama, January 1993.

3. *The Writers's Quotation Book*, edited by James Charlton (New York: Penguin Books, 1986), p. 19.

Chapter 12

1. Janice Lewis, "Redefining Critical Reading for College Critical Thinking Courses," *Journal of Reading* 34(6), March 1991, p. 421.

2. Louis Uchitelle, "Moscow Subway Defies the Odds," *The New York Times*, March 10, 1992, p. C2. Copyright © 1992 by The New York Times Company. Reprinted by permission.

Chapter 13

1. Paul A. Samuelson, *Economics*, 11th ed. (New York: McGraw-Hill, 1980), p. 551.
2. Vine Deloria, Jr,. *Custer Died for Your Sins* (New York: Avon, 1969), p. 35.

Texts for Analysis

1. Mary C. Simms Oliphant, *The Simms History of South Carolina*, "For Use in Schools," (Columbia, SC: State, 1932), pp. 245–247. Used by permission.
2. *Report of the National Advisory Commission on Civil Disorders* (New York: Bantam, 1968), pp. 213–214.
3. R. Jackson Wilson et al., *The Pursuit of Liberty, A History of the American People*, Vol. 1, 2nd ed. (Belmont, CA: Wasworth, 1990), pp. 554–556.
4. C. P. Hall II, Brookfield, IL, Letter to the Editor, *American Heritage*, October 1992, p. 8. Used by permission of C. P. Hall II.
5. Peter Kihss, *The New York Times*, February 22, 1965, p 1. Copyright © 1965 by The New York Times Company. Reprinted by permission.
6. From *Newsweek*, March 8, 1965. Copyright © 1965, Newsweek, Inc. All rights reserved. Reprinted by permission.
7. Thomas Skinner, "I Saw Malcolm Die," *New York Post*, February 22, 1965, p. 1. Used by permission.
8. *Congressional Record* 139(14), February 4, 1993, p. S1301.
9. Ken Corbett, "Between Fear and Fantasy," *The New York Times*, February 3, 1993, p. A15. Copyright © 1993 by The New York Times Company. Reprinted by permission.
10. Senator Carol Moseley-Braun, *Congressional Record* 139(14), February 4, 1993, pp. S1273–4.
11. Samuel Francis, "Issue of Gays Really Needs Deep Thought," *Insight on the News*, March 1, 1993, pp. 19–20. Reprinted from *The Washington Times*. Used by permission.
12. *Hastings Center Report* 6(1) pp. 20–22. This and similar case studies and commentaries are included in Carol Levine and Robert M. Veatch, eds,. *Cases in Bioethics from The Hastings Center Report* (Hastings-on-Hudson, NY: The Hastings Center, 1982). Used by permission.
13. "Public Statement of Eight Alabama Clergymen," issued April 12, 1963; originally appeared in *The Birmingham News*. Used by permission.
14. *The New York Times*, August 11, 1970, p. 30. Copyright © 1970 by The New York Times Company. Reprinted by permission.
15. Advertisement sponsored by Americans for Medical Progress Educational Foundation, *The New York Times*, February 7, 1993, p. E5. Used by permission.
16. Senator John Danforth, statement to the Senate, September 29, 1989. For a collection of documents surrounding the debate, see Richard Bolton, ed., *Culture Wars: Documents from the Recent Controversies in the Arts* (New York: New Press, 1992).

17. Earl Shorris, "Latino, Sí. Hispanic, No." *The New York Times*, October 28, 1992, p. A15. Copyright © 1992 by The New York Times Company. Reprinted by permission.

18. William F. Buckley Jr., "On Abortion," *Harper's Magazine*, November 1992, pp. 44–45. Copyright © 1992 by *Harper's Magazine*. All rights reserved. Reprinted from the November issue by special permission.

19. Paulette Mason (pseudonym), "I'm 38, and Running Out of Time," *The New York Times*, October 3, 1992, p. 15. Copyright © 1992 by The New York Times Company. Reprinted by permission.

20. Stephanie Strom, "One Size Fits All the Way to Middle Age," *The New York Times*, January 31, 1993, Section 4, p. 2. Copyright © 1993 by the New York Times Company. Reprinted by permission.

21. Elizabeth M. Whelan, "Alarm Clocks Can Kill You. Have a Smoke." *The New York Times*, September 8, 1992, p. A19. Copyright © 1992 by The New York Times Company. Reprinted by permission.

22. Jamie Ann Conway, "Let Women Fly in Combat," *The New York Times*, June 25, 1992, p. A23. Copyright © 1992 by The New York Times Company. Reprinted by permission.

23. Tracy Quan, "'Sex Work'?" Letter to the Editor, *The New York Book Review*, November 5, 1992, p. 61. Reprinted with permission from *The New York Review of Books*. Copyright © 1992 Nyrev, Inc.

Appendix B

1. Charles R. Hoffer, *A Concise Introduction to Music Listening*, 5th ed. (Belmont, CA: Wadsworth, 1992), p. 16.

2. Hoffer, *A Concise Introduction to Music Listening,* p. 46.

3. Serena Nanda, *Cultural Anthropology*, 4th ed. (Belmont, CA: Wadsworth, 1984), p. 69.

4. R. Jackson Wilson et al., *The Pursuit of Liberty: A History of the American People*, Vol. 1, 2nd ed. (Belmont, CA: Wadsworth, 1990), p. 247.

5. William K. Hartmann, *The Cosmic Voyage: Through Time and Space*, 1992 ed. (Belmont, CA: Wadsworth, 1992), p. 149.

6. Mary Ann Lamanna and Agnes Riedmann, *Marriages and Families: Making Choices and Facing Change*, 4th ed. (Belmont, CA: Wadsworth, 1991), p. 223.

7. Hartmann, *The Cosmic Voyage*, p. 74.

8. Michael A. Milburn, *Persuasion and Politics: The Social Psychology of Public Opinion* (Pacific Grove, CA: Brooks/Cole, 1991), p. 70.

9. Nanda, *Cultural Anthropology*, pp. 9–10.

Appendix C

1. Joan Ferrante, *Sociology: A Global Perspective* (Belmont, CA: Wadsworth, 1992), p. 383.

2. Shirley Biagi, *Media/Impact: An Introduction to Mass Media*, 2nd ed. (Belmont, CA: Wadsworth, 1992), p. 199.

3. James W. Kalat, *Introduction to Psychology*, 2nd ed. (Belmont, CA: Wadsworth, 1990), p. 14.

4. Charles R. Hoffer, *A Concise Introduction to Music Listening*, 5th ed. (Belmont, CA: Wadsworth, 1992), p. 75.

5. Kalat, *Introduction to Psychology*, pp. 36–37.

6. Rev. Martin Luther King, Jr., *Letter from the Birmingham Jail*, April 16, 1963.

7. Paul A. Samuelson, *Economics*, 11th ed. (New York: McGraw-Hill, 1980), p. 551.

8. R. Jackson Wilson et al., *The Pursuit of Liberty: A History of the American People*, Vol. 1, 2nd ed. (Belmont, CA: Wadsworth, 1990), pp. 186–87.

Appendix D

1. R. Jackson Wilson et al., *The Pursuit of Liberty: A History of the American People*, Vol. 1, 2nd ed. (Belmont, CA: Wadsworth, 1990), pp. 186–87.

Appendix E

1. R. Jackson Wilson et al., *The Pursuit of Liberty: A History of the American People*, Vol. 1, 2nd ed. (Belmont, CA: Wadsworth, 1990), p. 94.

2. Brian Urquhart, "A Double Standard," from a speech to the Cosmopolitan Club, published in *The New York Review of Books* 34(7), April 9, 1992, p. 42. Reprinted with permission from *The New York Review of Books*. Copyright © 1992 Nyrev, Inc.

Appendix F

1. James W. Kalat, *Introduction to Psychology*, 2nd ed. (Belmont, CA: Wadsworth, 1990), p. 14.

2. William V. O'Brien, "The Gulf War and Just War Doctrine," *Freedom Review* 22(3), May-June 1991, p. 17.

3. Ruth Benedict, *Patterns of Culture* (New York: New American Library, Mentor Edition, 1946), pp. 4–6.

4. Kalat, *Introduction to Psychology*, pp. 36–37.

5. Abstract for Gregory N. Connolly, C. Tracy Orleans, and Alan Blum, "Snuffing Tobacco Out of Sport," commentary in *American Journal of Public Health* 82(3), March 1992, p. 351. Used by permission.

6. As cited in Philip J. Hilts, "Blunt Style on Teen Sex and Health," *The New York Times*, September 14, 1993, p. B5.

7. Daniel Goleman, "Pollsters Enlist Psychologists in Quest for Unbiased Results," *The New York Times*, September 7, 1993, p. B5.

8. D. Bob Gowin, *Educating* (Ithaca, NY: Cornell University Press, 1981), p. 31.

Subject Index

Name Index